Knowing God, Knowing Emptiness

Knowing God, Knowing Emptiness

An Epistemological Exploration of Bernard Lonergan, Karl Rahner and Nāgārjuna

John N. C. Robinson

SHEFFIELD UK   BRISTOL CT

Published by Equinox Publishing Ltd.

UK   Office 415, The Workstation, 15 Paternoster Row, Sheffield, South Yorkshire S1 2BX
USA ISD, 70 Enterprise Drive, Bristol, CT 06010

www.equinoxpub.com

First published 2022

© John N. C. Robinson 2022

All rights reserved. No part of this publication may be reproduced or transmitted in any form or by any means, electronic or mechanical, including photocopying, recording or any information storage or retrieval system, without prior permission in writing from the publishers.

British Library Cataloguing-in-Publication Data

A catalogue record for this book is available from the British Library.

ISBN-13 978 1 80050 098 3 (hardback)
            978 1 80050 099 0 (paperback)
            978 1 80050 100 3 (ePDF)
            978 1 80050 170 6 (ePub)

Library of Congress Cataloging-in-Publication Data

Names: Robinson, John Neil Charles, author.
Title: Knowing God, Knowing Emptiness: An Epistemological Exploration of Bernard Lonergan, Karl Rahner and Nāgārjuna / John N.C. Robinson.
Description: Sheffield, South Yorkshire; Bristol, CT: Equinox Publishing Ltd., 2022. | Includes bibliographical references and index. | Summary: 'Knowing God, Knowing Emptiness examines the viability of the epistemology proposed by Bernard Lonergan in his seminal work Insight, particularly with regard to its possible application in the field of interreligious dialogue. It applies Lonergan's epistemological categories to Karl Rahner's Foundations of Christian Faith, and Nāgārjuna's Mūlamadhyamakakārikā'– Provided by publisher.
Identifiers: LCCN 2021047830 (print) | LCCN 2021047831 (ebook) | ISBN 9781800500983 (hardback) | ISBN 9781800500990 (paperback) | ISBN 9781800501003 (epdf) | ISBN 9781800501706 (epub)
Subjects: LCSH: Lonergan, Bernard J. F. Insight. | Knowledge, Theory of. | Rahner, Karl, 1904-1984. Grundkurs des Glaubens. | Nāgārjuna, active 2nd century. Madhyamakakārikā.
Classification: LCC B995.L653 I577 2022 (print) | LCC B995.L653 (ebook) | DDC 121--dc23/eng/20211006
LC record available at https://lccn.loc.gov/2021047830
LC ebook record available at https://lccn.loc.gov/2021047831

Typeset by Sparks – www.sparkspublishing.com

Contents

Preface	vii
Acknowledgements	ix
Introduction	1
1 Bernard Lonergan's *Insight* – A Methodological Examination	9
2 Karl Rahner's *Foundations of Christian Faith*: A Lonerganian Analysis	51
3 Nāgārjuna's *Mūlamadhyamakakārikā*: A Lonerganian Analysis	101
4 Dialectic Application of Lonergan's Epistemology	195
Conclusion	217
Bibliography	223
Index	229

Preface

The purpose of this book is to examine the viability of the epistemology proposed by Bernard Lonergan in his seminal work *Insight*, particularly with regard to its possible application in the field of interreligious dialogue. This enquiry was prompted by an awareness of the epistemological questions raised by the various dialogues taking place between different religions, and it was in light of this that Lonergan's claim to comprehensiveness in his epistemology was examined.

The method adopted was that of a dialectical experiment in which Lonergan's epistemology could be tested. Lonergan claims in *Insight* that as his epistemology is both based on and corresponds directly to the structure of human cognition, it is therefore intrinsic to all instances of thought. Accordingly, he claims, it is ideally placed to mutually relate any combination of differing positions.

In this work, I sought to test this claim by applying Lonergan's epistemological categories to Karl Rahner's *Foundations of Christian Faith* and Nāgārjuna's *Mūlamadhyamakakārikā*. Having critically reconstructed Lonergan's position as articulated in *Insight*, I did the same for both of the texts selected and then sought to parse them on the basis of the terms laid out by Lonergan in his epistemological system. I further sought to ascertain whether the thought contained in these two works could be fruitfully related on the basis of Lonergan's epistemology, and what, if any, were the implications for the field of interreligious dialogue. I considered these implications both in terms of the theology of religions and of the more recently developed comparative theology, typified by the approach taken by thinkers such as Francis X. Clooney and others. I concluded by considering what, if any, were the possible developments that could result from the attempted dialectic.

Lonergan's epistemology did prove viable both in terms of parsing the two texts selected and in mutually relating the positions expressed by them. His claim that his epistemology could be found as an underlying structure proved true in both cases, though the comprehensiveness of his epistemology did not prove absolute when applied to Nāgārjuna's thought. Equally, the attempt at fruitful mutual relation on the basis of Lonergan's system also proved successful, and the approach was found both to facilitate this process and to be open to further development. Overall, Lonergan's claims were largely substantiated, though it was found that the terms of his epistemology, emerging as they do from the Western philosophical tradition, did not prove to be entirely adequate when considering a crucial element of Nāgārjuna's thought in the *Mūlamadhyamakakārikā*.

Acknowledgements

Any work such as this is always a collaborative effort to a degree that is never apparent when one examines the final text. Yet there are many people without whose assistance and help I could not have completed this task. First and foremost, my parents, who have been unstinting in their love, support and assistance, and who continued to believe in this project even when my own faith in it was flagging. Second, I would like to thank the many friends and colleagues who have given constant support and encouragement throughout this research. While too numerous to mention individually, particular thanks are due to Dr Grant Cooper, Dr Fiachra Mac Góráin and Ms Niamh Ní Dhomhnaill for their comments and suggestions, and to Dr Albert Bradshaw, Mr Peter Colquhoun, Dr Jude Lal Fernando, Mr Gavin Elliott and Mr Steven Elliott for their encouragement and practical help. I would also like to acknowledge the helpful suggestions given by Professor Perry Schmidt-Leukel. I am grateful to the European Network of Buddhist Christian Studies for the opportunity to present some of the ideas contained in this work to the broader scholarly community, and to Dr John O'Grady for giving me the chance to do so in article form in 'Mining Truths: Festschrift in honour of Geraldine Smyth OP – Ecumenical Theologian and Peacebuilder' (ed. J O'Grady, C. Higgins, J Lal Fernando, Munich: St Otillien, 2015). Finally, I would like to thank the staff of the Irish School of Ecumenics, particularly Prof. John D'Arcy May and Dr Andrew Pierce who provided support, encouragement and inspiration. I would like to acknowledge the role and influence of Dr Denis Carroll and Dr Terence Mc Caughey who were both inspirational teachers and valued friends. I am grateful, too, to the team at Equinox for their professionalism and patience in the preparation of this text, and to the family of the Revd. Dr Lynn De Silva for their kind permission to use the cover image. I would like to conclude with a special word of thanks to Christine Houlihan, Aideen Woods and Mary Priestman whose constant graciousness, humour and kindness did so much to make the ISE a happy and pleasant environment in which to work.

Introduction

In this introduction, I will attempt to give an account of the questions that have spurred this experiment in philosophical theology, along with the methodology adopted and the reasons for the selection of the core texts which are examined in it. The context of this epistemological enquiry is that of religious pluralism, a phenomenon which is now the ineluctable context of all religious thought and which poses specific questions which go to the heart of religious belief itself. Specifically, in the light of the pluralism of religions, what is to be made of the range of competing truth claims in relation to each other? Are they to be viewed as competing systems or is each to be judged solely on its own terms, with the implication of incommensurability which goes with this approach? Are they all true, and if so, what is to be made of what appear to be contradictory beliefs? What does it mean to deem something 'true' in this context? Is one option truer than the others, and if so, how is it possible to know this, especially given the historical and social relativity of consciousness and the role of cultural conditioning?

A variety of answers has been given to these questions; until recently, most of these have fallen within one of the categories put forward by Alan Race in the threefold hypothesis formulated in his 1983 work *Christians and Religious Pluralism*.[1] This hypothesis characterised the range of approaches to religious diversity as falling within the three categories of exclusivism, inclusivism and pluralism. Yet as the ongoing debate has shown, each position contained in this hypothesis involves significant logical difficulties.

The exclusivist position, in which one religion is deemed correct and the others are viewed simply as error, is problematic on a number of grounds. Epistemologically such an approach relies on a fideistic form of circular reasoning which, while initially appearing coherent, does on further investigation suffer from a number of weaknesses. If it is indeed true, as Christian exponents of this position have claimed, that all human knowing is dependent on divine revelation, then it is hard to see how human subjects can understand this revelation without this approach moving into the transcendentalist arena. Any attempts to ground this approach transcendentally, however, imply a correspondence model of truth which in turn raises the question of whether other religions may not also correspond in similar fashion to the underlying transcendental conditions which allow revelation to be appropriated

---

[1] Cf. Alan Race, *Christians and Religious Pluralism: Patterns in the Christian Theology of Religions* (London: SCM Press, 1983).

by the human subject. To answer in the negative implies either a straightforward refusal of the question or the assumption of a 'God's eye' vantage point which enables each religion to be perceived free from the constraints of historically conditioned consciousness with all the relativity of perspective that this implies. Moreover, such an approach suffers from a credibility gap in its discounting of the manifest goodness and virtue to be found in other religious affiliations and in their adherents. In addition, for those who believe in God it is hard to reconcile such an approach with the universality of the divine salvific will of God as expressed in revelation.[2] The crux of this objection is the idea that a loving God would damn the majority of the world's population simply because they are not Christian while simultaneously desiring that all be saved. While such a view has been highly influential in the history of Christian thought, especially in the articulation of this position given by Augustine, it suffers from a credibility gap for many people who find such a view impossible to square with belief in a God of love.

Proponents of this approach will answer by pointing to some of the more exclusivist statements, particularly in the New Testament (e.g. John 14:6), yet theirs is far from being the only possible interpretation of these statements,[3] and in any case such a 'proof-text' approach is untenable on both theological and exegetical grounds.

Inclusivism suffers from the same epistemological problem relating to the absence of a 'God's eye' position of neutrality from which the different religions can be assessed in order to ascertain the different degrees of truth involved. Such an approach claims that while elements of revelation and/or salvation may indeed be found in other religions, these are found in their fullness only in Christianity. The problem of the impossibility of the kind of perspective required to make this judgement vitiates such an approach unless one is to rely on the type of fideistic reasoning already criticised above.

Finally, and counter-intuitively, the same may be said of pluralism, as the claim that all religions are equally valid paths also presupposes some means of examining them, free of any bias or cultural conditioning, along with the ability to experience them in their fullness, something which is arguably possible only for people within these traditions. Moreover, as critics of this

---

[2] E.g. 1 Timothy 2:4

[3] E.g. Perry Schmidt-Leukel, 'Uniqueness: a pluralistic reading of John 14:6', in *Ecumenics from the Rim: Explorations in Honour of John D'Arcy May*, ed. John O'Grady and Peter Scherle (Berlin: Lit Verlag, 2007), 303–10. For a more detailed discussion on this issue see Paul. F. Knitter, *Jesus and the Other Names: Christian Mission and Global Responsibility* (New York: Orbis Books, 1996)

approach have pointed out, in declaring that all religions constitute equally valid paths, it advocates a perspective that is common to none of them, and thus in seeking to declare them all valid in reality does so only by altering their own self-understandings.

An additional possibility is articulated in the thought of George Lindbeck, though this does not appear to be Lindbeck's own position, with his claim that different religious discourses can be viewed as simply incommensurable when they are viewed as cultural-linguistic systems. In this particular application of the cultural-linguistic interpretation of religion, the attempt to make sense of the 'other' is neither possible nor necessary, with each religion operating in, as it were, its own enclosed universe of thought and experience. In this view, Lindbeck considers the possibility that different religions are akin to different systems for making sense of reality and this in turn raises the possibility of incommensurability. In considering this possible implication of a cultural-linguistic approach to religious truth, he lucidly underlines the difficulties that would pertain to dialogue between different religions if this view were taken:

> In short, the cultural-linguistic approach is open to the possibility that different religions and/or philosophies may have incommensurable notions of truth, of experience, and of categorical adequacy, and therefore also of what it would mean for something to be most important (i.e., "God"). Unlike other perspectives, this approach proposes no common framework such as that supplied by the propositionalist's concept of truth or the expressivist's concept of experience within which to compare religions. Thus when affirmations or ideas from categorially different religious or philosophical frameworks are introduced into a given religious outlook, these are either simply babbling or else, like mathematical formulas employed in a poetic text, they have vastly different functions and meanings than they had in their original settings.[4]

In a sense, all of these questions rest on the more fundamental question of what it means to say something is true, how we can make such a determination, and how far such a judgement can enable us to further pronounce on the truth claims of others which we do not share. In this instance these questions take on concrete form specifically in relation to the religious realm and the question of the dialogue between different religions. It is in this context that

---

[4] George A. Lindbeck, *The Nature of Doctrine: Religion and Theology in a Postliberal Age* (London: SPCK, 1984), 47

Bernard Lonergan's claim in *Insight* will be examined, namely, that the epistemology he proposes is innate to all systems of thought and can, therefore, make sense of them in epistemological terms as well as serving as a means of dialectic relation between them.[5]

A number of factors have informed the choice of Lonergan's *Insight*: he proposes an epistemology which runs a Kantian gauntlet, while also providing a possible answer to the contention of a radical relativism which would reduce all truth claims to perspectives. The commonality he views as existing in human knowing, while not seeking to do away with the very real perspectival differences that inform different viewpoints, offers particular advantages in the project of interfaith dialogue. Finally, if his claim is that his epistemology can serve as an integrative framework in the attempt to dialectically relate any combination of viewpoints, then it becomes possible to conceive of a shared epistemological structure common to all participants in any given interfaith encounter.[6] This alone merits testing the claim made as the potential benefits of any such commonality would have considerable significance.

---

[5] Though as will become apparent Lonergan uses the term 'dialectic' somewhat differently from its normal application, a point that will be addressed in Chapter 1

[6] Lonergan is not, of course, without his critics, and while many of the criticisms pertain to his *Method in Theology* rather than to *Insight*, the continuity between the two works is such that criticism of *Method* frequently applies to *Insight* too. Lonergan's affirmation of intelligibility as a category came under sustained attack following the publication of *Insight* from a variety of writers, such as James Albertson ('Review of Insight', *The Modern Schoolman* 35 (1957–58): 238), Ronald Hepburn ('Method and Insight', *Journal of the Royal Institute of Philosophy* 48 (1975): 153–60), J. P. Mackey ('Divine Revelation and Lonergan's Transcendental Method in Theology', *Irish Theological Quarterly* 40 (1973): 7) and David Burrell ('How Complete Can Intelligibility Be? A Commentary on Insight Chapter XIX', *The American Catholic Philosophical Association Proceedings for the Year 1967*, Washington: Catholic University of America, 1967: 252). Lonergan's account of cognition and his claim to derive his metaphysics from it was criticised by Schubert M. Ogden ('Lonergan and the Subjectivist Principle', *The Journal of Religion* 51 Vol 3 (1971): 155–72). A further set of criticisms was levelled against *Method in Theology* which also has relevance to the position taken in *Insight* in the 1975 collection of essays *Looking at Lonergan's Method* ed. Patrick Corcoran (The Talbot Press LTD: Dublin, 1975). Noel Dermot O'Donoghue critiqued what may be termed Lonergan's introspection (pp. 42–54), Wolfhart Pannenburg pointed out the absence of engagement with the questions raised by Wittgenstein and more general hermeneutical questions (pp. 88–100), and Nicholas Lash maintained that Lonergan failed to appreciate the discontinuity that pertains between cultures in the formulation of his approach (pp. 127–43). Some of these criticisms are addressed from a Lonerganian perspective in Hugo A. Meynell's *The Theology of Bernard Lonergan* (Atlanta, GA: Scholars Press, 1986). For a contextual treatment of Lonergan's approach which also reviews some of the criticisms of it, see Neil Ormerod, *Faith and Reason* (1517 Media, Minneapolis, MN: Fortress Press, 2017), 75–118

Lonergan's approach can be summed up in a quotation from the book's introduction, in which he says: 'Thoroughly understand what it is to understand, and not only will you understand the broad lines of what is to be understood, but you will also possess a fixed base, an invariant pattern, opening upon all further developments of understanding.'[7]

The various building blocks of the system Lonergan will develop throughout the book are to be found *in nuce* in this quotation. Fundamentally his system is based on a thorough understanding of the process of understanding itself, and as understanding is involved in all thought, the structure that emerges from this is one that will be innate to all thought. As the contents of the act of understanding, that which is understood will share a structure with the act of understanding and this structure will be common to all positions, no matter how disparate they appear to be. This commonality will enable the dialectical relation of disparate positions as well as providing a template for perceiving where errors of understanding have taken place. In addition, once the structure of intelligent knowing is grasped, the structure of all subsequent thought is also thereby grasped, albeit prescinding from its specific content, thus enabling the anticipation of further developments.

These are undoubtedly far-reaching claims to make, and the aim of this work will be to test their validity by attempting to relate the transcendental theology of Karl Rahner in his *Foundations of Christian Faith* to the philosophy of emptiness put forward by Nāgārjuna in his *Mūlamadhyamakakārikā* on the basis of Lonergan's system. The work by Rahner has been chosen as the most systematic presentation of his theology that he wrote, while such is the sheer volume of commentary that has accumulated over the centuries in relation to Nāgārjuna's opus that consideration of his work will be restricted to the interpretation presented in the commentary and translation undertaken by Jay Garfield. This particular approach falls within the Prāsaṅgika-Mādhyamika school, and Garfield's secular interpretation of the text further sharpens the challenge involved in seeking to relate it to Rahner's approach in *Foundations*. Accordingly, given the desirability of maximising the tension of the dialectic undertaken and thereby providing a maximal challenge to Lonergan's epistemology, Garfield's translation and commentarial interpretation is particularly suitable for the task in hand. In terms of engagement with the *Mūlamadhyamakakārikā* itself, however, the translation by Mark Siderits and Shōryū Katsura[8] arguably represents an advance on Garfield's

---

[7] Lonergan, *Insight*, 28

[8] Mark Siderits and Shōryū Katsura, *Nāgārjuna's Middle Way: Mūlamadhyamakakārikā* (Boston, MA: Wisdom Publications, 2013)

translation which was based only on the Tibetan text. Yet no rendering of a text which is as sophisticated and subtle as the *Mūlamadhyamakakārikā* will ever be wholly adequate, and it is to be expected that all attempts to do so will give rise to a measure of scholarly disagreement.[9]

Further reasons for the choice of these two positions include the following points. First, the two positions appear to be incompatible with each other in their respective approaches, thus providing a rigorous test for the validity of Lonergan's claims. Quite simply, it does not seem possible to reconcile Rahner's affirmation of God with Nāgārjuna's positing of emptiness as an all-encompassing category. Second, despite Lonergan and Rahner sharing a basic philosophical orientation as transcendental Thomists, Rahner was famously critical of the approach Lonergan formulated in his writings, thus raising the intriguing question of whether Lonergan's system is applicable or even compatible with Rahner's thought. Certainly, as will be shown subsequently in the text, significant philosophical differences are indeed present in the two thinkers' approaches. Third, the *Mūlamadhyamakakārikā*, besides being a text of considerable complexity, also provides a challenge to the very categories in which Lonergan's thought is couched – it is hard to see, for instance, how the relationship between phenomena (the second of Lonergan's three stages) is compatible with Nāgārjuna's insistence on the emptiness of all existents, emptiness here defined as the absence of substantial essence, with the lack of ontological boundaries between phenomena that this would entail.

Thus the reasons for the choice of texts relate both to challenges pertaining to analysing them in terms of Lonergan's epistemology and to the challenges involved in using this epistemology to dialectically interrelate them.

Prior to seeking to dialectically relate the two works which will form the two poles of the dialectic, the attempt will first be made to critically reconstruct Lonergan's position in *Insight* with reference also to John Henry Newman's *Grammar of Assent*, a work which Lonergan had studied in depth and which by all accounts influenced the subsequent trajectory of his thought.

The methodology employed in the analysis of the works of Rahner and Nāgārjuna will encompass three elements: first, the relevant thinker's position will be critically reconstructed; second, the attempt will be made to parse the position in the terms proposed by Lonergan in *Insight*; finally, the attempt will be made to dialectically relate the two positions based on this structural

---

[9] For more on this, see Anne McDonald, 'The Quest for an English-Speaking Nāgārjuna', *Indo-Iranian Journal*, Vol. 58, No. 4 (2015): 375, and Koji Tanaka, 'On Nāgārjuna's Ontological and Semantic Paradox', *Philosophy East and West*, Vol. 66, No. 4 (October 2016): 1292–306

analysis, specifically seeking to bring into relation with each other elements that emerge as structurally correlate in the analysis of the texts based on Lonergan's schema. The purpose of the methodology will be to examine a number of questions pertaining to Lonergan's claims. Do the categories fit the two positions as they ought to if Lonergan is correct and the structure he proposes is indeed innate to all thought? Does mapping the thought of both thinkers in this manner facilitate the dialectical relationship proposed? Lastly, does mutual intelligibility result from the attempt at interrelation?

The structure of the book will largely follow these elements. Chapter One will seek to reconstruct Lonergan's thought in *Insight* and will attempt to apply his epistemological structure to Newman's *Grammar of Assent*. In Chapter Two Rahner's thought in *Foundations of Christian Faith* will be reconstructed and parsed in Lonerganian terms, and the same approach will be followed in Chapter Three for Nāgārjuna's *Mūlamadhyamakakārikā*.[10] In Chapter Four the resulting epistemological analysis of both thinkers will serve as the basis of an attempt to interrelate them, and this attempt will then be evaluated in terms of both its viability and its fruitfulness in seeking to establish this interrelation. In addition, the implications of the findings of this attempt will be examined in the context of the current state of the theology of religions and the more recent move to comparative theology on the part of some scholars. Finally, the conclusion will seek to adumbrate questions that arise from this enquiry and will seek to formulate directions for further research.

These questions will not focus specifically on the results that emerge from the dialectical interrelation between the thought of Rahner and Nāgārjuna, but rather will examine questions pertaining to Lonergan's system and its application, particularly in terms of how it might be developed in order to more fully fulfil the aims to which he aspired in its formulation.

---

[10] It may be argued that the parsing and analysis of the *Mūlamadhyamakakārikā* using Lonergan's categories constitutes a Western colonial approach to Nāgārjuna's thought which seeks to elide the distinctiveness of the system he elaborates. The intent in selecting Nāgārjuna's text as one pole of this dialectic, however, is not to force it into Western categories but rather to let it stand as a challenge to them. Indeed, it is hoped that the attempt made here to take the thought of Nāgārjuna seriously as a possible challenge to Lonergan's epistemology will make a small contribution to redressing the silencing of non-Western voices so characteristic of the colonialist project. Garfield's translation and commentary have been selected due to his translation of the Tibetan text and also to the fact that his interpretation is one which is particularly unsympathetic to the points Rahner seeks to make. It is hoped that this seeming incompatibility will provide a greater test for the epistemology that Lonergan sets forth in *Insight*

Key to the thesis being advanced is an accurate analysis and exposition of the positions advanced by Lonergan, Rahner and Nāgārjuna in their integrity in the key texts selected, along with an analysis of the specifically epistemological concerns contained within these. A further reason for the detailed exposition of each position undertaken is to ensure that the differences in the various positions are in no way obscured by the attempt to relate them on the basis of Lonergan's epistemology. A range of secondary literature has been consulted with the specific aim of ensuring that my reading of the texts fits with the mainstream scholarly apprehension of these arguments and has not been compromised by the terms of this experiment. Direct engagement with this literature has been intentionally limited in the relevant chapters, however, as the aim throughout has been to engage directly with the arguments advanced by the three thinkers in question.

It will be noted that the chapters are not of equal length – this is due to the various and varying degrees of complexity contained in the different works, as well as the different lengths of the texts in question. The various strands are drawn together in Chapter Four, and it is in this chapter that the results of the epistemological experiment undertaken are presented.

The three texts have been chosen as most fully representing the typical positions of the authors. While Lonergan's *Method in Theology* is more widely known, it is in *Insight* that he gives the fullest account of his epistemology. Equally, it is in his *Foundations of Christian Faith* that Rahner comes closest to offering a systematic presentation of his theology, in contrast to the unsystematic presentation of themes that one finds in his *Theological Investigations*. Finally, the topic of emptiness receives its most complete treatment by Nāgārjuna in his *Mūlamadhyamakakārikā*, a text which continues to occupy a central place in Buddhist thought and is seen as one of the most significant texts of Buddhist philosophy.

This introduction has sought to explain and give an initial justification of the choices governing this work and its examination of the core texts and positions of the thinkers selected. Chapter One will seek to set the stage for what follows by setting out the epistemology that Lonergan proposes in *Insight* and which will form the context for the chapters that follow.

1 Bernard Lonergan's *Insight* – A Methodological Examination

1.1 Introduction

The aim of this introduction to the chapter will be to set the context for Lonergan's epistemological project as set forth in the introduction to *Insight* and to outline the structure that this chapter will follow. Whilst no one would deny that Lonergan's *Insight* is a work of gargantuan proportions and represents a synthesis that is dizzying in its breadth and scope, in its essence it is an application and logical expansion of a basic insight into the nature of human insight itself. To say this is not to detract from the philosophical work – notoriously, simple principles do indeed become both intricate and complex when followed to their logical *terminus ad quem*. Rather, it is to draw attention to a structural factor of Lonergan's opus which will serve as a guiding principle in seeking to expose and examine the core of what he has to say in it.

In the introduction to *Insight* Lonergan clearly states what the goal of the book actually is:

…our aim regards

1. not the fact of knowledge but a discrimination between two facts of knowledge,
2. not the details of the known but the structure of the knowing,
3. not the knowing as an object characterized by catalogues of abstract properties but the appropriation of one's own intellectual and rational self-consciousness,
4. not a sudden leap to appropriation but a slow and painstaking development, and
5. not a development indicated by appealing either to the logic of the as yet unknown goal or to a presupposed and as yet unexplained ontologically structured metaphysics, but a development that can begin in any sufficiently cultured consciousness, that expands in virtue of the dynamic tendencies of that consciousness

itself, and that heads through an understanding of all understanding to a basic understanding of all that can be understood.[1]

In a manner reminiscent of the overture of an opera, Lonergan here sounds the principal themes which will comprise the rest of the work. In terms of the structure of this chapter, three points follow from the above schema: in line with Lonergan's aim in *Insight* the focus of the analysis will be the structure of knowing presented rather than the examples with which it is illustrated; attention will be focused in particular on Lonergan's use of cognitional structure as an epistemological foundation and the application of the 'basic understanding of all that can be understood' to the question of interreligious dialogue in the form of a methodology which will, in turn, inform the rest of the work. Accordingly, not every point adduced by Lonergan will be covered in the summary contained in this chapter – such an undertaking would in any case be impossible given the size and scope of Lonergan's opus. Rather, the attempt will be made to critically reconstruct the structure which he propounds through the many examples posited in the text and on which he bases the epistemology which results.

The chapter itself will fall into three sections: section one will seek to critically reconstruct the fundamental elements of the argument Lonergan proposes; section two will compare and contrast these with the markedly different approach taken to the question of knowing by John Henry Newman in his *Grammar of Assent* with the aim of seeing whether Lonergan's schema is indeed as universal as he claims it is by attempting to accommodate Newman's analysis within it; and section three will seek to provide initial pointers as to how Lonergan's schema could function in the dialogue between Buddhism and Christianity. Having set the scene for Lonergan's analysis, the next step taken will be to examine Lonergan's definition of insight and how this operates.

1.2   Lonergan's Study of Human Understanding

1.2.1   Insight as Understanding

This section consists in an examination of the two kinds of knowledge as articulated by Lonergan and seeks to outline the noetic structure involved in

---

[1] Bernard J. F. Lonergan, *Insight: A Study of Human Understanding* (London: Longmans, Green & Co., 1958), xxviii

insight as a component of human knowing. As stated above, the fundamental idea upon which Lonergan hangs all else in *Insight* is relatively simple and hinges, not surprisingly, on the structure of human knowing conceived around the phenomenon of insight. Crucial to his formulation of this structure is his positing of what he sees as an essentially psychological problem in human consciousness whereby the two kinds of knowing – that of mere sense experience and the intelligent grasp of what is experienced – become conflated. Terry Tekippe sums up Lonergan's point here in the following terms which aptly summarise what Lonergan is drawing attention to:

> Human beings share with the dog the ability to see the print, the dark marks on the white paper; but they have another power the dog does not, to understand, to confer upon those mute marks a meaning that refers to a signified, namely, the components of the stereo system, and the order of their assembly. Human beings have both kinds of "knowing," in the wide sense of the term by which dogs "know"; but the danger is to get them mixed up.[2]

Thus Lonergan, like Kant, affirms the role of the human mind in actively organising the phenomena presented to the senses in order to attain to knowledge. This process is presented as taking place in three stages: first, the knower experiences a range of disparate phenomena; second, she grasps the relationship between these phenomena leading to a formulation of a proposition; and third, she judges whether the proposition is true or false and whether it leaves other pertinent questions unanswered.

Thus, as Lonergan expresses it himself, the act of insight is both synthetic and *a priori* in a way which draws attention to the importance of what will follow:

'It is *a priori*, for it goes beyond what is merely given to sense or to empirical consciousness. It is synthetic, for it adds to the merely given an explanatory unification or organization.'[3]

This threefold structure is one which Lonergan sees not only operative in all branches of human knowledge but also unifying them and driving their dynamic development. In this light, still at the start of his inquiry, he introduces the concept of the higher viewpoint. A higher viewpoint occurs when the emergence of new insights leads to a recognition of the inadequacy of a

---

[2] Terry Tekippe, *Bernard Lonergan's Insight: A Comprehensive Commentary* (Lanham, MD: University Press of America, 2003), 15

[3] Lonergan, *Insight*, xi

previous position, leading to an expansion and revision of that previous position and the components of which it was comprised. Lonergan defines this process thus: 'Still further insights arise. The shortcomings of the previous position become recognized. New definitions and postulates are devised. A new and larger field of deductions is set up. Broader and more accurate applications become possible. Such a complex shift in the whole structure of insights, definitions, postulates, deductions, and applications may be referred to very briefly as a higher viewpoint.'[4]

Lonergan provides a number of illustrative examples throughout *Insight*, but the basic point is clear: phenomena occurring which cannot be accounted for in a position can and often do lead to the formulation of a new position transcending the old, in which both the old position and the aberrant data are accounted for.

Linked with this concept are those of the inverse insight and the empirical residue. An inverse insight consists in the realisation that there is no meaning where one would expect there to be; Lonergan expresses this point in precise terms:

> While direct insight meets the spontaneous effort of intelligence to understand, inverse insight responds to a more subtle and critical attitude that distinguishes different degrees or levels or kinds of intelligibility. While direct insight grasps the point, or sees the solution, or comes to know the reason, inverse insight apprehends that in some fashion the point is that there is no point, or that the solution is to deny a solution, or that the reason is that the rationality of the real admits distinctions and qualifications. Finally, while the conceptual formulation of direct insight affirms a positive intelligibility though it may deny expected empirical elements, the conceptual formulation of an inverse insight affirms empirical elements only to deny an expected intelligibility.[5]

Lonergan emphasises, however, that the absence of intelligibility affirmed by an inverse insight does not render such an insight useless; rather, it serves to eliminate mistaken questions and can also be observed in connection 'with ideas or principles or methods of quite exceptional significance'.[6]

---

[4] Lonergan, *Insight*, 13
[5] Lonergan, *Insight*, 19
[6] Lonergan, *Insight*, 25

In seeking to further tease out this significance, Lonergan ends up introducing a further, and somewhat wider, category, namely that of the empirical residue. Empirical residue has three characteristics. It:

1. consists in positive empirical data
2. is to be denied any immanent intelligibility of its own, and
3. is connected with some compensating higher intelligibility of notable importance.[7]

The difference between it and inverse insight lies in the third point, and in a sense one might say that it is precisely this residue, rather than inverse insights *per se*, which provides the dynamism which issues in higher viewpoints.

At this point Lonergan seeks to illustrate the points made with a lengthy examination of empirical method, with particular reference to physics, and then moves to a consideration of common sense, a section of *Insight* which, whilst amply illustrating the points Lonergan wishes to make, does not actually add any new elements to the framework he is constructing. Two points of relevance which he does introduce, however, are the distinction between common sense which seeks to relate things to us, and empirical method which seeks to relate them to each other, and the possibility of aberration in both fields.

The two final building blocks Lonergan introduces before moving from his consideration of insight *qua* activity to insight *qua* knowledge are the concept of the thing and a further development of the third of the above-mentioned stages, that of judgement.

For Lonergan the notion of the thing involves grasping not phenomena in terms of their relations to each other *qua* disparate phenomena but rather their concrete unity as part of a whole. Underlining this he comments, 'the notion of a thing is grounded in an insight that grasps, not relations between data, but a unity, identity, whole in data; and this unity is grasped...by taking them (data) in their concrete individuality and in the totality of their aspects...the reader...will find that object to be a unity to which belongs every aspect of every datum within the unity...Moreover, from this grasp of unity in a concrete totality of data there follow the various characteristics of things.'[8]

---

[7] Lonergan, *Insight*, 25
[8] Lonergan, *Insight*, 246

This consideration of the thing leads Lonergan to further emphasise the distinction between the two types of knowing already mentioned by distinguishing between things, which are 'the intelligible unities to be grasped when one is within the intellectual pattern of experience', and bodies, which are 'the highly convincing instances of the "already out there now real" that are unquestioned and unquestionable not only for animals but also for the bias of common sense'.[9]

In this sense, then, as Tekippe points out,[10] things cannot be seen, only comprehended, and understanding a 'thing' involves not only grasping disparate phenomena as a concrete whole but also becoming aware of, and carefully distinguishing between, the two types of knowing operative within human consciousness.

Lonergan closes this first section of the book with a reflection on judgement and in so doing introduces the concept of the virtually unconditioned (the 'virtual' here would appear to correspond with the archaic meaning of the word referring to the possession of particular virtues, with 'unconditioned' referring to the absence of any governing *antecedent* condition). He succinctly sets out the parameters of the question, stating:

Prospective judgements are propositions

1. that are the content of an act of conceiving, thinking, defining, considering, or supposing,
2. that are subjected to the question for reflection, to the critical attitude of intelligence, and
3. that thereby are constituted as the conditioned.[11]

Judgement is, then, the process whereby we reflect on the proposition in which the relation between phenomena is grasped, i.e. the insight, and either affirm it as true or repudiate it as false. This we do on the basis of whether the proposition fulfils what Lonergan calls the 'virtually unconditioned', which he defines as '(1) a link of the conditioned to its conditions, and (2) the fulfilment of the conditions'.[12]

If these criteria are met, then the proposition may be affirmed as true subject to the proviso that there are no relevant questions left unanswered by

---

[9] Lonergan, *Insight*, 267
[10] Tekippe, Commentary, 123
[11] Lonergan, *Insight*, 315
[12] Lonergan, *Insight*, 315

the insight in question. It is this third stage which Lonergan sees as distinguishing his position from that of Kant, a position which he criticises for not according sufficient weight to the role of judgement, and he sees the role he accords it as both avoiding what he terms the 'vestigial empiricism' often detected in Kantian and steering a course between the Scylla of materialism and the Charybdis of idealism.[13] With this initial definition of the dynamic of insight in human knowing in mind, the analysis turns to a teasing out of the significance of the role of insight, specifically in terms of insight into insight itself.

1.2.2 Insight as Knowledge

Having thus outlined the structure of insight, in the second part of the book Lonergan turns to, in his own terms, insight into insight. He begins by considering the self-affirmation of the knower. This involves the knower knowing himself as such, i.e. knowing that he is a concrete unity-whole and knowing that this concrete unity-whole is characterised by the activities proper to knowing. Outlining precisely what he means by this self-affirmation, Lonergan states the position, saying:

> Since our study has been of cognitional process, the judgment we are best prepared to make is the self-affirmation of an instance of such a process as cognitional. By the 'self' is meant a concrete and intelligible unity-identity-whole. By such self-affirmation is meant that the self both affirms and is affirmed. By 'self-affirmation of the knower' is meant that the self as affirmed is characterised by such occurrences as sensing, perceiving, imagining, inquiring, understanding, formulating, reflecting, grasping the unconditioned and affirming.[14]

Central to this affirmation of the self is the phenomenon of awareness: that we do not simply experience things unconsciously, as it were, but that we are aware of doing so.

Two further implications adduced by Lonergan are the incoherence of denying such self-affirmation and the arrival of conscious understanding at what can be termed the 'thing *in se*'. The denial of self-affirmation is self-refuting as the denial presupposes and makes use of the very phenomena it denies: the knowing, rational cognition of the unity-whole which is the

---

[13] Lonergan, *Insight*, 341
[14] Lonergan, *Insight*, 319

self. Therefore self-affirmation stands as a logically irrefutable tenet and, as Lonergan will go on to demonstrate, provides a solid basis for further development.

In addition, such a process of self-affirmation, by logical necessity, leads to a grasp of the thing *in se*, in this instance the thinking self. Lonergan expresses this by posing and then answering the question of what it is that is distinctive in this view, saying: 'What is the source of this peculiarity of cognitional theory? It is that other theory reaches its thing-itself by turning away from the thing as related to us by sense or by consciousness, but cognitional theory reaches its thing-itself by understanding itself and affirming itself as concrete unity in a process that is conscious empirically, intelligently and rationally. Moreover since every other known becomes known through this process, no known could impugn the process without simultaneously impugning its own status as a known.'[15]

Thus the firm foundation has been laid for all that shall follow in the self-knowledge of the knower as a knowing self. Two points in particular are to be noted in relation to this point. First, Lonergan does not seek to ground human knowing but rather takes it as a given and then proceeds to examine it. Commenting on this, Tekippe correctly points out that in the position Lonergan presents here:

> We have no knowing prior to our knowing, no knowing which could conceivably justify our knowing from outside. "Human knowing does not begin from previous knowing but from natural spontaneities and inevitabilities. Its basic terms are not defined for it in some knowing prior to knowing; they are fixed by the dynamic structure of cognitional process itself."[16]

Second, the self-affirmation of the knower represents, in the structure of the book, a drawing together of all that Lonergan has been seeking to say about insight up to this point in the book. Tekippe points out the importance of this point, stating: 'Lonergan has not hitherto explicitly asked the reader to make a judgment about cognitional process; but, at least implicitly, he has been making judgments about insight from the very first page of Chapter I, and inviting his reader to share in them. Further and most particularly, the performance of this judgment rests upon the judgments about judgment made in Chapter X, which explicates judgment as a grasp of the virtually

---

[15] Lonergan, *Insight*, 338
[16] Tekippe, *Commentary*, 181

unconditioned, which can be unfolded in an analysis of conditioned, links between conditioned and conditions, and the fulfilment of the conditions.'[17]

Having laid this foundation, Lonergan further draws upon what has been affirmed by examining the notion of being. Here the methodological significance of Lonergan's function on the knowing subject and her cognition starts to become more apparent. In seeking to answer the question 'what is being?', Lonergan gives an answer at one remove and does so by pointing once again to consciousness. He does so by:

> ...distinguishing between a spontaneously operative notion of being, and a later and formalized account of being, such as found in the ontologies of various philosophies. In doing so, Lonergan is pioneering a new way of doing philosophy. Instead of discoursing abstractly on being, he rather points to something in the knowing subject. This is part of what Lonergan means when he says he wants to make philosophy more empirical. If the "I," the structure of knowing, and the notion of being themselves have a prior existence within the data of consciousness, then Lonergan can base his own account of these realities by appealing to their prior presence and operation.[18]

Thus being is defined as the 'objective of the pure desire to know'[19] which pervades all contents of cognition and is the goal of all human thought.

Linked to it is the notion of objectivity which for Lonergan is a complex of judgements, based on the unconditioned, and viewed as determinations within the notion of being taken as comprising everything that is. Once the act of self-affirmation has been made, the knower knows himself as 'being and object'. If such knowledge is attainable in relation to the self, it is attainable in relation to other existents. Lonergan links this point with what is to come, saying, 'Hence we place transcendence, not in going beyond a known knower, but in heading for being, within which there are positive differences, and, among such differences, the difference between object and subject.'[20]

It is at this juncture that Lonergan's investigation moves into the realm of metaphysics proper. Like being, metaphysics is viewed as being already present in the human subject in an elementary form which Lonergan terms 'latent metaphysics' and which is contrasted with the specifically thought-out

---

[17] Tekippe, *Commentary*, 182
[18] Tekippe, *Commentary*, 188
[19] Lonergan, *Insight*, 348
[20] Lonergan, *Insight*, 377

'explicit metaphysics', the former referring to 'the department of human knowledge that underlies, penetrates, transforms, and unifies all other departments'.[21] Explicit metaphysics, in turn, is the 'integral heuristic structure of proportionate being'.[22]

Proportionate being is here taken to mean all that is but is not God, and the affirmation of the integral heuristic structure of proportionate being is premised on the isomorphism of knowing with its contents. His approach may be summed up in a quotation from the preface in which he states: 'Thoroughly understand what it is to understand, and not only will you understand the broad lines of what is to be understood, but you will also possess a fixed base, an invariant pattern, opening upon all further developments of understanding.'[23]

Quite simply, then, in this view what actually happens when we understand is universally the same for everyone, something that can be verified by becoming aware of the activities of the mind when we understand, and as what is understood, i.e. being itself, is related to the different stages of knowing as its contents, then the structure of being is isomorphic with the structure of knowing. Speaking of this correspondence between knowing and being, Lonergan draws attention to this point, stating: '…the major premise is the isomorphism that obtains between the structure of knowing and the structure of the known. If the knowing consists of a related set of acts and the known is the related set of contents of these acts, then the pattern of the relations between the acts is similar in form to the pattern of the relations between the contents of the acts.'[24]

The corollary of this is that metaphysics itself is one with the pure desire to know and is therefore to be approached *via* the same threefold pattern which runs through all authentic knowing: experience, insight, judgement. This in turn leads Lonergan to his formulation of 'positions' and 'counterpositions', the former being any view which is based on this threefold structure of knowing and which therefore invites development, and the latter being any view which violates this structure, basing itself on mere extroversion, and which therefore invites reversal. What we have in this section is essentially a deductive chain which begins with the self-affirmation of the knower. This leads to the definition of being as the object of the desire to know and objectivity as an interrelated complex of judgements, a definition

---

[21] Lonergan, *Insight*, 390
[22] Lonergan, *Insight*, 391
[23] Lonergan, *Insight*, 28
[24] Lonergan, *Insight*, 399

that is undergirded by the affirmation of the isomorphism of the known with the structure of knowing. This approach Lonergan views as comprising the content of metaphysics, and the concept of proportionate being – all that is not God – is introduced, as is the distinction between positions which correspond to the structure of intelligent knowing, and counterpositions which violate this structure and invite refutation. Having introduced metaphysics into his argument, Lonergan now moves to a consideration of the method involved in metaphysics.

1.2.3 Method of Metaphysics

At this point, Lonergan moves into a discussion of the method of metaphysics, a section that is of particular importance in any attempt to extract a methodology from his analysis which could be employed in any kind of dialogue. One of the crucial points Lonergan makes throughout but which is particularly germane at this point in his inquiry is that the integral heuristic structure provides a way to anticipatively define the as yet unknown contents of cognitive acts. To put it bluntly, such a structure should give us enough of an idea in advance of what the knowledge we are seeking will look like to enable us to remain on the right noetic track. A second important role of the use of such a structure is the potential integration of disparate branches of knowledge, an integration which takes place in an initial form when the common structure of the different branches in question is grasped.

Predictably, Lonergan again drives home the point that the grasp of such structure begins in the act of self-affirmation, the principle of isomorphism having already established that the structure of knowing will also be the structure of what is known, along with the insistence that being is what is known and intelligently grasped. As this structure, whilst a universal given, lies latent in the human mind, it is only through the reflexive self-affirmation of the knower that it comes to consciousness so to speak.

Again in the context of this discussion, Lonergan draws attention to the potential confusion that can result from a lack of awareness of what he terms the polymorphism of human consciousness, i.e. the two different knowings that are present in human consciousness and the danger of conflating them by confusing knowing with simply 'taking a look'. At this point Lonergan ups the ante, so to speak, with the claim that the method he here proposes is the only one which is not arbitrary, based as it is on the intrinsic structures of human cognition.

A further development of this point is his introduction of the concepts of analytical propositions and analytic principles, the former being statements on which the only restrictions are those pertaining to making a coherently logical statement and the latter adding to these the idea of concrete existence. It is on this basis that Lonergan criticises abstract logic as a basis for knowledge, a position, as will be seen later, he shares with Newman. Tekippe sums up this point succinctly, stating: 'A contingent universe cannot by its nature cooperate in corresponding to the necessity of a logical system.'[25]

Truth, for Lonergan, then, is grasped neither by simple sense experience in the manner of empiricism, nor in the critical realism of Kant, but by a grasp of the unconditioned, which is emphasised, saying: 'But once extroversion is questioned, it is only through a man's reflective grasp of the unconditioned that the objectivity and validity of human knowing can be established.'[26]

As mentioned, Lonergan grounds all of this in the structure of human knowing, awareness of which hinges on the act of self-affirmation, but he also devotes attention to what can distort the process of knowledge, the primary factor being the confusion of the two types of knowledge that pertain to human consciousness. Along with this, however, he also mentions the interference of other desires with the unrestricted desire to know, and states bluntly that one of the major tasks of philosophy has to be the examination of the functioning of human cognition with specific attention to where it can go astray:

> One is forced to the conclusion that philosophic method must concern itself with the structure and the aberrations of human cognitional process. Abstract deduction yields to concrete; the use of concrete deduction raises the question of its own possibility; and that possibility is found to lie in the genesis of a wisdom that is prior to metaphysics… our position is intellectualist, open, factual, and normative. It deals not with determinate conceptual contents but with heuristically defined anticipations. So far from fixing the concepts that will meet the anticipations, it awaits from nature and from history a succession of tentative solutions. Instead of binding these solutions by necessary relations, it regards them as products of a cumulative succession of insights and it claims that the succession follows neither a unique nor a necessary path; for identical results can be reached by different routes. And besides valid developments there are aberrations.[27]

---

[25] Tekippe, *Commentary*, 236
[26] Lonergan, *Insight*, 414
[27] Lonergan, *Insight*, 421

Having stated that, in terms of the role of the heuristic structure that constitutes metaphysics in anticipating what is yet to be known, only the content of the first of three stages remains an unknown, Lonergan's next move is to delineate the elements of metaphysics, and he begins by stating simply: 'We have to make explicit the latent metaphysics of the human mind, and the first step is to establish its elements. There are six of them: central potency, central form, central act, conjugate potency, conjugate form, and conjugate act.'[28]

Whilst the terminology Lonergan employs here has decided Aristotelian and Thomistic echoes, he proceeds to give these terms his own definition. Stated briefly, potency is the data which is known intellectually, form is the data considered in terms of the inner relationship of the different data in question to each other, and act is the affirmation of the truth of what has been understood based on the grasp of the unconditioned. Though the three are a unity, it is only when this last stage is reached that knowing proper has occurred. The further distinction of central and conjugate corresponds to the distinction between the two kinds of knowing; central potency, form and act are concerned with the intellectual pattern of experience whilst conjugate potency, form and act are concerned with the sensory pattern. Drawing on the conception of the thing, the former is seen as linked to the perceived whole that the mind understands when the concept of the thing is invoked, and the latter to the phenomena which are experienced by the senses prior to this mental move. This distinction is neatly and aptly summed up in Lonergan's use of mass-velocity as an illustration: 'To illustrate the meaning of the terms central and conjugate potency, form, and act, let us suppose that mass-velocity is a notion that survives in fully explanatory science. Then the mass-velocity will be a conjugate act; the mass, defined by its intelligible relations to other masses, will be a conjugate form; the space-time continuum of the trajectory will be a conjugate potency; what has the mass will be individual by its central potency, a unity by its central form, and existing by its central act.'[29]

It is important to emphasise that for Lonergan the formulation of these three elements is of huge importance and this becomes clear in the remainder of this section as Lonergan goes on to consider the dynamic character of the universe. It is the relation between these three elements which explains, for him, the relation between genera and species as well as the various other

---

[28] Lonergan, *Insight*, 431
[29] Lonergan, *Insight*, 437

components of the examples he has used throughout *Insight* in illustration of the points he has been making.

The argument at this point hinges on a further isomorphism – that between the dynamism of consciousness and the dynamism of the universe. The universe which we inhabit is a 'system on the move' and as such is constantly pressing forward to new developments, a process which can be affirmed since it can be observed.[30] This he expresses by invoking the concept of 'finality', seen as the dynamism due to which the universe continues to move forward into new developments, though he sees the ground of this continual development in potency, a move which, as Tekippe correctly points out, renders his analysis somewhat problematic at this particular point: 'In spite of what he has just said about nature, Lonergan finds the ultimate location of finality in potency…Lonergan is aware of the apparent contradiction in that he has just said potency is the principle of limitation, and he tries to answer that objection…But it strikes me that he is here according to potency a positive causality that would be foreign to Aristotle and Thomas, where prime matter is more a receptive and passive principle than an active cause…Lonergan remains an Aristotelian; but perhaps he is here bending the Aristotelian-Thomistic framework.'[31]

Finally, Lonergan introduces anticipatively the notion of dialectic which will become of importance later in the investigation.[32] In this section, Lonergan has teased out the implications of the posited structure of knowing and sought to establish on this basis the terms of a metaphysics which enables enquiry into the structure of being itself. He now moves to an application of this metaphysics and draws out its implications.

1.2.4 Metaphysics as Science and Dialectic

Crucial to this section of the inquiry are both the application of the metaphysics Lonergan has laid down and the consideration of the logical implications of this, particularly in terms of the intelligibility of being. The terms

---

[30] Lonergan, *Insight*, 445

[31] Tekippe, *Commentary*, 264

[32] 'Lonergan speaks, again by anticipation, of the fourth method to be placed in his toolbox, namely dialectic…As classical method studies system, and statistical method the "systematic lack of system," so genetic method studies growth, and dialectical method will study the tensions and lack of intelligibility introduced by the counterpositions. Moreover, Lonergan offers an argument that these four methods, taken together, are adequate to any investigation of proportionate being.' Tekippe, *Commentary*, 272

laid down at the beginning of the consideration of metaphysics *qua* science are those pertaining to distinctions. First, between the imagined and real, and then within the real between major (which pertains to things) and minor (which pertains to the components of things). Lonergan provides additional terminology within which distinctions can be stated, for example distinctions between the universal, the specific and the generic relating to individual things, species and genera, and between adequate distinctions (pertaining to distinctions between things) and inadequate distinctions (pertaining to distinctions between a thing and one of its components).

He develops this line of thought by reflecting on the nature of relations which he sums up thus: 'In this fashion we are brought to conceiving relations as involving two components: one component contains all the relativity of the relation, and it is necessary and permanent inasmuch as it is inseparable from its base in a thing of a determinate kind; the other component, however, is contingent; it is subject to variation in accord with successive schedules of probabilities in world process; but these variations change, not the primary component, but only the secondary determinations; they modify not the relative but the absolute.'[33]

Having established, then, the metaphysical elements and the parameters of their interrelation, Lonergan moves to the intrinsic intelligibility of being which flows from the definition of being as the objective of the pure desire to know, and receives concrete form in the threefold elements which correspond to the stages of intelligent knowing. Key to this operation, of course, is the transition in the human knower from the sensitive pattern of knowing to the intelligent pattern of knowing.

Lonergan at this point also adverts to the notion of metaphysical equivalence whereby the logical elements in a statement are paired with their metaphysical equivalents, thus allowing a control on the meaning of terms and helping to clarify the process of the integration of knowledge, a point which would seem to hold out definite possibilities for those engaged in the painstaking work of dialogue within the explanatory pattern of knowledge.

The two final points considered by Lonergan in this section are the unity of proportionate being and the unity of the human person. Lonergan introduces the unity of proportionate being by positing it in terms of the threefold

---

[33] Lonergan, *Insight*, 492. Here the term 'relative' seems to denote the abstractly conceived relation whilst 'absolute' denotes the actual occurrence of a given relation, governed by the various contingent factors that give rise to it.

metaphysical unity already mentioned and thus affirms a threefold unity within proportionate being itself. He states this point precisely, commenting:

> The unity of the universe of proportionate being is threefold: potential, formal and actual. Its actual unity is an immanent intelligible order, which we have found reason to identify with a generalized emergent probability. Its formal unity is constituted by its successive levels of conjugate forms which set up successive, intelligible fields. Its potential unity is grounded in conjugate prime potency, in the merely empirical conjunctions and successions that constitute the inexhaustible manifold of the merely coincidental that successive levels of forms and schemes bring under the intelligible control of system.[34]

Thus it is the same threefold structure that is invoked once again, driving home further the previously posited isomorphism between the knowing and the known.

At this point, Lonergan moves to consider the unity of man, which he sees as a unity of the material and the spiritual. He defines both in terms of intelligibility and further defines the spiritual as intelligibility which is itself intelligent, and material intelligibility as intelligibility which is not itself intelligent. The logical corollary of this is that the spiritual is independent of the material, though conditioned by it, for the spiritual comprises the material whereas the material does not comprise the spiritual.

In the final section of this chapter, that on metaphysics *qua* science, Lonergan sums up and draws out the implications of what he has been saying thus far. He reaffirms the centrality and all-pervasiveness of the notion of being and then reflects on the application of the metaphysical schema he has laid out in terms of clarification of claims made and the use of metaphysical structure to effect such clarification. He closes by summing up his position by speaking of humanity's existential situation in the following terms: 'If its confusion is to be replaced by intelligible order and its violence by reasonable affirmation, then the nucleus from which this process can begin must include an acknowledgement of detached inquiry and disinterested reflection, a rigorous unfolding of the implications of that acknowledgement, an acceptance not only of the metaphysics that constitutes that unfolding but also of the method that guides it between the Charybdis of asserting too little and the Scylla of asserting too much.'[35] While a number of points have been

---

[34] Lonergan, *Insight*, 510

[35] Lonergan, *Insight*, 529

adduced here, the central point to emerge in this section is that of the intrinsic intelligibility of being, defined as the object of the desire to know. This, coupled with the accompanying points about the correct functioning of this desire, leads into a consideration of metaphysics as dialectic in the next section.

1.2.5 Metaphysics as Dialectic

This section comprises a consideration of various forms of expression and their relation to truth, and, again seeking to tease out the implications of what has been posited, expands on the concept of truth and concludes by considering the implications of this. In many ways, the notion of metaphysics as dialectic can be stated in terms of forms of expression and the criterion of truth against which they are judged. The first issue examined is that of myth and mystery, and that against the backdrop of what Lonergan terms the 'known unknown'. The 'known unknown' is that to which knowledge is headed, and whilst its content it unknown, as we have seen in the examination of metaphysics as the integral heuristic structure of being, it can be anticipated in terms of, to use the metaphysical vocabulary Lonergan adopts, its form and act. Yet human consciousness is such that, as part of the heuristic structure, some way of relating to the 'known unknown' is required and this is provided by consciousness through the formation of images. Lonergan states this point by drawing attention to the different roles of images:

> The primary field of mystery and myth consists in the affect-laden images and names that have to do with the second sphere [that of the unknown]…so it will be well to distinguish between the image as image, the image as symbol, and the image as sign. The image as image is the sensible content as operative on the sensitive level; it is the image inasmuch as it functions within the psychic syndrome of associations, affects, exclamations, and articulated speech and actions. The image as symbol or as sign is the image as standing in correspondence with activities or elements on the intellectual level. But as symbol, the image is linked simply with the paradoxical 'known unknown'. As sign, the image is linked with some interpretation that offers to indicate the import of the image.[36]

In distinguishing between mystery and myth, Lonergan links myth with blind spots, and the interference of other desires with the pure desire to know,

---

[36] Lonergan, *Insight*, 533

citing anthropomorphic projection, which he views as the illegitimate coupling of emotion and insights, and the tendency to project one's own views onto others, coupling them with the reality of the views actually held by these others. Again, for Lonergan, this seems to boil down to a question of discrimination of knowledge and attention to the correct functioning of the cognitive process, a point he emphasises by drawing attention to the role of insight: 'Now I am no opponent of insight into the concrete presentations of one's own experience. But I would note that all the explaining is done by the insight and that, unless one distinguishes between the insight and the presentations, then one is open to the blunder of attributing an explanatory power to the presentations and even to associated feelings and emotions.'[37]

In a further emphasising of this point, mythic consciousness is contrasted with metaphysics *qua* the intelligent grasp of being as the object of the pure desire to know. Mystery, in contrast, is a case of dynamic images used within this latter context. Hence the issue is not the use of images, a necessity in relating to the known unknown, but rather a question of their use within the two different kinds of knowing.

Reflecting on this theme once again, Lonergan proposes, along with a proximate criterion of truth based on the grasp of the unconditioned, a remote criterion of truth contained in the correct unfolding of the desire to know.[38]

The formulation of the criterion of truth in terms of the unconditioned means that truth is independent of the individual subject, and this is taken a step further with the positing of ontological truth as a designation of the intelligibility intrinsic to being. This Lonergan states quite simply and clearly:

> The general theorem is, then, the identification with intrinsic intelligibility of
>
> 1 being,
> 2 unity,
> 3 truth in its ontological aspect, and, as will appear in the next chapter,
> 4 the good.[39]

There follows a reflection on the role of language and words in relation to truth, in which Lonergan discounts the view that words can refer only to

---

[37] Lonergan, *Insight*, 539

[38] Lonergan, *Insight*, 550

[39] Lonergan, *Insight*, 553

words and cites the possible as evidence that words are related to being grasped intelligently.

Finally, after a brief consideration of the types of interpretation, Lonergan sets forth his concept of a universal viewpoint in which all knowledge is dialectically ordered.

Lonergan defines this concept simply by stating: 'By a universal viewpoint will be meant a potential totality of generically and ordered viewpoints.'[40] This he bases on what he terms the protean notion of being defined as what is 'grasped intelligently and affirmed reasonably'.[41] Summing this up, he states:

> There is then a universe of meanings and its four dimensions are the full range of possible combinations
>
> 1. of experiences and lack of experience
> 2. of insights and lack of insights
> 3. of judgments and failures to judge, and
> 4. of the various orientations of the polymorphic consciousness of man.
>
> Now in the measure that one grasps the structure of this protean notion of being, one possesses the base and ground from which one can proceed to the content and context of every meaning.[42]

Commenting on this concept Tekippe points out that what we have in this concept of a universal viewpoint is 'simply the implication of a developed knowledge of the structure of cognition'.[43] Whilst allowing the universal viewpoint as a theoretical possibility, Tekippe cites a number of difficulties with Lonergan's thinking here. First, the notion that the sensitive and the emotional must be abstracted from in seeking to arrive at the universal perspective. Second, the inevitable historicity which Lonergan does not seem to take account of as something intrinsic. And third, the absence of information sufficient to allow what Lonergan is proposing here to take place in all cases. Tekippe draws attention to this difficulty, stating: 'Especially in interpreting ancient writers, there is simply not enough information about who they were and why they wrote, nor enough examples of their other writing, enough

---

[40] Lonergan, *Insight*, 564
[41] Lonergan, *Insight*, 567
[42] Lonergan, *Insight*, 567
[43] Tekippe, *Commentary*, 318

examples of their contemporaries' writing, and so of their intellectual context – to say with any great assurance what they meant.'[44]

Tekippe has a point here, and while Lonergan's universal viewpoint does still hold as a theoretical possibility, it is one very unlikely to be concretely attainable. It does, however, serve as a heuristic device to orientate the endeavour of human knowledge by proposing the concrete goal of relating all human knowledge together by dialectically ordering it. One is reminded of the words of Rabbi Tarfon in the Talmudic tractate Pirke Avot, who states: 'You are not expected to complete the work and yet you are not free to evade it.'[45]

As stated, Lonergan clearly sees the attainment of such a viewpoint in terms of dialectical ordering, though rather than dialectic as conceived with the aim of sublation in mind Lonergan states: 'Our development is both the accumulation of insights moving to higher viewpoints and the reversal of the aberrations that were brought about by the interference of alien desire.'[46] Thus the *terminus ad quem* proposed as the goal of such a dialectical process issues into an accumulation of higher insights leading to a higher viewpoint which embraces all of the relevant insights.

At this point Lonergan turns to a consideration of ethics, the most important of which in terms of this inquiry is his evolution of a notion of the good, though he also touches on the notions of human freedom and liberation. He bases his notion of the good and indeed of ethics in general on what he sees as the interpenetration of metaphysics and ethics, through the extension of the structure of the desire to know into the realm of action. Self-consistency emerges as a criterion of importance here.

The structure of knowing is paralleled with the structure of desire out of which Lonergan evolves a notion of the good in which what is considered good is considered so on the basis of an understanding of the objects of desire. He then extrapolates to the cosmic level on the principle of affirming of the whole what one affirms of the part, leading him to affirm a potential, a formal and an actual good:

The justification of this generalization of the notion of the good is that it is already implicit in the narrower notion. 'Objects of desire are manifold, but they are not an isolated manifold. They are existents and events that in their

---

[44] Tekippe, *Commentary*, 313

[45] Pirke Avot 2:16

[46] Lonergan, *Insight*, 422
This is linked to the concept of a 'moving viewpoint' applied by Lonergan to his own work in the introduction to *Insight*: *Insight* XXIII–VI

concrete possibility and in their realization are bound inextricably through natural laws and actual frequencies with the total manifold of the universe of proportionate being. If objects of desire are instances of the good because of the satisfactions they yield, then the rest of the manifold of existents and events also are a good, because desires are satisfied not in some dreamland but only in the concrete universe.[47]

Good, then, comes to be identified with the intelligible order of being, conceived in terms of the dual elements of intelligent order and rational being. He expresses this identification in distinction to the knower's emotional assessment of the good by saying: 'Accordingly, it will not be amiss to assert emphatically that the identification of being and the good by-passes human feelings and sentiments to take its stand exclusively upon intelligible order and rational value.'[48] After concluding this section with a brief excursus on freedom and liberation, Lonergan turns his attention to general and special transcendent knowledge in what may be considered the climax of his metaphysical analysis. This section has seen Lonergan's development of the concept of truth to include the formulation of his universal viewpoint, as well as his identification of being and goodness. This in turn sets the stage for a consideration of transcendence and the move from the consideration of proportionate being to his affirmation of God.

1.2.6 General and Special Transcendent Knowledge

The crux of this section of *Insight* lies in Lonergan's consideration of the contingency of proportionate being, something which he affirms on the basis of the isomorphism of the process of the knowing and the known. This in turn leads him to make the move to transcendent knowledge. Not surprisingly, the argument for general transcendent knowledge, defined as knowledge of transcendent being, begins with the idea of being itself. Transcendence is defined quite simply as a 'going beyond' and immanent transcendence is identified with the unrestricted desire to know. The desire to know is unrestricted as its object, being, is unrestricted as besides being there is nothing. The argument for transcendent knowledge hinges on the notion of the extrapolation from proportionate being to transcendent being, leading Lonergan to maintain that at least some elements of the idea of transcendent being will be verifiable.

---

[47] Lonergan, *Insight*, 605
[48] Lonergan, *Insight*, 606

The leap from proportionate being to transcendent occurs with the question, 'what is being?' As being is intelligible, it makes no sense to say that the question cannot be answered, to affirm that being simply 'is'. As a dynamic notion that 'unfolds through understanding and judgement, there can be formulated a heuristic notion of being as whatever is to be grasped intelligently and affirmed reasonably'.[49] Yet as an unrestricted concept, only an unrestricted act of understanding will be able to grasp it. Yet such a grasp, given the unrestricted nature of the idea of being, is something which is impossible for the finite human intellect. Hence the question 'what is being?', which demands of an answer *qua* that which is intelligible, can be defined only at one remove as 'the content of an unrestricted act of understanding'.[50]

Such an act of understanding would involve understanding everything about everything in which case it would also understand itself, and as intelligibility which is itself intelligent (because understanding itself), such an act of understanding would be spiritual.[51]

The primary component of such an act would, then, be the act's understanding of itself, and the secondary component would be its understanding of everything else through its understanding of itself. By its nature such an act would have certain properties intrinsic to it. These Lonergan logically sets forth, stating:

> Being is the objective of the unrestricted desire to know. Therefore, the idea of being is the content of an unrestricted act of understanding.
>
> Again, apart from being there is nothing. Therefore, the idea of being is the content of an act of understanding that leaves nothing to be understood, no further questions to be asked. But one cannot go beyond an act of understanding that leaves no questions to be asked, and so the idea of being is absolutely transcendent.
>
> Again, being is completely universal and completely concrete. Therefore, the idea of being is the content of an act of understanding that grasps everything about everything. Moreover, since that understanding leaves no questions to be asked, no part of its content can be implicit or obscure or indistinct.
>
> Again, being is intrinsically intelligible. Therefore, the idea of being is the idea of the total range of intelligibility.

---

[49] Lonergan, *Insight*, 642
[50] Lonergan, *Insight*, 643
[51] Cf. p XXX

Again, the good is identical with the intelligible. Therefore, the idea of being is the idea of the good.
Again, the unrestricted act of understanding is one act.[52]

The argument runs, then, that as being is intelligible, the question of what being is must admit of an answer. As a comprehensive notion encompassing all that is, the answer can only be given as the object of an unrestricted act of understanding. Therefore being is the object of an unrestricted act of understanding which, as understanding all that is, also understands itself. It is therefore an intelligibility which is itself intelligent and therefore it is spiritual.

Lonergan further bolsters this argument by examining the question of causality. In his account of finality in Chapter 15 he considers the elements of metaphysics (potency, form and act) in the context of the dynamism of the universe, with finality as the dynamism constantly driving or better drawing the development of the universe forward. These he here designates as internal causes as they are internal to proportionate being. Yet every instance of proportionate being affirmed through the grasp of the unconditioned is contingent for it depends on the fulfilment of conditions which themselves depend on conditions. Therefore proportionate being is not intelligible on its own, a point Lonergan emphasises:

> But proportionate being is being proportionate to our knowing, As our judgements rest on a grasp of the virtually unconditioned, so every proportionate being in its every aspect is a virtually unconditioned. As a matter of fact, it is, and so it is unconditioned. But it is unconditioned, not formally in the sense that it has no conditions whatever, but only virtually in the sense that its conditions happen to be fulfilled. To regard that happening as ultimate is to affirm a mere matter of fact without any explanation. To account for one happening by appealing to another is to change the topic without meeting the issue, for if the other happening is regarded as mere matter of fact without any explanation then either it is not being or else being is not the intelligible.[53]

Therefore, as proportionate being is not on its own intelligible yet being is that which is grasped intelligently and to which intelligibility is intrinsic, one can posit a transcendent being and do so in the context of external causes

---

[52] Lonergan, *Insight*, 644
[53] Lonergan, *Insight*, 653

– namely, exemplary, efficient and causal. Tekippe puts this point in more standard philosophical terminology: 'To present the material in a somewhat different way than Lonergan does, two principles appear to be involved in a proof of God's existence. The first is that the universe makes sense, to put it in non-technical language. The second is that finite being does not, by itself, make sense. When one meshes the two principles together, then one comes to the conclusion that finite being can only be explained by Infinite Being.'[54]

Equally, the order that lies within being, Lonergan maintains, cannot be simply stated as a matter of fact without lapsing into a counterposition in which being is no longer that which is intelligently grasped and thus has to be a rational choice. All of these arguments Lonergan pulls together to arrive at the affirmation of transcendent being, which in turn leads into a formal consideration of transcendent being itself, leading him to comment: 'But by asking what being is, already we have been led to the conclusion that the idea of being would be the content of an unrestricted act of understanding that primarily understood itself and consequently grasped every other intelligibility. Now, as will appear, our concept of an unrestricted act of understanding has a number of implications and, when they are worked out, it becomes manifest that it is one and the same thing to understand what being is and to understand what God is.'[55]

This section has concluded with the affirmation of Infinite Being. The following section seeks to articulate the characteristics of this Infinite Being based on what may be termed Lonergan's own version of *analogia entis*.

1.2.7 God

At this point in the inquiry, Lonergan further considers the metaphysical grounds for the affirmation of God and then seeks to establish what we can say about the characteristics of God *qua* Infinite Being on their basis. The basic principle in question in this section of Lonergan's investigation is that of the implications of affirming an unrestricted act of understanding which, as will be seen, corresponds in its characteristics to the classical conception of God. Drawing on the implications of what has already been said about the act of understanding, it follows that if there is an act of understanding, there is a corresponding object of such an act. The primary component in the unrestricted act of understanding has already been identified with the act itself, as in order to be unrestricted the act must grasp itself and in so doing grasp

---

[54] Tekippe, *Commentary*, 359
[55] Lonergan, *Insight*, 657

everything else. Therefore the primary intelligible is the act of understanding itself. As being is the objective of the desire to understand, the primary intelligible is the primary being. As good has already been identified with intelligible being, the primary being must also be the primary good. As the primary being is the objective of the unrestricted act of understanding, the primary being must be perfect, or the act of understanding would not grasp all that is and would not be unrestricted as there would be something of being which was lacking in this act and so was not understood in it.

Therefore the primary act is also the perfect act of loving and affirming truth.

Lonergan's teasing out of these implications then links up with what he had previously said about the primary being and causality as he deduces the unconditioned nature of the primary being: '…the primary being is unconditional. For the primary being is identical with the primary intelligible; and the primary intelligible must be unconditioned, for if it depended on anything else, it would not be self-explanatory. Finally, it is impossible for the primary intelligible to be completely independent and the primary being, identical with it, to be dependent on something else.'[56]

Equally, there can be only one primary being, for if there were more than one, they would differ from each other only empirically and consequently would not be self-explanatory which, as we have seen, the primary being must be. Further attributes are deduced: the primary being is simple, timeless, eternal, etc. A move similar to the previous move in ethics in which the structure of knowing being was extended into doing is made, as the primary being is posited as the 'omnipotent efficient cause';[57] this flows from the nature of the primary being as perfect, for if it were not possible that the primary being could ground all that is *qua* reality as well as *qua* object of thought, there would be a lack of perfection entailed, which would mean that the being in question could not be the primary being and some other being must be in reality the object of our investigation. Interestingly, though Lonergan, in the tradition of Aquinas, rejects Anselm's ontological argument for the existence of God, it does seem to keep appearing in his analysis in a way which corresponds to Lindbeck's definition of the cultural linguistic, namely as a regulative rule governing the correct use of religious language.[58] All in all Lonergan deduces twenty-six such attributes in this manner, including

---

[56] Lonergan, *Insight*, 659

[57] Lonergan, *Insight*, 661

[58] Cf. George A. Lindbeck, *The Nature of Doctrine: Religion and Theology in a Postliberal Age* (London: SPCK, 1984), 32–41

God as the exemplary cause of all that is, timeless, free, changeless, efficacious, creator, conserver and first agent of all that is.[59]

A particularly interesting move is the deduction of God's excellence and perfection as the cause of everything else. This argument proceeds again on the principle of the primary being as that which grounds everything else both as an object of thought and as reality, and the principle that what one affirms of any given part of reality one must ultimately affirm of all reality as any given part is dependent for its existence on a series of conditions which ultimately comprise reality as a whole. Lonergan expresses this relationship, stating: 'Inversely, then, the secondary intelligibles are intelligible because of the completeness of the primary; contingent beings are possible because of the perfection of primary being; and other instances of the good can arise because of the excellence of the primary good. But what is possible because of the perfection and excellence of another, also will be actual because of that perfection and excellence; and so God's perfection and excellence must be the final cause of everything else.'[60]

A further principle invoked in this development of the idea of God is that of the isomorphism with which Lonergan grounded his metaphysics of proportionate being. Just as the structure of knowing is isomorphic with the structure of being as the contents of what is known will correspond to the structure of the knowing, so here the move is from 'the contingent subject's unrestricted desire to know to the transcendent subject's unrestricted act of understanding'.[61]

At this point the notion of sin is introduced, not as a category extraneous to the logical development in hand but rather as a further logical development of it.

It has been established that God is the ground of the intelligible order in the universe and equally that being is that which is grasped intelligently by the unrestricted desire to know. Therefore action that is in accordance with being that is grasped intelligently is also action that is in accordance with and affirms the divine order of the world. Conversely, action which violates the intelligent grasp of being is a violation of the divine order of the world and hence is sin. Sin itself, therefore, is an absence of intelligibility, a point which Lonergan gives emphasis to, saying:

> In the first place, all that intelligence can grasp with respect to basic sins is that there is no intelligibility to be grasped. What is basic sin? It

---

[59] For a full treatment of these c.f. Lonergan, *Insight*, 658–669
[60] Lonergan, *Insight*, 665
[61] Lonergan, *Insight*, 679

is the irrational. Why does it occur? If there were a reason it would not be sin. There may be excuses; there may be extenuating circumstances; but there cannot be a reason, for basic sin consists, not in yielding to reasons and reasonableness, but in failing to yield to them; it consists not in inadvertent failure but in advertence to and in acknowledgement of obligation that, none the less, is not followed by reasonable response.[62]

Equally, sin has no cause: as sin is the failure to act in accordance with intelligent knowing it is devoid of intelligibility and therefore cannot be in any relation of 'intelligible dependence' on anything else, therefore it cannot have a cause. As such, God does not cause sin as sin by its nature is without any cause at all. Here Lonergan places his understanding of sin very clearly in the context of the Augustinian-Thomistic conception of evil as privation. To incorporate this understanding of sin into his metaphysics, Lonergan proposes a trichotomy: the being caused by God, absence of being, and what is not caused by God but permitted as a consequence of free will. Fundamentally, then, sin is without any intelligibility and there is nothing to be understood *in se*.

Lonergan then moves ahead to the question of the reality of the unrestricted act. Thus far he has considered the unrestricted act abstractly and teased out the logical consequences of affirming such an act in terms of the attributes which would pertain to it. Now he goes on to posit the unrestricted act as real on the basis of contingent being. The affirmation of truth, he states, rests on the grasp of the unconditioned, i.e. a proposition which is true as the conditions which would make it true are in fact fulfilled. The proposition here, i.e. that there is a necessary being, results from the contingence of proportionate being. Stating the case bluntly, Lonergan avers: 'If the real is completely intelligible, God exists. But the real is completely intelligible. Therefore, God exists.'[63]

Pointing out that his position coheres with that of Aristotle and Aquinas, and further locating his position in this particular lineage, Lonergan astutely points out that all of Aquinas' five ways for arriving at the existence of God also boil down to a consideration of the incompleteness of proportionate being, precisely the position that Lonergan deems himself to have been advancing.

Ultimately, Lonergan views his affirmation of God as real here in the same way in which he has viewed the other developments introduced in *Insight*:

---

[62] Lonergan, *Insight*, 667
[63] Lonergan, *Insight*, 672

simply as a teasing out of the logical implications of the ascertainable structure of human thinking: experience, insight and judgement.

At this point the transition is made from general transcendent knowledge which is knowledge of God to special transcendent knowledge which pertains to the solution to the problem of evil. The question is framed in terms of what God, as the author of all that is, does or has done about evil. As might be expected, the question of the nature of evil is dealt with in terms of the flight from knowledge, and yet a solution is affirmed as God exists and therefore the reality of evil must admit of further intelligibility. Such a solution will once again be a question of a higher manifold in which the problem of evil becomes a potential good as it is open to a solution which, as intelligible, will therefore be good and will be a part of the good of being which is willed by God.

Lonergan follows a similar methodology here to that followed in the last section and this time deduces a full thirty-one points. The principal contours of the solution as relevant to human consciousness lie in the heuristic anticipation of the solution as known to God. One of the most crucial points in the solution is that it must overcome the priority of living over learning, and that goodwill operative in this context is crucial to the solution. Basically the solution is based on the dialectical apprehension by human consciousness of the absence of intelligibility of evil and the returning of good for evil, thus bringing intelligibility into the situation and rendering it potential to a solution and thus a potential good. This Lonergan expresses by positing the role of love returned for evil as bringing what is evil into a situation of potentiality for good:

> Now the will can contribute to the solution of the problem of the social surd, inasmuch as it adopts a dialectical attitude that parallels the dialectical method of intellect. The dialectical method of intellect consists in grasping that the social surd neither is intelligible nor is to be treated as intelligible. The corresponding dialectical attitude of will is to return good for evil. For it is only inasmuch as men are willing to meet evil with good, to love their enemies, to pray for those that persecute and calumniate them, that the social surd is a potential good. It follows that love of God above all and in all so embraces the order of the universe as to love all men with a self-sacrificing love.[64]

---

[64] Lonergan, *Insight*, 699.

As the human being is a 'system on the move', repentance will provide the context for this returning of good for evil. Equally, the solution will entail hope as being based on the positions, as well as entailing a rejection of the despair of the counterpositions with their surrender of meaning and the hope of intelligibility.

Lonergan also includes a section on the nature of belief within this closing part of the book, but this will be considered here in the section comparing Lonergan's *Insight* with Newman's *Grammar of Assent*.

The solution proposed by Lonergan is given its clearest summary at the end of the section and is identified with the three traditional virtues of faith, hope and charity, after which he moves into the concluding epigraph of the book:

> It is a divinely sponsored collaboration in the transmission and application of the truths of the solution; it is a mystery in the threefold sense of psychic force, of sign, and of symbol; it moves from an initial emergent trend through a basic realization and consequent development to the attainment of an ulterior goal; it is operative through conjugate forms of faith, hope, and charity, that enable man to achieve sustained development on the human level inasmuch as they reverse the priority of living over the knowledge needed to guide life and over the good will needed to follow knowledge; it is a new and higher integration of human activity that, in any case, involves some transcendence of human ways and, possibly, complicates the dialectic by adding to the inner conflict between attachment and detachment in man the necessity of man's going quite beyond his humanity to save himself from disfiguring and distorting it.[65]

Thus, having considered the implications of affirming an unrestricted act of understanding which is identified as Infinite Being, and outlined what we can say about its characteristics, Lonergan considers sin and the solution to the problem of evil in the light of these considerations. The next section will look at the schema proposed by Lonergan up to this point, prior to moving ahead with its application in the rest of the text.

---

[65] Lonergan, *Insight*, 729

1.3 Insight – Some Preliminary Remarks

The epistemological system proposed thus far makes an impressive claim to completeness and has considerable strengths. Yet, as the following comments seek to show, there are weaknesses too, and the purpose of this section is to comment on both of these in preparation for putting Lonergan's system to work.

As Tekippe points out, Lonergan's analysis does not seek to ground human knowing in any way or indeed to establish its accuracy as yielding true knowledge of the world. Rather, it begins from human knowing as a given and points out that it is illogical to dispute the validity of human knowing as the very structures being disputed have of necessity to be invoked in order to launch such an attack. To be sure, grounding the analysis and consequent metaphysics in human knowing does have advantages. The structure of thought proposed by Lonergan certainly does seem to be indisputable (though with one caveat, which will be examined later) and is readily verifiable by anyone who becomes aware of their own thinking processes. Equally, such a common structure to human cognition should, in theory at least, be in a position to ground the desired interrelation of concepts and the work of rendering disparate discourses mutually intelligible, issues which would come into play in seeking to mutually interrelate Buddhism and Christianity.

A further strength is Lonergan's arrival at the concept of God. If one grants all the premises Lonergan proposes, and he makes a strong case for doing so, then the derivation of the concept of God is both tenable and defensible. Again, the invocation of proportionate being as leading logically to necessary being is also a strength in the analysis, and the coupling of this with what are shown to be the necessary consequences of the structure of human knowing seems to make for a very strong argument indeed.

The question of Lonergan's use of isomorphism does appear to pose certain difficulties, however. The isomorphism between knowing and being is posited on the grounds that the structure of what is known will correspond to what is known. This certainly seems to be something which can be affirmed of things as related to us, but the affirmation that it also refers to things as related to each other seems more problematic. Lonergan is surely correct in his affirmation of the structure of knowing as universal and ubiquitous, but this correspondingly means that were there a different structure pertaining to the relationship of things to each other, we would have no way of knowing it. Of course, as such, it could be dismissed as an academic question. Yet the question of how we know that the structure of things as related to us corresponds to the structure of things as related to each other remains. According to Lonergan's own criterion of truth, it is not enough simply to affirm the universality of the structure of knowing and our inevitable dependence on it, as the question of the grounds of affirming that the isomorphism can be extrapolated into the realm of things as related to each other remains a relevant question which cannot be answered, and therefore calls into question the truth of the insight affirmed.

A further weakness in Lonergan's analysis is his treatment of the unconscious. Though he does engage to some degree with depth psychology, even looking briefly at the thought of Freud and Jung, he does not adequately examine the question of how we know that the threefold structure of experience, insight and judgement also operates in the unconscious. The unconscious is not simply a particularly mysterious instance of the conscious mind, it is unconscious – radically unknown and only allowing of being inferred from the traces it leaves behind in conscious living. Yet its role in arriving at truth cannot simply be left out of the account. As Newman points out in his *Grammar of Assent*, the process of coming to affirm something as true and certain will most likely involve unconscious elements which may not correspond to Lonergan's threefold structure. Thus there may be other processes involved which cannot be accommodated by Lonergan's framework and which may be simply inescapable as elements in human knowing.

The two points above do not of themselves invalidate the veracity of what Lonergan is proposing here, though they do constitute lacunae within the framework in which he proposes it. It would seem that in order to affirm the truth of what Lonergan is saying, something more akin to Newman's illative sense would also have to come into play, though this may turn out to be the harbinger of further problems when the corresponding analysis is taken far enough. Having considered Lonergan's system as set forth in *Insight*, an initial attempt to test its viability will be made by applying it to a work that, itself, exercised a significant degree of influence on Lonergan, namely John Henry Newman's *Grammar of Assent*.

1.4 Newman's *Grammar of Assent*

1.4.1 Preliminary Considerations

Newman's *Grammar of Assent* was read by Lonergan and can be justifiably said to have exercised an influence on his thinking, despite the divergence of the two thinkers on various points. The methodology here will be to reconstruct Newman's argument and then to compare and contrast it with Lonergan's schema.

Newman's *Grammar*, in and of itself, constitutes an important moment in the ongoing enterprise of seeking to provide a ground and warrant for the act of faith which is, and always has been, central to Christianity. As has so often been the case, examination of this question leads beyond the ambit of the purely theological into wider considerations pertaining to human knowing in general. In an introduction written to the 1947 edition of Newman's *Grammar*, Charles Frederick Harold interestingly points out that Newman was very much aware of his ignorance of the vast body of metaphysical literature dealing with these questions.[66] Yet arguably it is this very factor which led to the originality of Newman's thinking and the distinctiveness of his contribution to the questions under consideration, an originality and distinctiveness which led Aldous Huxley to deem Newman's study of human cognition 'one of the most accurate, as it is certainly the most elegant, which has ever been made'.[67]

Newman bases his analysis of knowing around a series of distinctions and at the outset begins by drawing attention to the contrasting characteristics of assent and inference. For assent, understanding is needed; for inference, it is possible but not essential. Assent has an unconditional character to it, whereas inference is based on the conditional. Alongside this contrast he places the contrast between the real and the notional, correlating the former with assent and the latter with inference; crucially, assent is seen as pertaining to the *intrinsic* sense of a proposition rather than a sense bestowed on it by prior stages of a syllogism, something Newman articulates clearly, stating: 'By apprehension of a proposition, I mean, as I have already said, the interpretation of the terms of which it is composed. When we infer, we consider a proposition in relation to other propositions; when we assent to it, we consider it for its own sake and in its intrinsic sense.'[68]

Basically, in this analysis the real and the notional correspond to two types of thought, parallel to, though not corresponding with, Lonergan's two modes of thought. Both types arise in sense experience, but in one the experience is transformed by consciousness into an image, in the other into a notion, with real propositions pertaining to what is individual whilst notional

---

[66] John Henry Newman, *A Grammar of Assent* (New York: Longmans, Green and Co, 1947), xix

[67] Aldous Huxley, *Proper Studies* (London: Chatto & Windus, 1927), xix

[68] Newman, *Grammar*, 11

propositions abstract from individual being. Thus all thought has a mental object which is either an image or a notion.

Despite the correlation of assent with the real, however, assent can also be assent to notions (Newman will later cite assent to dogmas as an example of this) and inference can be inference of the real, though in both cases the respective forms of cognition may be deemed to be working in alien territory, a point supported by Newman's contention that:

> An act of inference indeed may be made with either of these modes of apprehension; so may an act of assent; but, when inferences are exercised on things, they tend to be conjectures or presentiments, without logical force; and when assents are exercised on notions, they tend to be mere assertions without any personal hold on them on the part of those who make them. If this be so, the paradox is true, that, when Inference is clearest, Assent may be least forcible, and, when Assent is most intense, Inference may be least distinct; – for, though acts of assent require previous acts of inference, they require them, not as adequate causes, but as *sine qua non* conditions; and, while the apprehension strengthens Assent, Inference often weakens the apprehension.[69]

Though Newman posits inference and assent as two distinctive modes of thought, he is careful not to separate them entirely and makes the point that inference is a necessary precursor to the act of assent not in the sense of causing it but rather in the sense of providing necessary conditions for it to take place, a relationship which becomes clearer later when he comes to examine the operation of the illative sense.

An example of notional assent comes in Newman's analysis of assent to mystery. A mystery is what we might term a compound proposition comprised of individual propositions and either involves what is impossible to conceive or entails an incompatibility between the individual propositions in which it consists.

It is possible to give real assent to the individual propositions that comprise a mystery, but we can only give notional assent to the mystery which together they comprise as, given the relationship between them is either inconceivable or involves seeming incompatibility, we can have no experience of the mystery itself as such.

At this point in the argument, Newman points out that credence, which he defines as the absence of doubt, corresponds to spontaneous assent, the

---

[69] Newman, *Grammar*, 32

occurrence of which in a mind constitutes the difference between the mind in its natural state and the mind which has been formed through education and the discourse named as civilisation. Developing this point further, opinion is designated the assent to the probability of a proposition, whilst credence is 'implicit assent to its truth'.[70] As opinion is assent to the abstract notion of the probability of a proposition's truth, it is notional rather than real.

The next crucial move in Newman's argument is his articulation of what he terms 'first principles'. Put simply, first principles are those principles from which one begins the reasoning process which cannot themselves be logically proved but upon whose acceptance all logical proof rests. First principles depend on abstraction from particular experiences and a trust in the reliability of the mental apparatus of human thought, a trust which Newman shares with Lonergan as being a necessary given if any reasoning is to take place at all and which he designates as being itself anterior to first principles.[71]

Reflecting on the nature of the abstraction through which first principles are arrived at, Newman states: 'These so-called first principles, I say, are really conclusions or abstractions from particular experiences; and an assent to their existence is not an assent to things or their images, but to notions, real assent being confined to the propositions directly embodying those experiences.'[72] Thus first principles also fall under the rubric of notional rather than real assent.

Reflecting further on real assent, the notion of imagination as a necessary ingredient in the reasoning process is introduced with the assertion that real assent is a case of assent to images left by things on the imagination. As dependent on these images, real assent is an intensely personal affair and by definition cannot be a communal activity as it depends on each individual consciousness taken individually.

At this point the source of real assent is located in the concatenation of factors which go to make up human consciousness, an act which will serve as the foundation for the formulation of illative sense later in the *Grammar*.

---

[70] Newman, *Grammar*, 46

[71] 'Our consciousness of self is prior to all questions of trust or assent. We act according to our nature, by means of ourselves, when we remember or reason. We are as little able to accept or reject our mental constitution, as our being. We have not the option; we can but misuse or mar its functions. We do not confront or bargain with ourselves; and therefore I cannot call the trustworthiness of the faculties of memory and reasoning one of our first principles.' Newman, *Grammar*, 47

[72] Newman, *Grammar*, 50

Newman emphasises this, saying: 'And in like manner that this or that person should have the particular experiences necessary for real assent on any point, that the Deist should become a Theist, the Erastian a Catholic, the Protectionist a Free-trader, the Conservative a Legitimist, the high Tory an out-and-out Democrat, are facts, each of which may be the result of a multitude of coincidences in one and the same individual, coincidences which we have no means of determining, and which, therefore, we may call accidents.'[73]

The parameters of assent and inference, and their correlation with the real and the notional, having been set forth, the focus will now move to a consideration of Newman's view of the relation between assent and religion.

1.4.2 Assent and Religion

The focus now turns to the role of assent in belief in God. At the outset of this consideration, Newman defines a dogma as a proposition which may designate either a thing or a notion, with real assent to dogma being a religious act and notional assent a theological act. It is faith in God, however, which is the fundament of belief in particular doctrines. This belief in God springs from a number of factors – creation, the analogy with the experience of human will as a causal factor, etc. But for Newman the principal source of belief in God lies in the experience of conscience, a reality Newman famously described as 'the aboriginal vicar of Christ'[74] and which he sees as, by its very nature, reaching beyond itself to a higher reality. Emphasising this, he states: 'But conscience does not repose on itself, but vaguely reaches forward to something beyond self, and dimly discerns a sanction higher than self for its decisions, as is evidenced in that keen sense of obligation and responsibility which informs them. And hence it is that we are accustomed to speak of conscience as a voice – a term which we should never think of applying to the sense of the beautiful; and moreover a voice, or the echo of a voice, imperative and constraining, like no other dictate in the whole of our experience.'[75] Developing this line of thought, he points out that the knowledge of God which emerges from the experience of conscience as the voice of God is similar in nature to other kinds of knowing, citing the innate ability

---

[73] Newman, *Grammar*, 65

[74] Newman, 'A Letter Addressed to the Duke of Norfolk on Occasion of Mr. Gladstone's Recent Expostulation', in *Certain Difficulties Felt by Anglicans in Catholic Teaching Vol. 2*, 248, accessed 2 September 2013, http://www.newmanreader.org/works/anglicans/volume2/gladstone/index.html

[75] Newman, *Grammar*, 82

to distinguish whole entities apart from the plethora of sense data which we experience as the underlying principle of this.

Newman next turns his attention to the nature of belief in mystery and begins by asserting that real assent to a mystery is not possible. This stems from his formulation of mystery as involving, among other things, an apparent contradiction in the principles which comprise it. Citing the doctrine of the Trinity as an example, he avers that one can give real assent only to the various propositions which comprise it, but once they are interrelated and constitute a mystery, by definition only notional assent is possible.

The role of assent having been considered, the following section will move to a more precise consideration of what Newman sees as being involved in assent as a noetic category.

1.4.3 The Nature of Assent

The focus now shifts to a more in-depth analysis of the precise nature of assent and in this regard a number of points are made. First, in a move similar to Lonergan's characterisation of the force of the unconditioned on the human mind, Newman affirms that a conclusive argument in which a truth is demonstrated has an inexorable force over our assent: 'I allow then as much as this, that, when an argument is in itself and by itself conclusive of a truth, it has by a law of our nature the same command over our assent, or rather the truth which it has reached has the same command, as our senses have. Certainly our intellectual nature is under laws, and the correlative of ascertained truth is unreserved assent.'[76]

A further distinction is then introduced between simple and complex assent, with simple assent happening spontaneously and complex assent involving a threefold structure which begins with simple assent, followed by consciously rehearsing the argument upon which the simple assent is based and ending by assenting to the initial simple assent. As part of this analysis, a distinction is also posited between truth and conclusiveness, a distinction which can be located within Newman's affirmation of the insufficiency of syllogistic reasoning and its ultimate dependence on first principles in contrast to what is entailed in full assent. The result of complex assent is seen as certainty and this results from the reflexive awareness of knowing that one knows a truth, something Newman affirms in emphatic terms: 'Certitude, as I have said, is the perception of a truth with the perception that it is a truth, or the consciousness of knowing, as expressed in the phrase, "I know that

---

[76] Newman, *Grammar*, 128

I know," or "I know that I know that I know," or simply "I know;" for one reflex assertion of the mind about self sums up the series of self-consciousnesses without the need of any actual evolution of them.'[77]

Whilst simple assent can yield what is termed here material or interpretive certitude, full certitude is attendant only upon the reflex act of assent to assent, which, as such, is by nature always notional. Certitude, whilst indefectible, is however, relevant to individual propositions and thus is not to be confused with infallibility as an attribute. Summarising his thought on the topic of assent, Newman affirms that there are three conditions for certitude: 'It seems then that on the whole there are three conditions of certitude: that it follows on investigation and proof, that it is accompanied by a specific sense of intellectual satisfaction and repose, and that it is irreversible. If the assent is made without rational grounds, it is a rash judgment, a fancy, or a prejudice; if without the sense of finality, it is scarcely more than an inference; if without permanence, it is a mere conviction.'[78]

The process by which we arrive at certainty is seen as possessed of a penumbral and indistinct character and rather than stemming from the processes of formal logic, it results more from the cumulative effect of principles on the mind, much of whose operation is not conscious. It is also a characteristic of this kind of certainty that, whilst absolute, it does not admit of logical criteria which can demonstrate the veracity of the assurance attained. As an example of this Newman cites our knowledge that we will die. We know at most that everyone not now living has died before us, but logically we cannot prove with certainty that the process will be repeated in us. Yet the cumulative effect of the accounts of the human experience of death along with our direct experience of the deaths of people close to us leads us to the certainty that ultimately we too will die. It is a certainty which remains logically indemonstrable as much as it is certain. Germane to this kind of knowing is the tendency of the human mind to grasp truth as a whole rather than in its individual parts. Equally, the process of arriving at truth is an individual affair which is existentially determined and is affected by elements such as the integrity of a given interlocutor and the formation of the relevant mental images within us in the process of seeking truth. Ultimately, then, more than anything else, truth can be seen as a matter of convergence. This noetic process leads in the following section to a consideration of Newman's illative sense, in which the foregoing considerations are condensed and set forth in a unified fashion.

---

[77] Newman, *Grammar*, 149

[78] Newman, *Grammar*, 195

1.4.4 The Illative Sense

All of these arguments are synthesised in Newman's formulation of the illative sense which is defined as the branch of judgement dealing with 'right judgment in ratiocination'.[79] He prefaces his examination of the illative sense by positing as a foundation for it the observable fact of the occurrence of certainty within human cognition. Like Lonergan, he also reiterates with emphasis that the human faculties themselves are the *sine qua non* of all thought and it is futile to seek to ground them as they are themselves what makes the grounding of anything possible:

> What is left to us but to take things as they are, and to resign ourselves to what we find? That is, instead of devising, what cannot be, some sufficient science of reasoning, which may compel certitude in concrete conclusions, to confess that there is no ultimate test of truth besides the testimony borne to truth by the mind itself, and that this phenomenon, perplexing as we may find it, is a normal and inevitable characteristic of the mental constitution of a being like man on a stage such as the world. His progress is a living growth, not a mechanism; and its instruments are mental acts, not the formulas and contrivances of language.[80]

As well as this, a theological import is given to the laws of the mind as a manifestation of God's will. The illative sense itself is deemed a surd of the mind and the ultimate arbiter in matters of truth, and this applies also to the first principles upon which all processes of thought are based. The role of logic is seen as that of providing some manner of common discourse between individuals, and in his approach to these questions Newman clearly locates himself among those who would assign to logic a central epistemological role.

Turning to the question of absolute truth in the context of differences of opinion, Newman asserts that the possibility of absolute truth is in no way disproved because it is not universally held, and that more than merely circumstantial differences are involved in differences of belief. In terms of theological claims, he further ups the ante by claiming that the truths of Christianity are divinely guarantored and so occupy a *sui generis* place within competing truth claims. As with other branches of knowledge, inference and assent in religion are both personal and individual and the primary ground

---

[79] Newman, *Grammar*, 260
[80] Newman, *Grammar*, 266

of these is a person's own reasons, with the assent of others functioning as a secondary ground.

Again returning to the point made above in relation to certainty, Newman states that affirming the truth of Christianity is akin to the affirmation that I was born. There is no strictly logical proof for either and yet the force of the certainty generated does not suffer any diminution as a result. He concludes this section by pointing out that, generally speaking, people do not differ in their use of logic but rather do so in the first principles upon which their reasoning is based. Having concluded this consideration of Newman's *Grammar*, an attempt will be made to apply Lonergan's categories to it as an initial test of the viability of Lonergan's epistemological structure.

1.5 Lonergan and Newman: Convergence and Contrast

The aim at this point will be to parse Newman's opus in Lonerganian terms, but prior to this the points of convergence and contrast will be noted. As is widely known, Lonergan read Newman early on in his career[81] and yet the relationship between the schema proposed in *Insight* and that proposed by Newman is not one that Lonergan engages with in *Insight* despite his readiness to engage with a range of other thinkers. Certainly there are points of similarity in both thinkers. Both distrust logic based on syllogism as an adequate means of arriving at truth. Both also base their epistemology on the foundation of experience. And just as Lonergan says that the grasp of the virtually unconditional commands absolute assent in its truth, Newman makes similar claims for assent, complex assent in particular.

Both thinkers can also be located very firmly among those who affirm the operations of the mind as a solid epistemological base, though here their divergence becomes apparent. For Newman, the foundations of knowledge lie within the first principles assented to through the operation of the illative sense. For Lonergan, it is the observable structure of human cognition which comes about in the self-affirmation of the knower which is the foundation of knowledge. Yet the conflict between the two, on this particular point at any rate, is not one that is of necessity irreconcilable. There is no *a priori* reason that the functioning of the illative sense may not also operate according to the threefold structure Lonergan proposes. Part of the problem, however, is the penumbral quality of the illative sense as defined by Newman

---

[81] Bernard Lonergan, 'Reality, Myth, Symbol', in Alan M. Olson (ed.) *Myth, Symbol, and Reality* (Notre Dame, IN: University of Notre Dame Press, 1980), 32–33

and the involvement of unconscious factors within it. Thus we may say that it is possible that the illative sense admits of being accommodated within Lonergan's framework, though we are still a step away from saying that this actually is the case.

The crux of the problem may be seen to lie in the role of the unconscious mind in knowing. This is of course a topic that Lonergan does discuss in *Insight*, but as we have seen, he seems to take insufficient account of the mysteriousness and unknown nature of the unconscious mind. Yet even a cursory glance at the findings of depth psychology leads to the logical conclusion that the unconscious does indeed have a role in knowing, a fact which, with notable prescience, Newman recognised in advance of the advent of Freud and the 'birth' of the unconscious. Here, then, it would seem that Newman's illative sense must be placed outside the threefold structure proposed by Lonergan which begins in consciousness with the self-affirmation of the knower. Yet Lonergan does define knowing as experience, insight and judgement which are conscious, hence positing reflexivity and awareness as constituent elements of the process. As a phenomenon which is experienced and yet not consciously understood, the operation of the illative sense can justifiably be placed in the category of experience, with the reflection on its nature in the category of insight. This is not to deny that there are realms within human consciousness that we cannot directly grasp, but rather to say that we can experience this to be the case and can posit these realms as operational in knowing (as Newman does) and thus come to a judgement about the structure of this knowing. The conflict, then, is one which admits of resolution and leads back again to the reflexive nature of conscious knowing expressed in Lonergan's threefold structure. A further example is the voice of conscience, which is the mainstay of Newman's affirmation of God. In Lonergan's framework, such a voice belongs within experience and the reflections and conclusions drawn from this experience within insight and judgement.

A similar state of affairs pertains in relation to the categories of the notional and the real. Again there is no direct correlation in Lonergan's thought, yet both categories are statements affirming something about the contents of knowing and as such constitute integrating insights which grasp a relationship between the occurrence of the mind's contents and objective reality. Hence they belong in the second of the three categories, namely that of insight.

Overall, the solution to the divergence of the epistemology of the two thinkers lies in Lonergan's distinction between the two kinds of knowing, with the experience in question that of the operation of the mind. Newman draws attention to and expresses the phenomena that constitute human knowing. This is similar to Lonergan's 'knowing-as-taking-a-look' as Newman does not go beyond description of mental phenomena, the accuracy of his description notwithstanding; Lonergan, in contrast to this, seeks to categorise and interrelate these disparate phenomena. One may say that Newman is concerned with giving expression to the content of the process of knowing whereas Lonergan focuses on the structure of the process – Newman delineates what happens in each stage of the structure, Lonergan posits the structure itself. As such, the thought of Newman does not contradict or invalidate the framework proposed by Lonergan and actually one serves to complement the other, with Newman's thought providing greater insight into what happens within the three stages of the process. Thus Lonergan's model proves adequate as an analytical framework for the analysis proposed in Newman's *Grammar of Assent*.

1.6 Lonergan's Structure of Knowing and Interfaith Dialogue

Having ascertained that Lonergan's framework does not fall at the first hurdle, so to speak, but does appear to be able to integrate a very different style of thought into its analysis, the question becomes what role this framework could play in the bigger questions raised by Buddhist–Christian dialogue. As already stated, the aim of this enquiry will be, first, to establish whether Lonergan's framework can function as an integrative framework in Buddhist–Christian dialogue, and second, if this does prove to be the case, what does the relationship between the two faiths look like in the light of such an integration?

The next steps will be to examine whether Lonergan's framework can successfully accommodate a systematic exposition of the fundamental claims of Christianity and Buddhism – this will be done by looking at the thought of a significant thinker from each religion (Chapters 2 and 3). Lonergan's method will then be used to attempt to interrelate the two positions on the basis of the dialectical method he proposes. This will involve retracing the three stages by which truth is grasped, i.e. experience, insight and judgement, and checking whether the process has operated correctly or whether it has admitted of distortions to the knowing process. If his method fails to integrate these thinkers and issues, attention will be given to wherein lies the method's defect, whether this defect can be overcome, and what it tells us both about Lonergan's thought and about the thinkers and issues under consideration. If it proves successful, then the conclusion will seek to adumbrate the possible implications Lonergan's schema may have for interfaith dialogue and delineate possible avenues of enquiry for future research. A second question will be that of relating divergent judgements by seeing whether one set already encompasses the other, whether a higher integration exists that may encompass both, or whether the only solution is an inverse insight affirming complete incommensurability.

2 Karl Rahner's *Foundations of Christian Faith*: A Lonerganian Analysis

2.1 Preliminary Remarks

As is clear from Lonergan's own view of the epistemology he proposes in *Insight*, the aim of his project is to formulate what, according to him, is the underlying structure of all knowing and hence to provide an epistemology which leaves nothing beyond its scope. It logically follows from this that such an epistemology, if valid, by explicitly formulating the underlying structure of knowing would provide an integrative frame for disparate positions which are opposed, or at least appear to be so, in their arguments and conclusions. This would be so, as any such epistemology would enable us to compare different positions and rule on the disagreements between them by assessing in which stage of the reasoning process a given thinker has gone astray or committed an omission. Such a view is logically demanded by a framework which claims to give an accurate delineation of the process through which *all* positions are arrived at and, moreover, makes the claim that it is the same process which is found in all instances of logical reasoning. Quite simply, if two conflicting positions using the same knowing process arrive at different conclusions, then either they are not actually in conflict, appearances notwithstanding, one of them has failed to be completely logically consistent, or it is an instance of what Lonergan terms an inverse insight where the insight is that of the absence of expected intelligibility.

This chapter tests this theoretical position by reconstructing the theology proposed by Karl Rahner in his *Foundations of Christian Faith* and then analysing the moves Rahner makes in terms of Lonergan's metaphysical method. The following chapter will do the same for Nāgārjuna's *Mūlamadhyamakakārikā*, and Chapter Four will attempt to interrelate dialectically the two above-mentioned works according to Lonergan's metaphysical method.

2.2 Rahner – *Foundations of Christian Faith*

Published in 1976, Rahner intended his *Foundations* as an introduction to the idea of Christianity and it is, arguably, the closest he ever got to writing a systematic theology. The book itself is divided into an introduction and nine chapters and closes with a short epilogue. Accordingly, the following reconstruction will be ordered according to Rahner's own chapter headings and will thus be organised into ten sections: one corresponding to the introduction, and one corresponding to each of the nine chapters, with an appendix corresponding to the creedal section at the end of the book.

2.2.1 Introduction

In the introduction to the work Rahner situates what is to follow in the context of Christian existence as it is in fact, and asserts that his method will be one which will seek to integrate philosophy and theology. Yet, as Karen Kilby points out, this should not be taken as an attempt to justify the claims of Christian faith on the basis of criteria that are exterior to it:

> *Foundations of Christian Faith* is best interpreted as a work of theology from start to finish, which in fact contains *no* independent philosophy. Many of Rahner's comments only make sense in this light. It is because *Foundations of Christian Faith* is a work of theology through and through that Rahner can affirm from the beginning of the volume that "[w]e are presupposing here the existence of our own personal Christian faith in its normal ecclesial form, and we are trying…to reach an *idea* of this" and it is because it is *not* a question of even partially justifying Christianity by an independent philosophy that he can describe his aim "to give people confidence from the very *content* of Christian dogma itself that they can believe with intellectual honesty."[1]

As will become apparent, then, the integration that he seeks is precisely that: a coherence of philosophy and theology rather than any attempt to establish theology on the basis of a relationship of dependence on philosophy.

He draws these elements together by positing human self-interpretation as the beginning of the theological task and thus introduces anthropology as a category which will be fundamental to his schema. He further provides

---

[1] Karen Kilby, *Karl Rahner: Theology and Philosophy*, (London: Routledge, 2004), 79

a structure for what is to follow by setting out the three steps according to which his introduction will proceed:

1. Reflection on the human person 'as the universal question which he is for himself'.
2. Reflection on 'transcendental and historical conditions which make revelation possible' within the parameters given as a result of the first step.
3. Reflection on 'the fundamental assertion of Christianity as the answer to the question which man is... hence we must do theology'.[2]

A particularly interesting point made in the introduction is the assertion that Rahner seeks to provide confidence in Christianity from the content of its dogmas, along with the further assertion that a mystery is not to be erroneously thought of as something which is simply unintelligible, a point he underlines by reflecting on human existence itself as mystery. Introducing an additional theme which will occur subsequently in the book, Rahner identifies God's self-communication in the depths of human existence with grace, and the divine self-communication in history with Christ. In the third section of the Introduction, Rahner turns his attention to reflecting on some epistemological problems, a section which he opens by considering the relation that pertains between concepts and reality and between reflection and self-reflection. Having been at pains earlier to distinguish reality from reflection upon it, he sharpens this line of thought by noting that the unity between reality and the self-presence of reality to itself in human consciousness is more than the unity which can be found between reality and concept, and that this former unity can never be entirely mediated by concepts.

Reflecting further on the necessary orientating of language to foundational experience, he places his approach within what Lindbeck describes as a synthesis between the experiential-expressivist and cognitive-propositional approaches,[3] though as will be seen, this in no way derogates from the propositional truth which can be thus derived in Rahner's view. Having made these points, Rahner now arrives at the nub of his theological approach. He states that Christian doctrines are to be understood as reflexive and explicit formulations of what has already been experienced in the existential depths of human life: '...we should show again and again that all these theological

---

[2] Karl Rahner, *Foundations of Christian Faith: An Introduction to the Idea of Christianity* (London: Darton, Longman & Todd, 1978), 11ff.
[3] C.f. Lindbeck, *The Nature of Doctrine*, 16

concepts do not make the reality itself present to man from outside of him, but they are rather more originally in the depths of existence.'[4]

Logically following on from this assertion, Rahner goes on to look at the fundamental existential dimensions of human existence. He draws attention to the self-possession which takes place as part of all knowing and defines human beings as 'pure openness':

> If we ask what the a priori structures of this self-possession are, then we must say that, without prejudice to the mediation of this self-possession by the experience of sense objects in time and space, this subject is fundamentally and by its very nature pure openness for absolutely everything, for being as such. This is shown by the fact that the denial of such an unlimited openness of the spirit to absolutely everything implicitly posits and affirms such openness. For a subject which knows itself to be finite, and in its knowledge is not just unknowing with regard to the limited nature of the possibility of its objects, has already transcended its finiteness. It has differentiated itself as finite from a subjectively and unthematically given horizon of possible objects that is of infinite breadth.[5]

The similarity between this formulation and Lonergan's notion of being as 'the objective of the pure desire to know'[6] is immediately striking.

These reflections issue in Rahner's definition of transcendental experience: 'We shall call *transcendental experience* the subjective, unthematic, necessary and unfailing consciousness of the knowing subject that is co-present in every spiritual act of knowledge, and the subject's openness to the unlimited expanse of all possible reality.'[7]

It is these components of transcendental experience which will provide the foundation of everything else which is to follow in the book, and again the similarity with Lonergan is clear as Rahner too seeks to run a Kantian gauntlet in the sense of seeking to affirm objective truths by basing them on the transcendental elements of the mind, and locates the foundation of knowledge in human knowing itself.

---

[4] Rahner, *Foundations*, 17
[5] Rahner, *Foundations*, 19
[6] Lonergan, *Insight*, 348
[7] Rahner, *Foundations*, 20

2.2.2 Chapter I The Hearer of the Message

Having thus laid his foundations, Rahner moves to consider the human being as the person who is the recipient of God's self-communication. He begins by developing the notion that what we have in Christianity is a reflexive articulation of what human existence actually is at its deepest level. Accordingly, philosophy, theology and anthropology are grouped together as the necessary components which such a reflection will entail. This move on Rahner's part is particularly interesting in the light of current debates between inclusivism and pluralism, and is one which does not seem to have significantly influenced the debate as yet.

Personhood is defined as comprising the three elements of human beings' self-presence to themselves, namely their unreflective awareness of the infinite horizon in every act of knowing, their responsibility for themselves and the fact that human beings cannot be derived. The important point is also made that 'the object of such a transcendental experience does not appear in its own reality when man is dealing with something individual and definable in an objective way, but when in such a process he is *being* subject and not dealing with a "subject" in an objective way'.[8]

Rahner then asserts that 'Man experiences himself as infinite possibility because in practice and in theory he necessarily places every sought after result in question'.[9]

This is a factor that, for Rahner, has implications both for the affirmation of God which he will make and for his evolutionary view of Christology. The crucial point to note at this stage, however, is the link between the presence to self in the human subject and the experience of transcendence this involves. Commenting on this, William Dych situates Rahner's thought in the context of transcendental Thomism: 'For, again with Maréchal, he finds in the self-presence of the human knower not a static presence, but an openness and a dynamism, a drive or a desire that reaches out beyond the actual object known to a larger horizon, indeed, an unlimited horizon. The world of our experience and our sense intuition, the thematic content of our knowledge, is always encompassed by this larger horizon of which we are also aware and which forms the unthematic content of our knowledge.'[10]

Rahner goes on, then, to posit humans as constituted as subjects by their experience of the infinite horizon encountered in the transcendental

---

[8] Rahner, *Foundations*, 31
[9] Rahner, *Foundations*, 32
[10] William V Dych SJ, *Karl Rahner* (London: Geoffrey Chapman, 1992), 43

component of subjectivity which he will later identify with God: 'But man is and remains a transcendent being, that is, he is that existent to whom the silent and uncontrollable infinity of reality is always present as mystery. This makes man totally open to this mystery and precisely in this way he becomes conscious of himself as person and subject.'[11]

Further elements of the human being as a transcendent being are formulated in the assertion of the person as both free and responsible for themselves. Rahner is, however, careful to assert that 'when freedom is really understood, it is not the power to be able to do this or that, but the power to decide about oneself and to actualise oneself'.[12]

The question of man's eternity is then introduced, with eternity viewed as freedom existing in its ultimate validity beyond time, a consideration which means that man's determination of his own destiny is, in the final analysis, a question of salvation. In addition, the prior assertion of Christian teaching as an explicit formulating of the conditions of human existence is sharpened in the assertion that Christianity addresses the human being in the transcendental elements of her experience. Moreover, historicity is posited as something that is intrinsic to man *qua* a historical being.

Chapter I closes with the assertion of man as a being who is dependent and whose origin and ultimate fate are hidden from him, a state of affairs that Rahner sums up simply and movingly by asserting of man that 'he comes to the real truth about himself precisely by the fact that he patiently endures and accepts this knowledge that his own reality is not in his hands'.[13] With this reflection on the nature of human existence, Rahner moves to consider the human being in relation to Absolute Mystery in the following chapter.

2.2.3 Chapter II Man in the Presence of Absolute Mystery[14]

Earlier, Rahner has spoken about the orientation towards mystery and here he expatiates on this theme and affirms that it is the Absolute Mystery towards which we are orientated that actually constitutes us as beings. It is this transcendence in man orientated towards Absolute Mystery that provides the foundation of human knowledge of God: 'At this point theology and anthropology necessarily become one. A person knows explicitly what is meant

---

[11] Rahner, *Foundations*, 35

[12] Rahner, *Foundations*, 38

[13] Rahner, *Foundations*, 43

[14] The chapter titles given are those used in the English translation of the *Foundations* and it is this factor which governs the use of 'man' where humanity is intended.

by "God" only insofar as he allows his transcendence beyond everything objectively identifiable to enter into his consciousness, accepts it, and objectifies in reflection what is already present in his transcendentality.'[15] Thus God is the infinite horizon against which categorical knowledge is possible and an implicit unformulated knowledge of God is present in every act of categorical knowing.

In an interesting development of this line of thinking, Rahner asserts that it is only in the objectifying of this transcendental knowledge in the word God that the objectification of all that is categorical, i.e. the totality of human existence, and all that humans are can take place: hence only in using the word God can man take responsibility for his existence. It is useful to note that, as Kilby points out, Rahner uses the word transcendental both in the sense of the necessary conditions which exist for knowing to take place and in the more usual sense of a 'going beyond' what is given: 'One way to put this is that Rahner employs the term transcendental in both a formal sense – to refer to the conditions of the possibility of experience, knowledge, action, and the kinds of investigation which uncover such conditions – and a material one – to refer to a movement or openness in us which reaches out beyond all that is finite. If you follow the formal procedure, however, according to Rahner, what you in fact discover – or one of the things you discover – is the material transcendence.'[16]

The objectification of the totality of all that is when the word 'God' is used also has the effect of objectifying language as the *modus* through which reality is present to us. As such a *modus*, and one that can take place only against the transcendental horizon, language, like the human subject, is constituted by God as this horizon.

In terms of the experience of human transcendentality as the ground of knowledge of God, Rahner cites our free acceptance of our orientation towards Absolute Mystery, and ultimately of the mystery itself, as that which establishes this transcendentality as a knowledge of God: 'But in order to remain true, all metaphysical ontology about God must return again and again to its source, must return to the transcendental experience of our orientation towards the Absolute Mystery, and to the existentiell practice of accepting this orientation freely. This acceptance takes place in unconditional obedience to conscience, and in the open and trusting acceptance of the uncontrollable in one's own existence in moments of prayer and quiet silence.'[17]

---

[15] Rahner, *Foundations*, 44
[16] Kilby, *Karl Rahner: Theology and Philosophy*, 34
[17] Rahner, *Foundations*, 54

The nature of human knowledge of the divine is named in terms of the *a posteriori* knowledge of God resulting from reflection on the transcendental element of human consciousness, divine self-disclosure in revelation and divine salvific activity in history.

In considering the as yet unthematic knowledge of God that Rahner puts forward here, it is important to bear in mind the distinction between his concept of knowledge and what he sees as the prevailing modern view. Dych sums this up, stating: 'To deepen our understanding of knowledge as including more than "the power of comprehending, of gaining mastery and subjugating", knowledge must be understood more fundamentally precisely as that wherein we stand before what is incomprehensible, as the "capacity to be grasped" by what lies always beyond us, or in the terminology of Aquinas, "as the capacity of excessus, of going out into the inaccessible".'[18] The import of all that has been argued until now comes in the assertion of the unity between the term of transcendence and transcendence itself in a 'unity between that which grounds and disposes freely and that which is grounded'.[19] Thus God and humanity are in union to begin with, a principle which will have far-reaching implications for the rest of Rahner's theology.

In line with the identification between God and the Absolute Mystery that is the transcendental horizon, Rahner points out that God ultimately cannot be directly named and that a further consequence of this identification is the logical mistake of thinking of God as one existent alongside another existent, a mistake which renders both naïve theism and atheism erroneous. Equally, the Holy Mystery is that which disposes, not that which it is in our power to dispose of, as we are constituted by it.

At this point Rahner adds love to freedom and willing as an experience of transcendence: just as presence to ourselves takes place against the background of the transcendental horizon, so too does presence to another person and 'for a subject who is present to himself to affirm freely vis-à-vis another subject means ultimately to love'.[20] Hence this transcendence is also the source of love in the subjects which it constitutes.

In this sense we can speak of the self-disclosure of Holy Mystery in the experience of transcendence – as that which constitutes us as subjects in freedom, willing and love, the Holy Mystery is free, exercises will and is loving. All of this is summed up succinctly in the formulation of the connection between the necessary conditions of our transcendence and the reality of the

---

[18] Dych, *Karl Rahner*, 19

[19] Rahner, *Foundations*, 58

[20] Rahner, *Foundations*, 65

term of this transcendence: 'The affirmation of the reality of the Absolute Mystery is grounded for us, who are finite spirits, in the necessity with which the actualisation of transcendence as our own act is given for us.'[21]

As the necessary condition of our own transcendence, we are always involved with the Holy Mystery whether we know it or not, whenever our transcendence is actualised in knowing, willing, the exercise of freedom, or in love. Equally, as finite being, man is unable to identify himself with the horizon which presents itself as infinite.

Like Lonergan, Rahner affirms all the traditional arguments for the existence of God as simply the making explicit of this relationship between absolute and finite being. This relationship and its presence to the subject he names as the principle of metaphysical causality.

Rahner then turns his attention to the conditions of speaking about God in language. As we can experience God only through secondary categorical realities, any statement about God is a statement which originates in the categorical and yet seeks to refer to the Absolute. Yet despite this linguistic distance, as subjects constituted by the transcendental horizon in our innermost being, there is a sense in which the analogous statement signifies 'what is most basic and original in our knowledge'.[22]

In an interesting furthering of this principle, Rahner sees human beings as also constituted analogously insofar as it is the transcendental horizon which constitutes us but is never immediately or directly apparent to us, but directs us towards categorical realities which serve to mediate it to us. In this sense he speaks of 'the self-communication of God to man in grace as the transcendental constitution of man'.[23]

Reflecting further on the human experience of finding our being given to us from another, the point is made that this other is sensed by us to be personal and not to be confused with an impersonal source. Again, the meaning of this constitution by a transcendent other is experienced by us in the process of transcendence itself. Creation is not, therefore, a moment in time but rather establishes time and that which is created and is their foundation. Creatures are called to live in this tension of analogy, in which we are free and responsible for ourselves, but are so before the Absolute Mystery which constitutes us and towards which we are oriented as our future. This Absolute Mystery is present to us through finite reality and is always mediated even, as in the most immediate experiences of God, when it is the finite subject's

---

[21] Rahner, *Foundations*, 67
[22] Rahner, *Foundations*, 72, C.f. Dych, *Karl Rahner*, 66
[23] Rahner, *Foundations*, 73

experience of herself which is the mediation. Such immediacy does not destroy human autonomy but rather constitutes human fulfilment and fullness, and human autonomy, far from being destroyed, is 'at once both the presupposition and the consequence of this absolute immediacy to God and from God'.[24]

All experience of God, then, though mediated through the categorical, is itself transcendental. God is present to us, however as 'absolute and forgiving closeness'[25] offered to us not of necessity, but by grace and the divine self-disclosure in freedom. Specific interventions of God are no more than 'the becoming historical and becoming concrete of that "intervention" in which God as the transcendental ground of the world has from the outset embedded himself in this world as its self-communicating ground'[26] and only have the function of revealing God in relation to a subject living out her subjectivity oriented towards the transcendental horizon. Linking this dynamic with the nature of creation, Rahner further posits matter as open to spirit, and spirit as open to God.

2.2.4 Chapter III Man as a Being Threatened Radically by Guilt

The third chapter considers the possibility of the subject saying 'no' to the divine self-communication and begins by stating that sin, redemption and their attendant notions are not to be interpreted in temporal succession. Man is affirmed as inextricably moral, but first and foremost in his transcendentality, with categorical realities the arena in which the ultimate decision which constitutes the exercise of human moral freedom is played out.

Guilt is a 'closing oneself to this offer of God's absolute self-communication',[27] an act which is done precisely in the context of God's offer of love and divine self-communication, thus making guilt something both fundamental and radical. Man is free and responsible for himself as a transcendental being who is able to view himself reflexively in his entirety and is able to dispose of himself as such. Thus, the exercise of freedom is ultimately a question of a unique act of self-actualisation, and freedom as such is both transcendentally given and transcendentally experienced.

Given freedom's actualisation in the world of concrete existence, freedom and necessity are always explicitly linked, and the subject herself exists

---

[24] Rahner, *Foundations*, 84
[25] Rahner, *Foundations*, 86
[26] Rahner, *Foundations*, 87
[27] Rahner, *Foundations*, 93

in a dialectic of self-presence (in both freedom and the very origins of the subject) and distance, as her reflexive presence to self has to be mediated through concrete categorical existents.

Thus fundamentally the exercise of freedom is an affirmative or negative response to the divine self-offer and constitutes a decision of ultimate validity involving the entire subject. Transcendence towards Absolute Mystery is that which constitutes our subjectivity and makes freedom possible: without such a horizon the subject cannot have the reflexive knowledge of itself necessary for the exercise of freedom and indeed cannot be reflexively conscious at all.

Whilst the 'no' to the absolute reality which constitutes us is self-negating and contradictory, such a 'no' remains a real possibility and an element of uncertainty remains in terms of the final outcome of individual and, indeed, collective destiny.

Rahner at this point turns to a consideration of the traditional doctrine of original sin and begins by pointing out that it is not a transmission of the guilt of others to us but rather 'this codetermination of the situation of every person by the guilt of others is something universal, permanent, and therefore also original'.[28]

Divine self-communication, identified with justification as grace, is prior to freedom and 'the *loss* of such a sanctifying self-communication assumes the character of something which *should not be*, and is not merely a diminishing of the possibilities of freedom as can otherwise be the case in the instance of a "hereditary defect"'.[29]

Knowledge of original sin is posited as dependent on 'reflexive knowledge about immediacy to God...radicalized in the instance of a positive relationship to him'.

In this sense, both grace and sin are prior to the human subject:

This universal state of sinfulness stands in dialectical relationship to God's universal saving will which imparts to everyone through Christ, at least as an offer, that sanctification which was not imparted through descent from Adam. As realities prior to a person's free decision, both original sin and redemptive grace in their dialectical relationship determine the situation into which everyone is born.[30]

---

[28] Rahner, *Foundations*, 109
[29] Rahner, *Foundations*, 113
[30] Dych, *Karl Rahner*, 142

2.2.5 Chapter IV Man as the Event of God's Free and Forgiving Self-Communication

Central to Rahner's reflection on the initiative of God towards human beings is the assertion that God's self-communication is ontological: 'The term "self-communication" is really intended to signify that God in his own most proper reality makes himself the innermost constitutive element of man.'[31]

This self-communication happens through grace and is not a part of man's natural constitution, even though it does constitute the deepest reality of the human being; accordingly, Rahner names this reality the 'supernatural existential'. At this point it is worth noting that despite the fact that this concept is present in a number of Rahner's works, it is used in a number of different ways that are not all compatible. Kilby sums up the view of the supernatural existential present in *Foundations of Christian Faith* as follows:

> In the fourth chapter of the *Foundations* Rahner takes as his theme that God communicates himself to human beings. This is a communication not of something *about* God, but of God himself, and what it means for the recipient is not a new piece of knowledge, nor that something new is possessed, but that the human being herself *is* something new: "God in his own most proper reality makes himself the innermost constitutive element of man." Now, what is described from God's side as self-communication is, viewed from the side of the human being, the supernatural existential. To be more precise, the supernatural existential is here identified as God's self-communication in the mode of offer.[32]

In doctrinal terms, this is expressed in the assertion that the doctrines of grace and the final vision of God are to be held together as parts of one event, namely the ontological divinisation of man through grace. This insight is further sharpened as the relationship between God and humanity is described as one of formal rather than efficient causality. In formal causality, through self-communication the causal agent participates in the being of that which is caused, as opposed to the distinction between the being of the causal agent and that which is caused that pertains in efficient causality. All of this is summarised by Rahner in the statement: 'In what we call grace and the

---

[31] Rahner, *Foundations*, 116
[32] Kilby, *Karl Rahner: Theology and Philosophy*, 55

immediate vision of God, God is really an intrinsic, constitutive principle of man as existing in the situation of salvation and fulfilment.'[33]

The possibility and actuality of the relationship of humanity with God in love and knowledge is based on this act of ontological self-communication on God's part, an act which is one of free love, but which remains intrinsic rather than extrinsic to us. As the recipient of such a free act, the human being is constituted as one who is potentially the one addressed by God in revelation. This line of thought issues in the affirmation that God's desire to give himself is the very reason for creation.

Rahner sees Christianity as different from and surpassing other religions if, and only if, 'it is a profession of faith in this immediacy to God'.[34]

Part of the formulation of this immediacy of God to us is the affirmation of grace and the vision of God, in which the most radical experience of the transcendental horizon is experienced in the mode of promise and we are borne by the self-communication of the transcendental horizon as Holy Mystery which is both the future of humanity and the absolute fulfilment of our transcendence. Reflecting on the implications of this, Rahner states: 'The doctrine about this grace and its fulfilment, therefore, bids us keep ourselves radically open in faith, hope and love for the ineffable, unimaginable and nameless absolute future of God which is coming, and bids us never close ourselves before there is nothing more to close, because nothing will be left outside of God, since we shall be wholly in God and he shall be wholly in us.'[35]

Reflecting on the role of Christianity, Rahner posits Christianity as the reflexive expression of what we already know and experience unreflexively. In addition, God's offer of himself is that which makes our acceptance of this possible *via* our acceptance of our own finitude in a way that does not diminish God. The fact that all of this is present in us as the depths of our being means that 'in principle…the original experience of God even in his self-communication can be so universal, so unthematic and so "unreligious" that it takes place, unnamed but really, wherever we are living out our existence'.[36]

A further interesting extension of this, conceptualised in terms of the traditional teaching about the unicity of God's essence, is Rahner's refutation of the idea of human beings as different and distinct centres of consciousness.

---

[33] Rahner, *Foundations*, 121
[34] Rahner, *Foundations*, 125
[35] Rahner, *Foundations*, 125
[36] Rahner, *Foundations*, 132

Rather, as subjects constituted by the same Transcendental Horizon which is present to all of us, we are united fundamentally not only with God but also with each other, an idea which resonates deeply with the Buddhist conceptions of not-self.[37]

This chapter finishes by correlating Trinitarian terminology with our experience of God: insofar as God is holy and ineffable mystery God is father, as the Logos present in Christ God is the son and as divinising us in our essence God is Spirit. Finally, as God gives himself in reality and not merely in appearance, the three persons are equally and fully God and the economic trinity is identical with the immanent trinity.

2.2.6 Chapter V The History of Salvation and Revelation

This chapter opens with the definition of Christian proclamation as proclamation of a salvific history comprising God's revelation and salvific action on and for us. According to Rahner, Christianity claims fundamentally 'that it is salvation and revelation for every person; it makes the claim that it is a religion of absolute value'.[38]

Linking this with Rahner's formulation of the supernatural existential, Dych comments: 'For then this presence is as universal as God's saving will itself, and salvation becomes a concrete possibility for everyone. It is not confined to particular times and places and to a small minority of the human race. In this way the philosophical concept can help theology express Christian faith in a more universal and less particularistic, exclusivistic way.'[39]

A further dialectic is introduced at this point between the transcendentality of our relationship with God and the historical character of salvation and revelation. Humans are historical beings, but are so as transcendental beings constituted by the transcendental horizon; hence in human beings historicity and transcendentality meet, and, indeed, our transcendentality is mediated to us by history.

Linking these two, Rahner states that 'history is ultimately the history of transcendentality itself; and conversely, man's transcendentality cannot be understood as a capacity which is given and lived and experienced and reflected upon independently of history'.[40]

---

[37] Damien Keown, and Charles S. Prebish, eds. *Encylopedia of Buddhism*, (Oxon: Routledge, 2007), 568–575

[38] Rahner, *Foundations*, 138

[39] Dych, *Karl Rahner*, 40

[40] Rahner, *Foundations*, 140

Further underlining the previously-stated unity of humanity, which flows of necessity from the doctrine of the unicity of the divine nature, Rahner posits salvation history as history on God's part also, and this for three reasons: first, it is God as the transcendental horizon who constitutes us as subjects; second, this is done through the divine self-communication; and third, we are intrinsically historical beings. Hence the divine self-communication assumes history in us as a precursor to the hypostatic union in Christ, a point which Rahner will make explicitly later in the book.

In the consideration of history and revelation, a dialectical structure is once again adduced between God's presence in the divine self-disclosure and God's absence as Holy Mystery.

In line with the emphasis he places on transcendentality, Rahner states that revelation can take place only in the context of the faith of its recipient: 'There is no revelation which could take place in any other way except in the faith of the person hearing the revelation. To this extent it is clear that the history of salvation and revelation is always the already existing synthesis of God's historical activity and man's at the same time, because the divine and the human history of salvation cannot be understood as joining together in a sort of synergistic cooperation.'[41]

Thus as a synthesis which is written into the very structure of creation, the history of salvation is coextensive with world history, though not identical with it, as world history also encompasses guilt and the rejection of God, i.e. the opposite of salvation.

Accordingly, salvation *qua* God's offer of godself in revelation is lost only through consciously exercised volition. As both history and humanity are ultimately one, God's offer of salvation extends to all people in all their dimensions and all history in a sense is the acceptance or rejection of God's salvific offer of Self. In light of this, revelation and salvation may be considered as simply the temporal manifestation of God's offer and our response. All of human life is potentially the historical concretisation of salvation and revelation as long as it constitutes the actualisation of our transcendentality.

Developing his earlier statement about Christianity in this chapter, Rahner builds on the above view and states that Christianity understands itself as the actualisation of the self-awareness of both salvation and world history. An important conclusion then follows: 'If, then, there can be salvation and hence also faith everywhere in history, then a supernatural revelation of God to humankind must have been at work everywhere in the history of the human race. It must have been at work in such a way that it actually touches

---

[41] Rahner, *Foundations*, 142

every person and effects salvation in him through faith, every person who does not close himself to this revelation by a failure to believe through his own fault.'[42]

This omnipresence of salvation and faith is of a piece with the presence of transcendental revelation and has implications for Rahner's formulation of the 'anonymous Christian' as well as for his assertion that salvation history is coextensive with all history. Kilby draws attention in this regard to:

> The absolute *generality* not only of transcendental revelation but also of its historical mediation. Transcendental revelation is in fact God's self-communication to the human being in grace, and this is present at least as an offer at all times and to all people – hence the phrase 'supernatural existential.' And not only is this transcendental revelation omnipresent, but so are its categorical mediations: "supernaturally elevated transcendentality is…mediated to itself by *any and every* categorical reality in which and through which the subject becomes present to itself," and as we have seen the subject becomes present to itself in every act of knowing and willing.[43]

Thus both faith and salvation are always already omnipresent and represent an intrinsic rather than extrinsic dimension of human existence in creation.

Our constitution as subjects by the Holy Mystery as transcendental horizon is named as the original revelation, and it is this original revelation which is the foundation of all subsequent revelation. Just as revelation is dependent on faith, which in this unthematic sense is a faith in one's own existence in self-realisation opposite the transcendental horizon, faith is an act of God's freedom.

From this, Rahner considers explicitly the role of the transcendental horizon in human knowing as ordinarily understood: 'A proposition never appears only as an individual proposition all by itself on the *tabula rasa* of a consciousness, but is always dependent on man's transcendentality, on the a priori horizon of his understanding, and on his universal language field.'[44] The transcendentality of humans, which can be correctly named supernatural, is mediated to us through any and every categorical reality in which our presence to self becomes actual; such presence is already happening in an unthematic way in human self-appropriation in knowledge and freedom.

---

[42] Rahner, *Foundations*, 148

[43] Kilby, *Karl Rahner: Theology and Philosophy*, 125

[44] Rahner, *Foundations*, 150

A further twist is given to the recurring theme of mediation, when the world is adduced as our mediation to God, a statement that logically chimes with the earlier assertion about history also being history on God's part. Given that transcendental experience is omnipresent, its self-reflexive knowledge and articulation in historical revelation and religious faith is not strictly necessary for salvation. History itself, however, is the objectification of the original revelation of God and the interpretation of this original revelation; thus of necessity it is simultaneously the history of revelation.

Introducing the Bible in this context, Rahner cites the Old and New Testaments as 'the valid self-interpretation of God's transcendental self-communication to man, and as the thematization of the universal categorical history of this self-communication'.[45]

In the prophetic literature something universal is coming to expression, and the prophet is one who expresses with accuracy the transcendental depths of human experience, and it is this which constitutes the prophet's authority. Reflecting on the constitution of the world as intrinsically interpersonal, Rahner adduces an interpersonal element to transcendental self-interpretation which he identifies with the category of tradition spanning past, present and future.

Yet another dialectic is introduced at this point, as creation is seen as rendering us both distant and distinct from God whilst grace simultaneously renders us close. Revelation as God's self-disclosure in grace, however, precedes us. Rahner speaks of this in terms of primeval revelation: 'Insofar as man's transcendental constitution, his origins, always involves being situated in a concrete history as in a beginning and within a horizon which is prior to him in his freedom, and insofar as this constitution is both logically and really, although perhaps not temporally and tangibly, antecedent to his free and sinful self-interpretation, we can speak of the beginning of God's transcendental and categorical revelation in paradise, that is, of a primeval transcendental and categorical revelation.'[46] Both transcendentally and categorically, grace is viewed here as being prior to sin because of God's desire to communicate himself in, and because of, Christ.

Reflecting on the fullest meaning of the actualisation of human transcendentality, Rahner here states that whenever someone engages in an act of transcendental self-interpretation which grasps the finitude of categorical reality, we directly approach the boundary with the transcendental horizon *qua* Holy Mystery: 'Wherever we really find a being of absolute transcendence

---

[45] Rahner, *Foundations*, 158

[46] Rahner, *Foundations*, 162

who places the biological and the interpersonal realm as a whole in question, there we find a man with freedom, with self-determination, and with an immediate boundary with absolute mystery.'[47]

At this point the relationship between natural and historical revelation is broached in more detail. The Old Testament, for Rahner, is relevant to us only because of Christ, and it is in Jesus that the definitive event of God's self-disclosure takes place. Jesus is 'the absolute historical objectification of its (humanity's) transcendental understanding of God. In this objectification, namely, in Jesus Christ, the God who communicates himself and the man who accepts God's self-communication become irrevocably one. And the history of revelation and salvation of the whole human race reaches its goal'.[48]

In natural revelation the divine is present *qua* questions and it is only in Christ that the answer is given. Christ discloses God's inner reality and the nature of the divine relationship with us in freedom. This answer has the character of revelation as event and is not something that can be derived from our being as transcendental subjects.

In this answer Godself approaches us as the answer to our 'unlimited transcendentality'.[49] Ultimately, as is the case with original revelation, as both humanity and history exist as unified realities, this answer is intended for all of us in all aspects of our being.

Finally, as all self-disclosure of God is mediated, we can speak of a history of mediation, a history that is directed by God 'which is nothing else but the dynamism of God's transcendental self-communication towards its historical realization and mediation, and hence this mediation is itself God's revelation'.[50] Moreover, as Dych points out, in Rahner's view transcendental revelation may not be sundered from history and thus ultimately of necessity entails historical revelation, too. Reflecting on the relation between transcendental and historical revelation, Dych states:

> One can speak, therefore, of the transcendental element in revelation. It refers to what Rahner calls the 'new formal object' or the 'new horizon' within which we exist. But there can be no formal object without a material object nor a horizon without the content for which it is the horizon. Hence there can be no such thing as transcendental revelation

---

[47] Rahner, *Foundations*, 166
[48] Rahner, *Foundations*, 169
[49] Rahner, *Foundations*, 172
[50] Rahner, *Foundations*, 173

by itself, but only as an element in our historical experience. Human beings are always transcendence within history, always spirit in world. Transcendental revelation, therefore, is not a purely interior illumination freeing one from the particularities of history, including the particular history of the Judaeo-Christian tradition. It always takes place within and as a dimension of our encounter with historical realities.[51]

The attempt to mediate reflexively original revelation and express it is made in all religions, and despite the omnipresence of revelation and faith, Rahner states that the unifying law and structure in the history of religions is not readily discernible.

2.2.7 Chapter VI Jesus Christ

With Chapter VI we arrive at what may be viewed as the crux of the book in a wide-ranging reflection on the significance of Christ that spans a full 144 pages in all. Rahner begins by locating the significance of Christ within an evolutionary view of the world in which there is a dynamic movement from matter to spirit and then ultimately to self-transcendence into the divine life of God. Carefully distinguishing Christological reflection from concrete experience of Christ, Rahner points out that we reflect on the conditions of possibility of the realities we encounter, and that this serves to clarify our understanding and adds to our intellectual conviction. This is precisely what he proceeds to do.

Linking this idea specifically with Christology, Dych comments: 'In one of his favourite examples, Rahner says that it is only when Beethoven has actually created his music that one realizes what the possibilities of music are. Likewise, it is only an encounter with Jesus as man and God that reveals what the God-given possibilities of human existence are'[52] Man is once again cited as that being in which spirit and matter meet, and for whom transcendence into God is made possible by revelation, understood here as the revelation of God in Christ, although this awaits fulfilment.

Speaking of the incarnation in the context both of the unity of the world and of the evolutionary dynamic of cosmic history, he introduces the idea of the inexorability of the process of divinisation, a process which is absolute in that it is not itself one element in creation alongside others. In humans, as beings of matter and spirit (indeed the only beings thus constituted), unity

---

[51] Dych, *Karl Rahner*, 45
[52] Dych, *Karl Rahner*, 65

precedes differentiation, and spirit, here identified with self-presence, is the necessary starting point of all knowledge: '*Spirit* is the single person insofar as he becomes conscious of himself in an absolute presence to himself, and indeed does this by the fact that he is always oriented towards the absoluteness of reality as such, and towards its one ground whom we call God.'[53]

This orientation to absolute reality is itself located within the aforementioned evolutionary dynamic, viewed as a process in which evolution takes place to an ever-fuller plenitude of being through the process of divinisation. The source of this becoming must be absolute being, otherwise nothingness would be the foundation of its own becoming, a state of affairs which, in the view adopted here, would be both logically and metaphysically absurd.[54] Equally, the fullness of being as occasioning self-transcendence, whilst intrinsic to finite being, is not essential to it, as if it were then finite being would not be such but would itself be absolute being. Moreover, it is in this context, as will become clear, that Rahner locates the doctrine of the incarnation, linking it to the universal offer of grace on God's part which meets the universal tendency to transcendence in human beings. George Vass underlines this link, commenting:

> All this sounds rather abstract and speculative. It can, however, be tested, if we translate the relationship between man's transcendence and the self-communication of God as an offer of grace for the whole of mankind. This offer of grace, as we have seen elsewhere, means man's destination to the vision of God, to the immediacy of his presence to him, or simply, the union of God and man. Now, the precise question is whether the Incarnation in Christ means a union which is on a higher level than the vision as offered to every individual or 'is it a singular and unique moment in the universal bestowal of grace'? Is the grace present in the humanity of Jesus the Christ the same as is offered to every other creature? Rahner's answer is affirmative...[55]

Thus, reflecting Rahner's ongoing concern to ground fundamental Christian doctrines in human anthropological reality, the incarnation is seen as part of the fundamental dynamic of transcendence present in creation as a whole

---

[53] Rahner, *Foundations*, 183

[54] This view would provide a very interesting point of discussion and comparison with Buddhist views, albeit one which lies outside the purview of this study.

[55] George Vass, *A Pattern of Doctrines 1: God and Christ: Understanding Karl Rahner Volume 3*, 121

rather than considered as an isolated reality that comes from without, so to speak.

As the human being is the being in which nature transcends into spirit, nature and spirit are seen by Rahner as a unity and, indeed, nature attains both its goal in the human spirit and its freedom whilst always remaining a constituent of this history of spirit. Given the element of freedom involved, this history is also one of 'guilt and trial',[56] yet despite this, Christianity affirms the consummation and fulfilment of the cosmos as a whole.

Developing further this evolutionary view, Rahner points out that natural science effectively contradicts the idea of humanity as a merely random occurrence, and further points to the uniqueness of the facticity of self-transcendence in each person given our individuality in the cosmos. The cosmos is:

> ...the *single* body as it were of a *multiple* self-presence of this very cosmos and its orientation towards its absolute and infinite ground. If this cosmic corporeality of countless personal self-consciousnesses in which the cosmos can become present to itself has become self-present only in a very incipient way in the self-consciousness and in the freedom of individual persons, it exists nevertheless in every person as something which can and should come to be. For man in his corporeality is an element of the cosmos which cannot really be demarcated and separated, and he communicates with the whole cosmos in such a way that, in and through the corporeality of man as what is other to spirit, the cosmos really presses forward to this self-presence in spirit.[57]

In this dynamic of cosmic evolution, it is Godself who is the innermost being of the world: 'the absolute ground itself becomes immediately interior to what is grounded by it.'[58] The many points of self-consciousness within the cosmos are also bound together inextricably in intercommunion, and accordingly it is into this context of intercommunion that God's salvific word of self-communication is spoken.

Turning to look more specifically at the notion of an absolute saviour, Rahner distinguishes between the assertion that the absolute saviour is the beginning of God's self-communication with an atemporal view of such a beginning. The absolute saviour he defines as follows: 'We are calling saviour

---

[56] Rahner, *Foundations*, 188
[57] Rahner, *Foundations*, 189
[58] Rahner, *Foundations*, 191

here that historical subjectivity in which, first this process of God's absolute self-communication to the spiritual world as a whole exists *irrevocably*; secondly, that process in which this divine self-communication can be recognised unambiguously as irrevocable; and thirdly, that process in which God's self-communication reaches its climax insofar as this climax must be understood as a moment within the total history of the human race, and as such must not simply be identified with the totality of the spiritual world under God's self-communication.'[59]

Such a self-communication, whilst irrevocable, is not yet consummated and is viewed as a final cause, conceived as that which bears the movement of things towards itself as their goal through its power and potency; as such the absolute saviour is the final cause of God's self-communication. The irrevocability of God's offer of self-communication is present in the absolute saviour as both offer and acceptance. Dych sums up this view thus:

> Jesus of Nazareth is seen by Christian faith as the person in whose total openness to God this offer met with a free and perfect response, so that in his life and death the history of grace reaches its irreversible and unsurpassable triumph over sin. Since the history of sin is the history of separation and alienation from God, the perfect union with God that he achieved in his free response is the undoing of sin and the entrance into history of its opposite, that is salvation. He *is* salvation and saviour in his very being, and not just in his actions. Moreover, since his union with God is irrevocable and cannot be surpassed by a still greater union, he is the 'absolute saviour'.[60]

This view, in turn, leads Rahner into a discussion of the import of the hypostatic union and leads to the situating of the traditional Christological formulas within the context of what has been presented so far.

The Logos, viewed as God's expression of himself within himself, is affirmed as present in the human being Jesus who is the expression of the Logos: 'He (the Logos) establishes it (this corporeal part of the world) as what is different from himself in such a way that this very materiality expresses *him*, the Logos himself, and allows him to be present in his world.'[61]

---

[59] Rahner, *Foundations*, 194

[60] Dych, *Karl Rahner*, 72

[61] Rahner, *Foundations*, 196

This presence of the Logos in Jesus is seen as part of an overall dynamic in which 'God becomes world'.[62]

Such a conceptualisation represents what is traditionally termed 'Christology from above', but the hypostatic union can just as legitimately be conceived 'from below' in terms of human self-transcendence into the life God, in which the highest point of this transcendence becomes identical with the self-communication of God in an absolute sense. Moreover, this process is 'to be understood as taking place in *all* subjects'.[63]

Thus, given this dynamic and the unity between the highest point of human self-transcendence and God's offer of self in an absolute sense, the incarnation becomes a necessary moment in cosmic history.

Christian tradition has asserted that the incarnation took place for our sake; reflecting on this, Rahner points out that what is intrinsic to Jesus' human reality in the hypostatic union is the same as what is intended for all of us through grace. Jesus is the offer, we are the recipients of the offer and, in a sense, the beneficiaries of Jesus' yes.

Moving more deeply into the experience of the believer as the starting point for the Christological enterprise, this experience is formulated in terms of faith and free decision. The relationship is defined as follows: 'We can say in a phenomenological description of this common Christian relationship to Jesus Christ: this relationship to Jesus Christ is present in and through the "faith" that in the encounter with him in the unity and totality of his word, his life and his victorious death the all-encompassing and all-pervasive mystery of reality as a whole and of each individual life, the mystery which we call God, "is present" for our salvation, offering forgiveness and divine life, and is offered to us in such a way that God's offer in him is final and irrevocable.'[64] Expanding again on the concept of the unity of the world, the absolute saviour is seen by Rahner as having an 'exemplary' significance, though there is much more involved in his conception of the significance of the absolute saviour than is articulated here.

Rahner next turns to the interpretation of some of the terminology used by the tradition in the light of what he has said so far. Framing his comments by saying that the very truth of faith is contained in Christology, he looks at what it means to say that God became human and not surprisingly he locates the discussion in the orientation towards Absolute Mystery. The Incarnation becomes the point at which human transcendence meets divine self-offer, and

---

[62] Rahner, *Foundations*, 197
[63] Rahner, *Foundations*, 198
[64] Rahner, *Foundations*, 204

from our point of view this entails abandonment into the mystery of God: 'Seen from this perspective, the Incarnation of God is the unique and *highest* instance of the actualization of the essence of human reality, which consists in this: that man is insofar as he abandons himself to the absolute mystery whom we call God.'[65] The logical corollary of this, he points out, is that becoming is a possibility for God: 'He who is not subject to change in himself can *himself* be subject to change *in something else.*'[66]

What is primarily placed before us in Christian faith, then, is God's kenosis in which he becomes what is other to himself whilst retaining his essential being; accordingly, the whole humanity of Jesus is the expression of God, and as human beings we are all 'the grammar of God's possible self-expression'.[67] Linking this with the previously articulated notion of the absolute saviour as final cause, humanity is viewed as resulting from the incarnation. Equally, also underscoring a point made previously, the hypostatic union is presented as necessitating the conceptualisation of theology as anthropology, and in the incarnation, the infinite presents itself as the depths of the finite. The final cause also means that the earlier acceptance of revelation by those who accepted their lives is here given a Christological interpretation.

Speaking of the act of faith and its relationship to grace, the point is made that of necessity this takes place at a depth in us that cannot be made entirely reflexive: 'For what is meant by the grace of faith as an unconditional presupposition of believing and being able to believe also implies that a moment of synthesis, which ultimately cannot be made completely reflexive, is necessary for faith in order that there can come to exist that unity in which subjective willingness to believe sees the objective ground of faith, and hence this objective ground justifies the willingness to believe which the subject must bring.'[68] Lack of belief in one to whom the message is proclaimed is viewed as either a purposive closing of the subject to God's offer of grace or else as something which is itself God's providential will; one way or the other, grace and understanding are always already present in a person to some degree.

Rahner openly acknowledges that there is an incongruity between the historicity of the events proclaimed by Christianity and the existentiell significance attributed to them, but this incongruity is ultimately located in the dialectic between the transcendental and the historical. The relationship between

---

[65] Rahner, *Foundations*, 218
[66] Rahner, *Foundations*, 220
[67] Rahner, *Foundations*, 223
[68] Rahner, *Foundations*, 231

logical certitude and existentially absolute commitment is also considered and located within the existence of any number of such relationships in the life of the individual. Rahner also proposes that, strictly speaking, the identity of Christian affirmation with Christ's pre-resurrection consciousness is not necessary, though he does not rule this out and seems to hint at it, at least to some degree, in his assertion that for the pre-resurrection Christ the presence of God's offer was inextricably linked with his own person. He does state explicitly, however, that the self-interpretation of Jesus corresponds so well to the search for transcendental experience of God's self-communication that it contains the ground of credibility within itself.

Another instance of Rahner's explicitly-stated attempt to provide a basis of credibility for Christianity from Christian doctrine itself is his use of the traditional doctrine of grace to argue against an extrinsic view of faith: 'There are dogmatic reasons against such an extrinsic relationship, for the Catholic doctrine of faith maintains that faith and the knowledge of faith are not possible without grace, and that they entail the personal and *free* assent of the believing subject. A real and effective grasp of the historical grounds of faith takes place only within the process of faith itself in grace and freedom.'[69] Reflecting further on the character of faith, Rahner uses the contrast between the words *Geschichte* and *Historie* to underscore that salvation history is not something the import of which can be grasped by merely looking at a set of historical events from a hermeneutically disinterested perspective. Returning to the theme of transcendentality, he affirms that all knowledge is 'under the law of a subjective apriority'.[70]

Turning to the resurrection as the lynchpin of Christian proclamation, the assertion is made that the resurrection is not speaking about something which pertains to this-worldly categorical reality. Parenthetically, the topic of miracles is concerned with the points being made that miracles are fundamentally instances of divine self-communication and that the laws of the cosmos are themselves contained within the dialogue between God and human beings, and that as God is intrinsic to the cosmos to begin with, logical problems arising from the notion of a suspension of the laws of nature from without need not detain us further. The resurrection, however, is viewed as qualitatively different from the miracles recorded in the gospels, and this is given further emphasis with the statement that the miracles of Christ did not form

---

[69] Rahner, *Foundations*, 240
[70] Rahner, *Foundations*, 243

part of what we may call the fundamental theology of the apostolic period, whereas the resurrection did.

The resurrection is the core meaning of Jesus' life and is the answer to the human question of meaning. Death is that which in some ways bestows 'final and ultimate validity',[71] but the death of Jesus is a 'death into the resurrection'.[72] The ambit of the resurrection is widened, as Rahner asserts that a person and the cause for which they lived cannot be separated, and accordingly the cause for which Jesus lived is also involved in his resurrection which is the 'eschatological victory of God's grace in the world'[73] and 'a liberation from all the powers of finiteness, of guilt and of death.'[74]

Corresponding to the actual occurrence of the resurrection in history is the transcendental anticipation of it, manifest as the desire for ultimate survival which is a dimension of our transcendentality, especially in the exercise of freedom and responsibility. Again, the continually operative circle between the transcendental and the categorical is invoked, here in terms of the relationship between us and Jesus.

The resurrection as eternal life implies a view of eternity, and this is defined simply but profoundly as 'a mode of spirit and freedom which have been actualised in time'.[75]

An interesting implication is adduced from this, namely that the self-actualisation of eternity towards fulfilment occurs in finite life as it moves towards death. Given the transcendental hope which is part of our transcendentality, the news of the resurrection does not come to us as something which has been completely without expectation.

Our experience of the risen Christ takes place in the Spirit and entails four elements:

1. Apostolic witness.
2. Experience of the Risen Christ in faith.
3. Transcendental hope in the resurrection as horizon of freedom and responsibility.
4. Dynamics of grace in our own life leading us to 'stand beyond death'.[76]

---

[71] Rahner, *Foundations*, 266
[72] Rahner, *Foundations*, 266
[73] Rahner, *Foundations*, 267
[74] Rahner, *Foundations*, 269
[75] Rahner, *Foundations*, 271
[76] Rahner, *Foundations*, 275 ff

In the resurrection there is a move beyond the previously-cited dialectic between the transcendental and categorical to a manifested identity of structure. This section of the chapter reaches its conclusion with the affirmation of the Easter experience as the ground of faith and the resurrection experience, along with the historical claim of Jesus, as the starting point for Christology.

Attention now turns to the relationship between the forgiveness of sins and Christ's death, a germane topic both when the book was written and today given the difficulty people have with the traditional account of this as a substitutionary atonement or, as often as not, modern misrepresentations of these accounts. Rahner views the relationship between Christ's death and God's forgiveness by analogy with sacramental thinking, with Christ's death a sign which effects what it signifies: 'In this causality what is signified, in this case God's salvific will, posits the sign, in this case the death of Jesus along with his resurrection, and in and through the sign it causes what is signified.'[77]

Two presuppositions necessary for soteriology are cited: the solidarity of humankind and the previously mentioned unity of history – Rahner makes the point that while these are present implicitly in the New Testament, they are not given explicit interpretations and hence a number of different soteriological readings are possible. He does, however, state that functional Christological statements have ontological implications, thus tying in his conception of the soteriological function of Christ's death with what he has said about the Incarnation.

In terms of what all of this means for the believer, Rahner states that discipleship is a unique call rather than an injunction to exact imitation, and involves a participation in the life, death and resurrection of Christ through which 'everything finite enters into the infinity of God, and in the immediate experience of this the finite in Jesus and in us does not perish, but rises to its fulfilment'.[78] Christ's presence in history is of a particular density, however, in the poor and oppressed, and it is through these that Christ 'lives' in our world.

The chapter closes with a consideration of the relationship between Jesus and the non-Christian religions, viewed in terms both of human transcendentality and of the presence of Christ in all people for whom salvation can be actualised without being made thematically explicit. Two presuppositions are provided for what follows, namely the universality of God's salvific will and the role of non-Christian religions in the salvation of their adherents, a role

---

[77] Rahner, *Foundations*, 284

[78] Rahner, *Foundations*, 310

which follows of necessity from the communal nature of human being. The conclusion reached is that Christ is present in the 'non-Christian religions' in the Spirit who proceeds from the Logos and the Father and is 'the universal self-communication of God to the world which we call the Holy Spirit',[79] thus again grounding a progressive interpretation in traditional Christian teaching. The relationship between the Spirit and Christ is expressed by Rahner in terms of the relationship between an efficient and a final cause.

He concludes this chapter with a brief reflection on the role of *memoria*, citing Plato and Augustine, and speaks of it as a principle of expectation (transcendental hope) which enables recognition in subjects and which leads to the anticipation of an absolute saviour in history: 'Saviour figures in the history of religion can readily be regarded as an indication of the fact that mankind, moved always and everywhere by grace, anticipates and looks for that event in which its absolute hope becomes irreversible in history, and becomes manifest in its irreversibility.'[80] With this reflection, Rahner turns to a consideration of the ecclesial nature of Christianity in the following chapter.

2.2.8 Chapter VII Christianity as Church

In line with the theological view held by Rahner, the chapter on Jesus is directly followed by the chapter on the Church. Linking the two themes together, Rahner defines the Church as 'the Historical continuation of Christ in and through the community of those who believe in him'.[81] As such, Christianity is of its very essence ecclesial, as the transcendental communication of God with people takes place in the context of a history that is located in space and time. Equally, human beings are quintessentially social beings, hence love of neighbour does not take place solely on an individual basis but encompasses the political and social, further tying into the above-mentioned history. At the same time, however, it is pointed out that the doctrine of the Church is not at the centre of Christianity. In its simplest sense it is the continuation of the Jesus movement in the light of the caesura in salvation history brought about by the non-acceptance of Jesus as messiah on the part of Israel. As well as being rooted in Jesus, the Church is founded in the power of the Spirit and recognises a legitimate process of development in its history.

Considering the Church in the New Testament, Rahner points out that in spite of the disjuncture brought about by Israel's stance on Jesus, the Church

---

[79] Rahner, *Foundations*, 371

[80] Rahner, *Foundations*, 321

[81] Rahner, *Foundations*, 322

does stand in continuity with Israel. Despite the presence of many different images for the Church in the New Testament writings, there is a deep unity present also: 'Ultimately the same basic convictions and the same basic theological structures are found everywhere. There is the one church which was founded by Christ and was won by Christ and is united with Christ. It is at the same time a visible and an invisible church, it has an earthly and a heavenly mode of existence, and it possesses both an exterior form and an interior, Spirit-filled and mysterious essence.'[82] In its role as the historical continuation of Christ's presence in the world, the church is 'co-constitutive of his (man's) relationship to God'.[83] It is in the Church that the universality of the offer of grace is realised and the Church is 'a part of Christianity as the very event of salvation'.[84]

Central to these convictions is the notion of the intrinsic role of the interpersonal in our constitution as subjects. Indeed, as God is the source of all our aspects, the interpersonal itself, written as it is into our very being, ultimately comes from God as its source also. Hence there is a necessity for a norm of objectivity for human subjectivity, in salvation history as in every other aspect of life, and this role is fulfilled by the Church. The Church as the community of believers, then, is a necessary part of the salvation of human beings who realise their transcendentality as subjects in history.

Rahner next considers the claim advanced by the Catholic Church to be the Church of Christ. Central to his method is the assertion of the necessary oneness of the Church, and he asserts that the Church is present whenever baptism and the Eucharist are celebrated. This could mean, accordingly, that the various ecclesial manifestations of Christianity are united to begin with, but this unity has, of necessity, to come to social expression. In relation to the question of this pre-existing unity, Rahner simply points to the fact that no consensus has been reached on these questions. Real differences do exist, however: such divergences are not compatible with the Church's essence. For the individual, though, it is possible and legitimate to have confidence in the ecclesial body which one finds oneself part of through birth, upbringing, etc. It is the place where grace, salvation, Christian life and consolation are experienced, and, as such, it has a validity because of this. Put simply: 'Every genuine experience of Christianity may and must be regarded as an

---

[82] Rahner, *Foundations*, 341
[83] Rahner, *Foundations*, 342
[84] Rahner, *Foundations*, 343

experience of the power of our existence which is really grounded in the mystery of God.'[85]

Rahner formulates three criteria against which the Catholic Church's claim is to be judged: the institution of a church must not contradict the essential teaching of Christianity, it must have the closest possible historical continuity, and it must function as an objective authority in the life of the individual. Rahner points out first that the historical continuity involved in the Catholic Church's relationship with the early Church is closer and more direct than is the case with the churches of the Reformation, and asserts that nothing was definitively taught in pre-Reformation Catholicism which can be shown to be in inherent opposition to the fundamental essence of Christianity. Equally, through its teaching authority, the Catholic Church does indeed fulfil a role as an objective norm which addresses the conscience of the individual in her subjectivity.

He next considers three planks of the teaching of the Reformation, namely *sola scriptura*, *sola fide* and *sola gratia*. He points out that such is the Catholic teaching on grace that it is axiomatic that a person does not bring something of her own to contribute to her salvation, but that all is received through God's grace, something which is in no way abrogated by the Council of Trent's teaching on human freedom: 'Freedom does not abolish the absolute gratuity of salvation, and the doctrine of grace intends to say nothing else but that by an act of God, by a free act of God which cannot be coerced, a person really and truly is changed interiorly from being a sinner to being justified. He is a justified person who can never judge about this justification because it is constantly threatened, and because it is a hidden reality in him. To this extent even as justified he cannot assume an autonomous position in relation to God.'[86] *Sola fide*, he says, is simply the obverse side of *sola gratia*, seen this time from our point of view rather than God's.

Equally, in considering the Catholic teaching about the role of tradition in relation to the idea of *sola scriptura*, Rahner points out that scripture is effectively the result of a process of tradition and that it is inherently connected with the community of the Church; indeed it would not be possible to establish the canon of scripture were it not so. Neither can the notion of scripture on its own be maintained once the notion of a direct verbal inspiration of the words of scripture has been abandoned, something which he claims has happened in mainstream Protestantisms. Finally, if scripture is self-interpreting through the Spirit, then we are left having to account for

---

[85] Rahner, *Foundations*, 351

[86] Rahner, *Foundations*, 360

the divisions caused by variant readings of it. Fundamentally, the question of the essence of scripture is a question pertaining to the already mentioned relationship between the transcendental and the categorical. In any case, the mediation of salvation takes place not primarily in the words of scripture but in salvation history as a whole.

In terms of the relationship between the Catholic Church and the churches of the Reformation, whilst the Catholic Church does not and cannot recognise an *identical* salvific significance in other churches, Rahner points out that this is not the same as saying that they have *no* salvific significance – this they do, both for those who are members in them and for Catholic Christians also. The unity between the churches is also something that is deeper than that which divides them, and this unity can be asserted as existing in both the categorical and the pneumatological realms.

Turning to consider the role of tradition in more detail, Rahner notes both that the principle of a legitimate development of the unchanging substance of faith is allowed for in Catholicism and that the possibility of believers giving an interpretation of the Bible that is binding on Christians exists. Neither is tradition to be considered in any way as a source parallel to that of scripture; scripture remains the one norming norm. The doctrine of the inspiration and inerrancy of scripture means that it is guaranteed that the form of revelation does not corrupt the substance. At the same time, since scripture exists as something derivative, its canonicity can be viewed as determined by God through the Church, founded as it is on the cross and resurrection of Christ. It is in this light that God can be understood as the author of scripture: 'If the church was founded by God himself through his Spirit and in Jesus Christ, if the *original* church as the norm for the future church is the object of God's activity in a qualitatively unique way which is different from his preservation of the church in the course of history, and if scripture is a constitutive element of this original church as the norm for future ages, then this already means quite adequately and in both a positive and an exclusive sense that God is the author of scripture and that he inspired it.'[87]

The inerrancy of scripture is a question of understanding a given statement in the light of the totality of the scriptural writings and it can be legitimate also to distinguish between the truth and the correctness of a statement. The teaching office of the Church exists solely to give witness to what is contained in scripture, and the guarantee present in the doctrine of the Church as the historical continuity of God's offer in Christ is that, taken as a whole, the Church cannot definitively lose God's love or truth. Linking

---

[87] Rahner, *Foundations*, 374

the teaching office of the Church with the current eschatological status that comes post the event of God's offer in Christ, Rahner states: 'From this perspective, the perspective of this eschatological situation which is the situation of Christ himself, the Catholic understanding of the Church says that when the Church in its teaching authority, that is, in the whole episcopate along with the Pope, or in the personal head of this whole episcopate, really confronts man in its teaching with an *ultimate* demand in the name of Christ, God's grace and power prevent this teaching authority from losing the truth of Christ.'[88] Speaking of the infallibility of the Pope, it is simply pointed out that there can be no *a priori* opposition from the substance of Christianity to this quality adhering to an individual and that, insofar as the role of the Pope is that of an individual, some special charism of teaching is to be expected.

There follows a brief consideration of the Marian dogmas in which it is emphasised that nothing is affirmed in these dogmas which we do not also affirm of our own ultimate destiny in the creeds. Finally there is a consideration of the role of church authority in relation to the individual, with a consideration of the claim the teaching office of the Church has on the individual on the one hand and the legitimate and, occasionally, even obligatory dissent which the individual may exercise on the other. The Church is also considered as the place where both God and neighbour are loved, and it is affirmed that we experience both of these loves coming to us from without rather than as something which we ourselves generate from our own resources.

2.2.9 Chapter VIII Remarks on Christian Life

This chapter begins with a number of observations on the nature of the life of the Christian and then moves to consider more specifically the role of the sacraments in this life. Freedom is adduced as a *sine qua non* in the openness to existence that Christian life entails, and this insight is taken further in the identification of Christian life with human life, a move which mirrors the posited relationship between world history and salvation history: 'The real and total and comprehensive task of a Christian as a Christian is to be a human being, a human being of course whose depths are divine. These depths are inescapably present in his existence and open it outwards.'[89] In this sense it can be said that Christian life is human life lived with its implicit transcendental depths made explicit. Accordingly, there is an ultimacy to the fundamental decision made in the way one chooses to live this life, a decision

---

[88] Rahner, *Foundations*, 381
[89] Rahner, *Foundations*, 403

which in this very ultimacy is a decision to accept or reject the divine offer of grace, even if this is never made conceptually explicit.

In relation to the characteristics of this earthly life, Christianity entails what Rahner terms an optimistic pessimism – there is a non-denial of death and the incomprehensibility of our existence. Hope, however, comes from faith in God as our future, and it is this which is also the source of our existential freedom. Within this freedom, there is a genuine pluralism present in the life which we live, that which, in our self-abandonment to it, mediates God to us. The constant temptation by which we are beset is to absolutise that which is not God, namely to sin, and the corollary of this is that we are called to love God above all else. There is, then, no refuge from the irreducible plurality of this existence, and no refuge to be found in making any aspect of temporal reality our fount of meaning: 'A Christian, then, is distinguished from someone who really is not a Christian either reflexively or anonymously by the fact that he does not turn his existence into a system, but rather allows himself without hesitation to be led through the multiplicity of reality, a reality which is also dark and obscure and incomprehensible.'[90] Against this background, morality becomes a question of what we should be, and the realm in which, in this plurality of existence, our ultimate decision for or against God is played out. Put positively: 'The objective norm which Christianity preaches, but preaches, however, in a form which to some extent is historically conditioned, is the sum of what a person basically should become and can become if he is open to God and gives himself over to the movement of his existence with trust and courage.'[91] In the constant tension to achieve this goal, Rahner points out that we remain always *simul iustus et peccator*.

The focus of consideration now switches to the sacramental life and in a sense one could say that Rahner's theology of the sacraments is a case of a series of derivations of formal causality. God's self-communication takes place by divinising human nature and pervading all dimensions of human existence with divine grace which then means that the history of salvation and grace is one with world history. The history of salvation proper is the making explicit of this history of salvation and grace, and this happens with particular density in history in Jesus Christ, whose presence is then continued in the Church which is the basic or primary sacrament. Indeed, all of life can be seen as having a sacramental character with the exception of those instances where humans refuse the offer of divine grace.

---

[90] Rahner, *Foundations*, 407
[91] Rahner, *Foundations*, 408

Rahner defines a sacrament in terms of the primary sacramentality of the Church, stating: 'Wherever the finality and the invincibility of God's offer of himself becomes manifest in the concrete in the life of an individual through the church which is the basic sacrament of salvation, we call this a Christian sacrament.'[92] God's offer of self is bound up through grace with human acceptance of this offer, and in the same way the sacraments are effective only when the offer contained within them is met by an acceptance and openness manifest in particular in faith, hope and love.

Reflecting on the seven sacraments, Rahner states that these take place when the offer of divine grace, historically present and manifest in the Church, is addressed by the Church to the individual in relation to an existentially significant moment of her life. The question of the sense in which it can be claimed that Jesus instituted the seven sacraments as we know them is situated in the context of Rahner's previously mentioned principle of development under the Holy Spirit, which he adduced when addressing the question of the sense in which Jesus founded the Church. In the context of the Reformation disputes surrounding the number of sacraments instituted by Christ, Dych comments: 'Rahner considers this "positivistic" approach to the question unnecessary, and, in view of our knowledge of the historical Jesus and what he did or did not explicitly institute, impossible in any case.'[93] Thus Rahner states: 'We can say that the origin or the institution of the sacraments has to be understood, and also *can* be understood, in a way which is analogous to the institution of the church itself by Jesus. The sacramentality of the church's basic activity is implied by the very essence of the church as the irreversible presence of God's salvific offer in Christ. This sacramentality is interpreted by the church in the seven sacraments.'[94]

He thus sums up his view of sacraments before considering the seven sacraments as present in church life, stating: 'Sacraments are nothing else but God's efficacious word to man, the word in which God offers himself to man and thereby liberates man's freedom to accept God's self-communication by his own act.'[95]

The seven sacraments are now considered and they are grouped into the sacraments of initiation, sacraments of states of life, and penance and the anointing of the sick, with the Eucharist considered separately.

---

[92] Rahner, *Foundations*, 412
[93] Dych, *Karl Rahner*, 122
[94] Rahner, *Foundations*, 413
[95] Rahner, *Foundations*, 415

Two poles of the sacramental life are posited as being present in each of the sacraments, namely the life of the individual in her existential history and the Church as the basic sacrament in which the offer of God's grace is made historically manifest and tangible. The grace for salvation is given first and foremost in baptism, in which a person becomes a member of the body of Christ that is the Church through being initiated into Christ's death. In baptism, the individual also becomes a part of the ecclesial dynamic of manifesting the offer of divine grace in history and accordingly shares in the mandate of the Church as a result of being baptised. Confirmation is the positive side of this reality in which the Holy Spirit is given in a sacramental way to the individual to empower him to live out this mandate and to resist the contrary voices and influences which mitigate against it. Orders and matrimony both entail the sacramental manifestation of the call of God which is present when a person makes an existentially definitive decision to enter into a particular state of life. Again, the union between the existential and the manifestation of the transcendental sacramentally is fundamental.

Whilst the sacramental nature of ordination flows in an obvious way from the nature of the Church as that basic sacrament in which God's offer of grace in Christ continues to be present in history, the sacramental nature of marriage is formulated in relation to the covenantal dynamism of human history. Rahner states that creation exists as a potential to be a covenantal partner with God, and that the definitive expression of this covenantal union between God and humanity is present historically in Christ as a final cause. All of creation is drawn forward by this possible union with God and its development is directed and moulded accordingly. Grace, in this view, is 'the most real unity among persons' and it is grace which unites people when two human beings come together in love and offer themselves to each other in a definitive way. Indeed, we might say that the coming together of people united by grace is an integral part of the covenantal dynamic referred to here.

Penance is defined as the sacrament in which the forgiving love of God, present in history in the Church, is addressed to the individual in the situation of her guilt, and again the sacramentality of penance is bound up with the involvement of the individual in the Church *qua* the presence of God's offer in Christ in history.

Sickness, as that moment in which the reality of death casts its shadow over the life of the individual, is discussed as another moment of decisive significance. Both in his attitude to death and the decision for or against God which the prospect of death presents, and in the fundamental loneliness which man experiences as he approaches the end of life, man is again in a situation of decisive existentiell significance, and it is to this situation that

God's word of grace, present through the Church, is addressed in the sacrament of the sick.

The Eucharist is considered separately as it is the sacrament which, more than any other, is of decisive significance for the Church: 'The sacrament of the Eucharist should not simply be counted among the seven sacraments. However much it involves the individual and brings him time and time again into the community with Christ, it is nevertheless the sacrament of the church as such in a very radical sense. It is precisely the institution of the Lord's Supper which is of decisive importance for the founding of the church and for the self-understanding of Jesus as the mediator of salvation.'[96] It is the sacrament in which the sacrifice of the cross becomes present once again, along with the incarnation, resurrection and glorification of Christ and, indeed, the sacrament in which Christ offers himself sacramentally in a way that involves a particular density of his presence in history. Accordingly, the Eucharist is intrinsically bound up with the constitution of the Church as the ongoing presence in time and space of God's offer to human beings in Christ.

Turning finally to look at the common aspects of the sacraments, Rahner draws attention both to the intrinsic link between divine offer and human response in the sacraments and to the fact that the grace of a sacrament can be present without the presence of the usual elements involved in it. The sacraments are significant in the life of the Christian as the means through which human salvation is rendered explicit and as the explicit manifestation of the ultimate depths of human existence itself.

2.2.10 Chapter IX Eschatology

The final chapter of the book deals, appropriately, with the Church's teaching about the last things, namely eschatology. Rahner defines eschatology simply, stating: 'It is the doctrine about man insofar as he is a being who is open to the absolute future of God himself.'[97] He begins his consideration of the content of eschatology by reflecting on what he terms 'the hermeneutics of eschatological statements'.[98] The crux of Rahner's theory here is that as the horizon of death remains impenetrable to us this side of eternity, we are left to extrapolate from our current reality and experience of salvation to beyond this horizon. Linked with this is our orientation towards the future: 'For man

---

[96] Rahner, *Foundations*, 424
[97] Rahner, *Foundations*, 431
[98] Rahner, *Foundations*, 431

cannot understand his present in any other way except as the beginning and the coming to be of a future and as the dynamism towards it.'[99]

In this context, the recognition of Jesus' full humanity ought to prevent us from reading statements in the scriptures as prophecies about what *will* happen rather than as images of what will be the final outworking of human acceptance or rejection of God. Reflecting on the apocalyptic worldview, which is the mode in which these insights are expressed in the Bible, Rahner comments: 'These are images which intend to say something very essential and very real. But they intend to say just what can be said by Christian anthropology about the last things, and nothing else. And we can say at least in principle: whatever we cannot arrive at in this way about the last things belongs to the mode of representation in eschatological statements and to the realm of images, and not to the content.'[100]

Part of what it means to make this distinction is the affirmation that ultimately the precise nature of our fulfilment in eternity remains a mystery, though a mystery in which human freedom plays a role that is both real and decisive. In connection with this freedom, Rahner broaches the traditional teaching of hell as the possibility of ultimate loss. Basically, this amounts to the affirmation that a person can, in the exercise of their freedom, choose definitively against God. The articulation of such a possibility in the tradition, however, is not to be equated with the articulation of the possibility of salvation, as in Christ the acceptance of God's offer to humanity reaches an irreversibility so that even though it cannot be affirmed with certitude that every human being *will* attain to salvation (though this is a very real possibility), it can be affirmed that 'the history of salvation as a whole will reach a positive conclusion for the human race through God's own powerful grace'.[101] Equally, the witness of scripture in no way obliges us to affirm that any individual has or will be definitively lost.

At this point Rahner draws attention to the traditional affirmation that in some way our body will be involved in our final fulfilment and he links this to the fact that human being cannot be abstracted from our corporeal reality. Also, the inherently social nature of being human means that eschatological statements must address the collective destiny of humanity as well as a person's individual destiny. It is impossible to resolve this individual-collective dialectic, but it must also be borne in mind that the two kinds of eschatological statement do not posit or refer to two different and separate

---

[99] Rahner, *Foundations*, 432
[100] Rahner, *Foundations*, 433
[101] Rahner, *Foundations*, 435

realities. Dych links this dynamic to the dual nature of human existence as both individual and social:

> We must speak of the eschatological consummation of history in both an individual and a collective sense because the human person is both an individual and a social being. As unique individuals we are endowed with freedom and responsibility for our own destiny, and as members of the larger history of the human race our individual destiny is related to the destiny of all. This collective history is not merely the place where individual dramas are played out on the stage of the world, but 'the *whole* is a drama, and the stage itself is also part of it'. For the history of God's offer of salvation and the individual's free acceptance of it does not take place alongside the history of the world, but within it as its innermost meaning.[102]

Moving to a consideration of death, Rahner makes the intriguing point that both theology and philosophy are involved in the Catholic position, a point which he will develop more explicitly when considering the affirmation that death does not simply mark the end for a human being. He affirms that death does not involve any kind of seamless continuation of a person's temporal life but rather posits a relationship between time and eternity which he defines in the following terms: 'In reality eternity comes to be in time as time's own mature fruit, an eternity which does not really continue on beyond experienced time. Rather eternity subsumes time by being liberated from the time which came to be temporarily so that freedom and something of final and definitive validity can be achieved. Eternity is not an infinitely long mode of pure time, but rather it is a mode of the spiritual freedom which has been exercised in time, and therefore it can be understood only from a correct understanding of spiritual freedom.'[103]

In thinking about the relation between human existence and eternity, abstraction is a necessity given the impenetrability of death. We can affirm with certainty, however, that human fulfilment is achieved not by avoiding death but through death. Reflecting on the affirmation that death is not the absolute end for a person, Rahner speaks of God's word elucidating the human self-understanding which has continually affirmed that death does not constitute such finality. Eternity is realised in time through experiences such as the absoluteness of the moral law and risking oneself for another in radical love.

---

[102] Dych, *Karl Rahner*, 139

[103] Rahner, *Foundations*, 437

God as our absolute future is the ineluctable horizon against which these and other such experiences take place, and it is in this way that we can affirm that eternity and time are not two distinct and unrelated modes of being. Rahner sums all of this up, stating:

> In an act of free and absolute obedience and in an act of radical love this act is willed as something which is set over against a merely passing moment, and this truth which survives time can be doubted outside the act, but not within the act itself...there could be no appearance of eternity if there were no eternity at all, if time did not live by eternity and not vice versa. No, wherever a person exists in self-presence and in this self-possession risks himself in freedom, he is not actualizing a moment in a series of mere nothings. Rather he is gathering time into a validity which is ultimately incommensurable with the merely external experience of time.[104]

Reflecting on the traditional Catholic doctrine of purgatory, Rahner states that given that we can reasonably affirm some kind of interval between death and the fulfilment of a person in their corporeality, the possibility exists of a purification, a 'maturation', as he puts it prior to ultimate fulfilment.[105] He further makes the point that this could provide Christians with a way of making sense of the idea of reincarnation which is taken for granted in many contexts in the East, and states that reincarnation is indeed possible, providing one affirms the final coming to fulfilment of the person in God. One could argue that this statement raises certain problematic questions, but it certainly does constitute a viable starting point for consideration of these questions, particularly in the context of interfaith encounter.

Rahner closes the chapter by placing all of what has come before in the context of the affirmation of 'grace as the reason for creation',[106] an affirmation which he develops, stating:

> The absolute future of man and of man's history is God himself as the origin of its dynamism and as its goal, God himself, who is not just the mythological cipher for a future which is eternally outstanding, a future which man creates from out of his own emptiness in order to let it fall back again into the nothingness from out of which it arises.

---

[104] Rahner, *Foundations*, 440
[105] Rahner, *Foundations*, 442
[106] Rahner, *Foundations*, 445

But nevertheless *as* the event of God's *self*-communication, this inner-worldly history means everything for man even with regard to his salvation. For it is within this history and not alongside it that there takes place the event of God's self-communication to creatures and the history of the free acceptance of this infinite God.[107]

Thus the relationship between eschatology and history takes the same form as the relationship between God and humanity in the traditional Christological formulas:

There is, therefore, between inner-worldly utopia and eschatology the same unity and difference which is found in the ultimate and basic axiom of Christology: in Christology man and God are not the same, but neither are they ever separate.[108]

2.2.11 Epilogue

The book as a whole concludes with three short modern creeds which take the form of a theological creed, an anthropological creed and a future-orientated creed. The first emphasises transcendence as the experience of forgiving closeness. Expressing things from an anthropocentric point of view, the second of the creeds emphasises the experience of loving and conceives of God as the one who makes the risk of loving another possible. Finally, the future-orientated creed confesses God as the absolute future which has been irreversibly established eschatologically in Jesus Christ.

2.3 Analysis of Rahner's *Foundations* According to Lonergan's Metaphysical Method

As stated, the next stage in this chapter is an examination of Rahner's opus according to the metaphysics laid out by Lonergan in *Insight*. Accordingly, the focus will be primarily on the metaphysical moves made by Rahner rather than on the theological positions which result from them.

Rahner lays out the lynchpin of his approach at the very beginning of *Foundations* with the statement that the location of his work is in lived Christian existence. Straightaway, then, we are in the first of Lonergan's three

---

[107] Rahner, *Foundations*, 446
[108] Rahner, *Foundations*, 447

stages – experience, or to use the metaphysical terminology, potency. A further point made right at the start is Rahner's averral that he seeks an integration of philosophy and theology in what could be described in Lonerganian terms as a higher viewpoint. In a move that mirrors Lonergan's insistence on the self-affirmation of the knower as fundamental in developing his epistemology, Rahner posits human self-interpretation as the beginning of the theological task. Theology, then, is an attempt at grasping the relationship (insight, form) between the various facets of human experience (experience, potency) and Rahner presents Christianity as the answer to the question which the human being is in her very being – the sought-after insight, or form.

In terms of the dynamics of the divine engagement with humanity, two aspects are presented, both falling into the category of experience/potency: namely God's self-communication in the depths of human existence and God's self-communication in history in Christ; the relationship between these two mirrors exactly Lonergan's implicit and explicit metaphysics, a point which will be relevant later in this examination. Rahner's formulation of the unity of reality and the self-presence of reality to itself in human consciousness corresponds exactly to Lonergan's self-affirmation of the knower and here again it becomes apparent that both are seeking to spell out the implications of the reflexive self-knowledge of the human being. In Lonergan's framework, then, Rahner's theological project is aiming at intelligent knowing, what metaphysically Lonergan terms central potency, form and act.

Taking the insight further, Rahner cites Christian doctrine itself as the reflexive expression of the depths of human existential experience. Christian doctrine, therefore, is the intelligent insight (central form)[109] which makes sense of and grasps the relationship between the different aspects of fundamental human existential experience. It is central rather than conjugate form as it does not merely describe the experiences in question but interprets them and gives meaning and sense to them.

For Rahner, one of the most fundamental data of the self-possession of human beings is the pure openness to being, the infinite horizon. Again, this is an experience – potency – and it is an experience made reflexively present and intelligently appropriated, and therefore it is central rather than conjugate potency. This openness, along with the reflexively present consciousness of the knowing subject, present in every act of knowing, comprises what Rahner terms transcendental experience; both aspects of this can be described as central potency. With this we arrive at the first major conclusion in seeking to parse Rahner's theology in *Foundations* according to Lonerganian

---

[109] Cf. 1.2.3

metaphysics: transcendental experience reflexively grasped is central potency. Further aspects of human transcendentality are added as Rahner proceeds with his exposition, e.g. responsibility for self, the experience of love and freedom, but all of these cohere with the assertion that transcendental experience is to be identified as central potency.

As the reflexive articulation in meaning-bestowing interpretation of the various experiences which Rahner names as transcendental, Christian doctrine then assumes the role of central form. Central form interprets central potency in the light of the higher viewpoint necessitated by these insights, namely the affirmation of the Absolute Mystery which constitutes us as human beings and the presence of which is verifiable in transcendental experience. The affirmation of these doctrines *qua* central form, in the context of the affirmation of Absolute Mystery as the higher viewpoint in which is grasped the relationship between the multifarious aspects of what is experienced in transcendental experience, corresponds to Lonergan's virtually unconditioned – the conditions of the affirmation are fulfilled and in the move from contingent being to absolute being that this affirmation involves, no further questions are left unanswered.

In terms of the fundamental transposition from the categorical to the transcendental in Rahner's approach, this corresponds to the insight into insight, the understanding of what it is to understand that is involved in Lonergan's method in *Insight*. Both thinkers, then, are grounding their affirmations, epistemologically speaking, on the self-affirmation and reflexive presence of the thinker to herself; what is experienced in this self-affirmation and reflexive presence leads Rahner to the affirmation of God *qua* Absolute Mystery. Interestingly, though, for Rahner, God as the infinite horizon is a necessary precondition of the perception of potency, act and form. Thus God is simultaneously the higher viewpoint derived from central potency and the striving for central form through which the relationship between the various aspects of transcendental experience is grasped, as well as the very condition of their existence to begin with.

At this point the content of central form becomes fleshed out somewhat more as Rahner articulates three elements of human knowledge of the divine: *a posteriori* knowledge of God derived from transcendental experience, divine self-disclosure and divine salvific activity in history. Again, all three of these articulations constitute central form as they are the intelligently grasped relationships between disparate phenomena, the attempt at which grasp necessitates the higher viewpoint of the affirmation of God as Absolute Mystery in which they become intelligently grasped. This higher viewpoint involves the identification of the transcendental horizon experienced by human beings with God as the Absolute Mystery. As the transcendental horizon which makes possible all our knowing, God cannot be directly known and hence Rahner is careful to insist that the appellation 'God' is a term relative to us and that the higher viewpoint arrived at (in terms of the comprehensive attempt to grasp the relationship between the multifarious aspects of proportionate being this higher viewpoint is itself central form) involves the affirmation of God as mystery which is fundamentally incomprehensible to us.

This does not constitute an inverse insight, however, as what is in question is not a lack of intelligibility *in se* but rather, *via* explicit metaphysics *qua* heuristic structure of being, the affirmation of form and act without a direct unmediated grasp of potency. Accordingly, Rahner affirms that as the Holy Mystery constitutes us as subjects in will, freedom and love, the Holy Mystery itself wills, exercises freedom and is loving.

In terms of the metaphysical correlation involved in what Rahner is doing here, the crucial point remains that for Rahner as for Lonergan, the affirmation of God comes as a result of the logical consequences of understanding the depth phenomena of human experience. Again, for both thinkers, the traditional arguments for God's existence are boiled down to a reflection on the relationship between finite and absolute being, a relationship which Rahner names as metaphysical causality. In Lonergan's metaphysics, this designation corresponds to what he calls external causes; namely, exemplary, efficient and causal. Interestingly, Rahner spells out the implications of this insight for human speech as he reflects on the analogical character of all language used in relation to God, an aspect which is missing from Lonergan's analysis in *Insight*. Interestingly, too, for Rahner the affirmation of the Holy Mystery as personal issues from what is sensed by us of this reality in our constitution by it as subjects, an affirmation which constitutes a move from conjugate potency to central potency, form and act. As divine experience is mediated to us through human experience, central form, as our experience intelligently grasped and lived is fundamentally related to our autonomy as human beings for Rahner; indeed, the experience of freedom is itself a dimension of transcendental experience.

The result of all of this is that the second fundamental affirmation resulting from the analysis of Rahner's thought according to Lonergan's metaphysical method can be stated in terms of the self-presence of the human subject to herself, resulting in the shift from knowing as mere extroversion to intelligent knowing (conjugate potency, form and act to central potency, form and act) and issuing in the higher viewpoint of the affirmation of absolute being as a result of an intelligent grasp of our experience.

Chapter III of *Foundations* centres on an examination of sin and guilt, which Rahner defines as a refusal of the divine self-offering present in human experience. Just as for Lonergan sin is an absence of intelligibility and a refusal to yield to reason in the realm of action, for Rahner sin, as defined above, is a self-refuting and self-contradictory act, premised as it is on that which it seeks to repudiate. Thus sin is, for Rahner also, an absence of intelligent grasping of reality, and it is notable that both thinkers' notions of sin are in continuity with the Augustinian tradition of evil as *privatio boni*.

In line with this notion of evil as a lack is Rahner's affirmation of the primary experience of justifying grace, along with the experience of the transcendental horizon as holy and as promise in the divine self-communication, sin then being the refusal of all of this. From the point of view of Lonergan's metaphysics, what is involved here is a further fleshing out of the data of central potency grasped in central form (a further example is the articulation by Rahner of the human experience of being borne by the Holy Mystery). Accordingly, there is a real sense for Rahner, as for Lonergan, of sin and evil as ontological lack, as an absence of being. To this degree, we may speak of their articulation as an inverse insight – what is grasped is absurdity and the absence of any intelligibility.

Reflecting further on notions of ontology, Rahner makes the assertion that God's self-communication to human beings is ontological, that the relation between God and humans is one of formal causality in which the causal agent participates ontologically in that which is caused. As subjects constituted by the ultimate horizon which is present to us only as mediated by categorical reality, this assertion belongs to central form *qua* the grasped relationship between elements of our experience, which form is ultimately located in the higher viewpoint entailed by the movement from proportional to absolute being. As beings who are formally caused by the Holy Mystery, our experience, beginning in time but ultimately finishing beyond it, is one of being borne forward by this mystery. This leads to the affirmation of God as our future, again an articulation which is an element of the central form, in which the grasp of central experience leads to the affirmation of absolute being.

The metaphysical designation of Christian doctrine as central form has already been encountered above and this concept becomes further developed in Rahner's view of the Trinity. Rahner insists that the economic Trinity is the same as the immanent Trinity and thus, in Lonerganian terms, we can name the doctrine of the Trinity as the insight that grasps the relationship between the different elements of our experience of God.

Equally, the threefold structure of potency, act and form pertains in each aspect of our experience of the divine, including the historical manifestation of God in Christ – in each aspect, we experience phenomena, the relationship between them is grasped issuing in an insight and in a higher perspective (or reinforcing a higher perspective already arrived at), and the conditions of the insight are seen to be fulfilled in it, leaving no further questions to be asked and the insight is affirmed as true.

For both Lonergan and Rahner, the idea of transcendence is crucial and, indeed, both view it in similar terms. Fundamentally, both view transcendence as heading for being, so to speak; and, in a manner reminiscent of Augustine, finding its term in God. This in turn is what drives history, leading Rahner to speak of history as the history of transcendentality itself. Rahner's assertion of salvation history as history on God's part too is a further insight corresponding to central form, as he unifies the experience of God as the transcendental horizon who constitutes us as subjects, the divine self-communication and our intrinsic historicity.

As already observed, the notion of dialectic runs through Rahner's thought and at this point it is formulated in relation to God's presence in revelation and his absence *qua* Holy Mystery. Given that no sublation is offered, we must assume that, in existentialist manner, a Kierkegaardian dialectic is intended in which the two terms are kept in tension, with no resolution being proposed. Here we stumble on an anomaly in the metaphysical pairing of Rahner's thought with Lonergan's metaphysics, as the model of dialectic used by Lonergan, in which different insights are ordered together in a process of metaphysical equivalence issuing in coherent insight affirmed as act, does not seem to encompass what is intended here. The only option offered in terms of Lonergan's schema in *Insight* seems to be that of an inverse insight, yet this implies we have sufficient knowledge to close off the possibility of a higher viewpoint, something which here would seem to require a 'God's-eye' view.

Chapter IV continues with an examination of the phenomenon of revelation. Revelation is cited as taking place in the faith of the recipient, again placing it firmly within the threefold structure of central potency, form and act, a point that is underlined by the insistence that the miracles of Jesus were essentially phatic events. This designation mirrors Lonergan's taking of the processes of consciousness as fundamental. Thus the history of salvation and revelation can be viewed as a synthesis between the divine and human. Given that this synthesis occurs within human experience *qua* central potency, Rahner asserts that the incarnation is a process which, if not blocked through sin, happens in all human subjects and not just in Christ. A further consequence is that salvation history can be seen as corresponding to history in the usual sense, as central form corresponds to conjugate form. In this sense, we can speak of Jesus as God's Logos – the divinely offered insight which enables us to move beyond mere extroversion to a grasp of the meaning of our life and experience as human beings. Thus the *kerygma* of Jesus as God's revelation bears within itself an intrinsic credibility, as it provides the relationship between existentiell experience and human transcendentality.

In his soteriology, the same process of garnered insight can be observed on Rahner's part, especially as he formulates the relationship between the unity of humanity, the unity of history and the explicit revelation of Christ. Thus the revelation in Christ is intended for all people everywhere, in all of our dimensions.

Like Lonergan, Rahner proposes an evolutionary dynamic in his view of human development, but here applied to the historical process of divinisation; whereas Lonergan offers what are, in his own metaphysical terminology, analytic propositions (logic), Rahner proposes analytic principles (logic with existence) in his formulation of Christian doctrine in terms of salvation history. The assertion of the inexorability of this process is also central form, as it grasps the significance of the observed evolutionary dynamic in the fullness of its meaning. This evolutionary dynamic is perceived in the higher viewpoint of the affirmation of God as absolute being manifest in Christ as the saviour figure in whom both divine offer and human acceptance of this offer exist irrevocably and absolutely. A similar metaphysical observation can be made in relation to Christ as the final cause, bearing the movement of all things forward as their goal.

Like Lonergan, for Rahner the spiritual is defined as being which is present to itself in consciousness. In light of this definition, the traditional affirmation of Christ as the Logos (self-awareness) of God appears with particular clarity. Coherent with the threefold metaphysical pattern already adduced, Rahner cites the believer's experience of God in Christ as the starting point for the Christological enterprise. The observation is made that the roots of faith and the relationship of these roots to grace cannot be made entirely reflexive. This makes good sense in light of the observation that we ourselves are a part of what is experienced in the potency which issues in form and act, though it does imply absence of complete reflexiveness of consciousness. Arguably, though, such complete reflexiveness belongs to the domain of God alone, so we are left with the effects of the hidden roots of our experience as the potency which enables us to move to form and then to act.

For Rahner, grace and understanding are already present in the human person to some degree. Lack of faith, then, is a closing of oneself to grasping the significance of certain phenomena which are part and parcel of the experience of being human. It is an instance of knowing *qua* mere extroversion in which intelligent grasp is absent, and, in its most extreme form, of scotosis as a structuring refusal of insight.

Reflecting on the role of Christ's death and resurrection, the resurrection is presented as the insight *par excellence* in which is manifested an identity of structure between the transcendental and categorical (central form). In the formulation of Christ's death as working our salvation in a manner analogical to that of a sacrament (effecting what it signifies), the same threefold structure can be observed which has already been presented as running throughout Rahner's opus. We experience the forgiveness of sins and God's salvific will for us in our experience of the death and resurrection of Christ as a reality that is present to us. The drawing out of what the co-presence of these two dimensions means (forgiveness of our sins and the experience of our salvation with the death and resurrection of Christ) takes us into the area of insight in the intellectual pattern of experience, or central form. A similar dynamic pertains to the experience of the particular density of Christ's presence in the poor and oppressed of our world.

Rahner's consideration of the significance of the other religions is framed in the dialectic that pertains between the transcendental and the categorical, and between Christ and the Spirit. In Lonerganian terms, Rahner's analysis at this point exhibits a lacuna, as Rahner does not consider whether or not the other religions can constitute central rather than conjugate potency, form and act, or whether it is universally the same set of phenomena that is being reflected upon in the various religions.

The reflection on the Church in Chapter VII exhibits a by now familiar working out of the same threefold structure of potency, act and form that we have seen to be operative throughout Rahner's analysis in *Foundations*. Again, in relation to the Church, the transcendental is experienced in the categorical and part of this experience of the Church as the ongoing, historical presence of God in Christ is the dynamic presence of the Spirit. This presence of the Spirit leads to the affirmation of a legitimate principle of development which leads to the continual impetus towards developing theological higher viewpoints. Rahner cites as important the role of the Church as a norm for the subjectivity of the individual, something which is necessary given the intrinsically interpersonal character of our existence. In Lonerganian terms, this ideally should mean a template of the correct unfolding of the unrestricted desire to know (remote criterion of truth) and possibly even the attempt at a dialectically ordered universal viewpoint – an approach which accords perfectly with the traditional Catholic positing of natural theology as the first point of departure in the theological enterprise. As with Christology, what is crucial in ecclesiology is our experience of the presence of Christ historically manifested in the Church (potency), the significance of this and its relationship with the multifarious elements of our experience, both within the life of the Church and in the world generally (form), and our affirmation of this relationship and its ultimate significance in faith (act).

Chapter VIII turns to a consideration of the life of the Christian and opens with an identification of Christian life with human life, a relationship which in Lonerganian terms can be conceived of as being the relationship between the central and the conjugate. What Rahner terms 'optimistic pessimism' results from the experience of living being understood according to the intelligent pattern of experience, with its transcendental depths being made explicit through the categorical in intelligent insight. Like Lonergan, Rahner views the lack of necessary insight in contingent being alone as being a factor which turns our faces to God.

Morality, in this light and in a *modus* which corresponds perfectly to Lonergan's conception, is a question of the correct unfolding of understanding transferred into existentiell mode. Moving on to consider the sacraments, the emphasis is once again on our experience as the starting point. The experience of the transcendental in the categorical corresponding to central potency, act and form is further underlined by Rahner in his assertion that the sacraments are bound up with a person's acceptance of the divine offer, an acceptance that can be unthematically realised in a person's acceptance of their life in its myriad circumstances.

In Chapter IX Rahner turns to consider eschatology and starts by defining this as human life in the context of God as the future of humanity. This can be paired with Lonergan's notion of explicit metaphysics, functioning as a heuristic structure given that we have not yet experienced what the future will be. Rather, as Lonergan states at the start of *Insight*: 'Thoroughly understand what it is to understand, and not only will you understand the broad lines of all there is to be understood but also you will possess a fixed base, an invariant pattern, opening upon all further developments of understanding.'[110]

This quotation from Lonergan effectively sums up what Rahner has to say about eschatology; whilst the potency is not something we can have access to, the form and act can be anticipated. Thus Rahner formulates his hermeneutics of eschatological statements in terms of eschatology as an existentiell extrapolation of Christian anthropology into the future (he further supports his point by drawing attention to the necessary limitations of Jesus' human consciousness).

Speaking of death not being the absolute end for human beings, Rahner speaks of God's word elucidating human subjectivity in terms of a fusion of experience and insight which takes the form of God's presence in his word.

---

[110] Lonergan, *Insight*, xxvii

This dynamic is isomorphic with the hypostatic union, and in it our finite experience is subsumed and led to a higher viewpoint. All of this is located in the basic and fundamental experience of God as the transcendental horizon grasped intelligently through the central act that is faith.

The reality of this 'being borne into God' as our absolute future issues in Rahner's affirmation of grace as the very reason for creation, an affirmation which can be viewed as the pinnacle of the central act of faith which rebounds and frames our ongoing experience of finite existence.

The book closes with an epilogue in which Rahner presents three creeds: a theological creed, an anthropological one and a future-orientated one. It is interesting to observe that each of the creeds bases itself on a different noetic superstructure. It is this heterogeneity present at this point in Rahner's analysis which may prove the key to using Lonergan's metaphysical method to dialectically relate the different religions. Such an approach could potentially do so in a way which goes beyond an all-embracing inclusivism in which the many are, without further ado, subsumed into an all-encompassing one.

2.4 Conclusion

In the light of the above considerations, it is now possible to sum up Rahner's theological project in *Foundations* in the following terms: the foundation of Rahner's theological project is human experience: in metaphysical terms, potency. He is aiming at a higher viewpoint in which philosophy, theology and, we may say, anthropology are integrated and he is also aiming at what Lonergan calls the intelligent pattern of experience. The transcendentalist foundation of Rahner's project is the self-affirmation of the knower. Transcendental experience (experience of the infinite horizon, of love, freedom, etc.) can be designated central potency. Corresponding to this, as the reflexive articulation of the nature and meaning of this experience, stands Christian doctrine *qua* central form.

The higher viewpoint of the affirmation of God as Absolute Mystery results from the attempt to intelligently grasp the potency that is transcendental experience along with the experience of revelation in history. In Christian doctrine, the relationship between the different elements of the central potency that is transcendentalist experience, along with God's salvific activity in history, is formulated and grasped in the light of this higher viewpoint. The virtually unconditioned pertains here (the fulfilment of the conditions of central form and the absence of further questions to be answered). This leads on to the central act – what in traditional Christian terms is designated faith.

The principle of *analogia entis* is invoked in the posited isomorphism between the nature of human beings, as constituted by the Absolute Mystery as subjects who are free and loving, and the Absolute Mystery as itself free and loving.

The self-presence of the human subject to herself is what leads from knowing as mere extroversion to the intelligent knowing that is faith, and to the affirmation of the Absolute Mystery *qua* higher viewpoint in which central potency, form and act take place. Equally, history and salvation history stand in relation to each other in the same way that conjugate and central potency, form and act are related. The other religions are also considered in terms of the relationship between the transcendental and the categorical and arguably, by extension, also fall under the category of the relationship between the conjugate and the central.

Morality, as for Lonergan, is correct understanding transposed into existentiell mode and evil is viewed as *privatio boni*. The good is further identified with existence, resulting in an inverse insight where evil is concerned: namely, absurdity and lack of intelligibility in place of the intelligibility which occurs where insights are formulated.

The relation of God to human beings as formal cause is formulated as an element of central form and this issues also in the designation of God as our future. The Trinity stands as the intelligent insight which grasps the relationship between our various experiences of God and the threefold pattern of intelligent knowing is the form which our knowledge of God takes. This threefold pattern also constitutes our knowledge of Christ, our theology of the Church, the sacraments and indeed all other branches of theology. In addition, the resurrection stands as the insight *par excellence* when grasped as central form. The grasping of the significance of the experience of the evolutionary dynamic present in creation also constitutes an element of central form. The spiritual is defined as the self-presence of the knowing subject to herself and this is the phenomenological nature of central potency.

Lack of faith constitutes a refusal of insight, most often in terms of the failure to move from conjugate to central patterns of knowing, but with the possibility of scotosis also. Linking in with this, the Church is seen, among other things, as a norm for the subjectivity of the individual, in a way that corresponds with Lonergan's remote criterion of truth as the correct unfolding of the unrestricted desire to know. Rahner's eschatology functions in a way that corresponds to Lonergan's citing of explicit metaphysical structure as heuristic insight. Finally, the three creeds may be seen as a parsing of Christian doctrine as central form according to different aspects of transcendental experience.

3 Nāgārjuna's *Mūlamadhyamakakārikā*: A Lonerganian Analysis

3.1 Preliminary Remarks

For any student of the Mahāyāna, and indeed of Buddhism more generally, the significance of Nāgārjuna is surely unparalleled in the history of the development of Buddhist thought. In terms of the systematic setting forth of the implications of the basic tenets of Buddhism in philosophical terms, this significance has earned him the title of 'the second Buddha' in Mahāyāna circles. Though relatively little is known about his life other than that he was a monk who lived in India around the second century CE, and the list of texts he authored is disputed, the authorship of his most influential and significant work, the *Mūlamadhyamakakārikā*, is undisputed. Comprising twenty-seven chapters treating the various elements of perceived existence, Nāgārjuna's magnum opus comprises a work at once penetrating in its analysis and formidable in the demands it makes of the reader.

Whilst a central and crucial figure in the evolution of Buddhist philosophy, Nāgārjuna emerged from the remarkably fertile context of the early period of Indian Buddhism which saw a flowering of reflection on the teachings preserved in oral form in the centuries subsequent to the death of the Buddha. Of particular significance in contextualising the thought of Nāgārjuna are the development of Abhidharma and the views contained in the Prajñā-pāramitā sutras.

The Abhidharma reached its climax in the fourth century CE but it can be traced back as far as the third century BCE and represents the systematising scholastic approach of the pre-Mahāyāna period of Indian Buddhism known as Nikāya Buddhism. It involved an attempt to both standardise and elaborate on Buddhist doctrine and embodied a concern with philosophical rigour that included a hermeneutical awareness that resonates with many of the philosophical concerns of our own era.

The core of the Prajñā-pāramitā sutras was composed between 100 BCE and 100 CE and two concerns which were to become particularly important in the development of Mahāyāna Buddhism are expounded: the Bodhisattva ideal and the elaboration of the concept of śūnyatā. It is the latter of these two which is particularly important for understanding the concerns that motivated Nāgārjuna. Śūnyatā, or emptiness, played an important role in earlier Buddhist teaching, particularly with regard to the teaching of not-self, but it is in the Prajñā-pāramitā sutras that insight into emptiness assumes a new prominence along with the assertion that all dharmas are empty. It is notable that this assertion is not restricted to conditioned dharmas alone but includes dharmas such as Nirvāṇa.

It is out of this dual context that Nāgārjuna sought to elaborate his 'middle way'. This way lay between the abhidharmic teaching that ascribed essences to the dharmas which were the building blocks of compound phenomena on the one hand and a nihilistic interpretation of śūnyatā on the other. In addition, Nāgārjuna engages with the view that mental dharmas, though also contingent, were possessed of a particular reality, a view which also emerged from the context of Abhidharma.

Through the centuries the *Mūlamadhyamakakārikā* has given rise to divergent schools of interpretations, the differences between which still perdure today. For the purposes of this work, the reading that will be considered is that of Jay L. Garfield, a modern Western interpreter rooted in the Prāsaṅgika-Mādhyamika tradition. At the outset, I must point out that I have chosen Garfield's reading of the text despite having strong reservations about what I would argue is a reductionist reading of Nāgārjuna's opus. It has been selected, however, as such a reading proves much less convivial to Rahner's position, and indeed to any position advancing a spiritual viewpoint, and accordingly provides a stronger test for Lonergan's epistemology. Garfield's interpretation of the text as set forth in his commentary on it has been chosen both because of its lucidity and completeness along with his fine translation of the work itself from the Tibetan, and also because, for the purposes of providing a test of the capacity of Lonergan's *Insight* to integrate disparate positions, Garfield's position falls within the category of those modern interpretations of Nāgārjuna that are less congenial to positions seeking to affirm belief in Absolute Being. Garfield situates his reading within the extensive commentarial literature based on the text describing his position in the following terms: 'The interpretation I offer is situated squarely within a Prāsaṅgika-Mādhyamika interpretation of Nāgārjuna (the philosophical school that reads *Mūlamadhyamakakārikā* through the commentaries of Buddhapālita and Candrakīrti). But more specifically, my reading is heavily influenced by the Tibetan Geluk-pa tradition that takes as central the commentaries of dGe-'dun-grub, mKhas-grub-rje and especially Je

Tsong Khapa.'[1] The place of Garfield's analysis in the wider constellation of interpretation lies beyond the scope of this work and accordingly it will be treated as a freestanding reading of the text.

The text itself is written in a terse style in which each verse consists of four lines, sometimes setting forth Nāgārjuna's own position, sometimes that of his opponent, sometimes expressing the underlying philosophical point through positing questions. It is fair to say that Nāgārjuna's style is frequently terse and cryptic and terms such as existence, nonexistence, etc. assume a particular meaning in the context of the text specifically related to the doctrine of the two truths that he expounds. The crux of the text, philosophically speaking, is the assertion of the contingent nature of all dharmas, expressed in Nāgārjuna's designation of them as empty, a designation which is then declared to be itself empty of inherent existence. In this respect, Nāgārjuna seeks to philosophically delineate the 'middle way' proposed in Buddhist tradition by the Buddha himself, a middle path between nihilism and the assertion of the inherent existence of dharmas. In between these two philosophical extremes lies the contingent nature of phenomena as set forth in the Buddhist doctrine of *pratītyasamutpāda*, frequently translated as 'dependent co-origination', and it is this that Nāgārjuna terms the emptiness of dharmas.

The methodological stratagem he adopts to prove his point is that of reductio ad absurdum, through which he seeks to expose the contradictions inherent in the delusory perspective that lies at the heart of *saṃsāric* existence. In this way he seeks to use these contradictions to explode the illusions contained in a naïve realist perspective that assumes the accuracy of our customary mode of perception and moves from this to assuming that reality corresponds to these perceptions. Noting the similarity between Nāgārjuna's approach and that of the Deconstructionists in twentieth-century thought, Klaus Klostermeier comments: 'Nāgārjuna also writes "under erasure" – he denies any essential relationship between word and reality, but he is using the customary reality-referring words nevertheless. Similarly the strange adherence to metaphysics while denying it with so many words that "free us from and guard us within the metaphysical enclosure" has its parallel in the *prasaṅga* method as well.'[2]

---

[1] Jay L. Garfield, *The Fundamental Wisdom of the Middle Way: Nāgārjuna's Mūlamadhyamakakārikā: Translation and Commentary by Jay L. Garfield* (Oxford: Oxford University Press,1995), 97

[2] Klaus K. Klostermaier, *Buddhism: A Short Introduction* (Oxford: Oneworld Publications, 1999), 180

Perhaps inevitably, comparisons have also been made between Nāgārjuna and the early work of Ludwig Wittgenstein, though these comparisons have not gone unchallenged.[3] The aim in this chapter will be to reconstruct Nāgārjuna's argument following his own chapter headings and then to parse this argument according to Lonergan's categories. The attempt will then be made in the next chapter to test the viability of Lonergan's thesis by attempting to dialectically relate Rahner's position with Nāgārjuna's on the basis of Lonergan's categories.

3.2.1 Dedicatory Verses

The text itself opens with dedicatory verses which, in this case, far from being a mere textual formality, contain *in nuce* the entire programme of what is to follow. On a first reading they seem to be cryptic, even contradictory. In them Nāgārjuna pays homage to the Buddha who is cited as teaching that:

> Whatever is dependently arisen is
> Unceasing, unborn,
> Unannihilated, not permanent, not coming, not going,
> Without distinction, without identity,
> And free from conceptual construction.[4]

With the juxtapositioning of 'dependently arisen' with 'unceasing, unborn', etc. Nāgārjuna immediately plunges the reader into the heart of a paradox which will be fundamental to his analysis and is encapsulated in his doctrine of 'two truths'. Throughout, the distinction is made between conventional reality and ultimate reality, with designations being assigned, albeit often implicitly, to one perspective or the other. In these verses, the relevant designations are made from the ultimate point of view. Dharmas, as the products of dependent arising, are ultimately empty of any substantial being. Thus, as Garfield points out: 'To say that "whatever is dependently arisen is unceasing

---

[3] Tyson Anderson, 'Wittgenstein and Nāgārjuna's Paradox,' *Philosophy East and West*, 35 (1985), 157–169

[4] *Mūlamadhyamakakārikā*: Dedicatory Verses
All quotations from the *Mūlamadhyamakakārikā* (MMK) are taken from Garfield's translation contained in *The Fundamental Wisdom of the Middle Way: Nāgārjuna's Mūlamadhyamakakārikā: Translation and Commentary*

and unborn" is to emphasize that dependent arising amounts to emptiness, and emptiness amounts to nonexistence in the ultimate sense.'[5]

Here, too, we see an example of the seemingly contradictory use of language as terms evolved in reference to conventional reality are pressed into action to designate that same reality as it is ultimately. Behind all of the negations in these verses lies the idea of essence as inherent existence, the ultimate purpose of the text being to show that there is no such thing, and indeed there cannot be. Garfield sums up this paradoxical use of language in his gloss on the final line of the dedication:

> The final remark – that the phenomenal world is free from conceptual imputation – raises a tension that is central to Mādhyamika philosophy and that animates the whole of the text: The tension between the desire to characterize the ultimate nature of things and the recognition that all characterization is conventional…This dynamic philosophical tension – a tension between the Mādhyamika account of the limits of what can be coherently said and its analytical ostension of what can't be said without paradox but must be understood – must constantly be borne in mind in reading the text. It is not an incoherent mysticism, but it is a logical tightrope act at the very limits of language and metaphysics.[6]

3.2.2 Chapter I Examination of Conditions

The first chapter of the work is essentially an attack on a naïve realist view of causation in which Nāgārjuna's argument hinges on the distinction between causes *qua* inhererently existing phenomena containing causal power as part of their essence and conditions *qua* phenomena which are themselves empty of inherent existence and, in various combinations, combine to give rise to equally empty effects. The chapter presents its conclusions at the outset:

> Neither from itself nor from another,
> Nor from both,
> Nor without a cause,
> Does anything whatever anywhere arise.[7]

---

[5] Garfield, *Fundamental Wisdom*, 101
[6] Garfield, *Fundamental Wisdom*, 102
[7] MMK 1:1

In this verse Nāgārjuna rules out four alternatives which would have been espoused by various rival schools at the time, but the underlying point remains the same: nothing is caused by any inherently existent factor, nor is anything that inherently exists brought into being. The third line emphasises also that things do not spontaneously arise. Having cited the different kinds of conditions, Nāgārjuna points out that as there is no such thing as essence, the basis for making any ultimate distinctions between phenomena disappears. Equally the notion of 'power to act' understood as causal power (verse 3) is deemed contradictory as it would involve an infinite regress which leaves unsolved the question of how a power to act comes to be:

> Causal powers, according to those who posit them, are meant to explain the causal nexus – they are meant to explain how it is that causes bring about their effects, which is itself supposed to be otherwise inexplicable. But, Nāgārjuna argues, if there were a causal power, it itself, as a phenomenon, would either have to have conditions or not. If the former, there is a vicious explanatory regress, for then one has to explain how the powers to act are themselves brought about by the conditions, and this is the very link presupposed by the friend of powers to be inexplicable. One could posit powers the conditions have to bring about powers and powers the powers have to bring about effects. But this just moves one step further down the regress.[8]

On the other hand, if such powers are deemed to be without conditions, the logical absurdity of deeming them to exist without any explanation as well as the falsifying of the doctrine of dependent origination is involved. Nāgārjuna answers by saying that conventionally phenomena do have power to bring about other phenomena but ultimately such power is not something which can be coherently ascribed to phenomena as a property. Here, as throughout the text, the argument hinges on the doctrine of the two truths pertaining to the conventional realm of designation and what is deemed to be ultimately true respectively.

The rest of the chapter is a fleshing out of this view with respect to the different forms of 'condition' current in the philosophical milieu of the time. Two further salient points emerge: Nāgārjuna points out the incompatibility of phenomena existing inherently with the doctrine of *pratītyasamutpāda* as what exists inherently can, by definition, neither arise nor cease to exist. This in turn leads him to state that conditions and effects are both therefore

---

[8] Garfield, *Fundamental Wisdom*, 113

deemed to be empty of inherent existence, thus setting the stage for the next element of the argument.

3.2.3   Chapter II Examination of Motion

In the second chapter the argument moves to an analysis of motion and specifically aims to refute the notion that motion can be characterised as having itself any kind of intrinsic existence. This argument takes the form of refuting the notion that motion can be considered an entity, that it is an independent property or that it can be viewed as an element within the essence of moving things. Whilst the range of applicability of the argument is a disputed point in the interpretation of the *Mūlamadhyamakakārikā*, Garfield asserts that the mention of change in the opening line of verse 2[9] gives the argument a further significance:

> This verse is important not only because it announces the obvious reply that motion exists in presently moving things, but because it introduces the connection between change in general and motion. Though this interpretative point is controversial, and several scholars have given widely different interpretations, it is highly plausible that Nāgārjuna is calling attention to the fact that the attack on motion as an inherently existent phenomenon is a general attack on seeing change or impermanence as inherently existent. This suggests that even the properties that according to Buddhist philosophy characterize all things – being dependently arisen and being impermanent – are not themselves inherently existent.[10]

In Garfield's view, then, the argument being made here feeds into much more fundamental conclusions which arise later in the text. The crux of the argument is a consideration of the idea of motion as a property of the mover; though the other points adduced above are also considered, they are treated by extending the logical argument relating to this point to the analogous categories they entail. The argument rests on a number of fundamental points.

---

[9] Verse two reads: 'Where there is change, there is motion.
  Since there is change in the moving,
  And not in the moved or not-moved
  Motion is in that which is moving.'
                                   MMK 2:2

[10] Garfield, *Fundamental Wisdom*, 125

First and foremost, it is pointed out that if motion and the mover are conceived of as existing independently of each other, one is left in the position of having to posit two subjects: one which moves the motion and one which moves the mover. This in turn leads to an infinite regress and the logical absurdity that such a proliferation of subjects entails. Affirming the independent existence of movement and the mover also means that it is possible to conceive of a mover that lacks the property of motion and thus has the contrary property, i.e. that of being non-moving, or of movement without a mover, both of which involve further logical absurdity. 'Property' here, as elsewhere in the text, denotes that which is intrinsically so, the very view which is under attack by Nāgārjuna in this chapter and, indeed, throughout the text. The question of when precisely motion can be viewed as beginning is also raised, drawing on the view that the present lacks any actual duration, thus relegating motion to the past and the future, a position which also lacks coherence. The argument is rehearsed again in relation to stasis with similar conclusions being drawn.

Ultimately Nāgārjuna replies to the questions raised as one would expect: by positing movement and the mover as conventionally existent and mutually constituting but lacking any inherent self-existence from the ultimate point of view. Garfield sums up this view thus: 'Motion can only be understood in relation to movers – as a relation between their positions at different times. Movers can only be understood as movers in relation to motion so understood. But to understand motion and movers this way is not to reify them as entities – and so to escape the dilemma of their identity or difference.'[11]

3.2.4 Chapter III Examination of the Senses

The next topic under consideration is sense perception and in approaching this topic Nāgārjuna employs the standard Buddhist typology which posits six senses rather than five, the mind being viewed as a sense in and of itself, particularly in terms of introspection. In verse one, the ground is laid for what follows by stating that each of the senses requires an object, though the question of any possible reflexivity involved in mental introspection is not treated in this chapter. The key argument occurs in verse two in a somewhat cryptic piece of reasoning which seeks to debunk the idea of vision having any intrinsic existence. The argument runs that if vision existed inherently, it would not require an external object and therefore could occur even in the absence of such. Yet as vision must be vision *of* something, the only logical

---

[11] Garfield, *Fundamental Wisdom*, 132

possibility left in the absence of any external object would be that vision sees itself, something which is clearly not the case. Therefore, Nāgārjuna argues, if vision cannot see itself then it clearly does not exist as something with inherent being. The opponent's voice is heard implicitly as the objection that vision is like fire – not consuming itself yet existing in and of itself – is dismissed.

This particular argument was often employed in early Buddhist debates and it is treated more fully in Chapter X where the notion of the inherent existence of fire is refuted. Here, however, it is dismissed through drawing out the logical implications of temporal categories. As something must be burned in the past, present or future, and it is logically absurd to state that something *is* being burned in the past or future, the only option is to say it is being burned in the present. Yet for Nāgārjuna the present is not a possibility either as the absence of sufficient duration in which the present has not already receded into the past or is yet to happen does not provide sufficient time for anything to be consumed by fire or, indeed, for anything to be seen. In addition, the actual act of seeing takes time, which means that nothing is seen in the present except a sense impression which has been formed of something which is now in the past. Therefore one only ever immediately sees sense impressions and not those phenomena from which such impressions are formed.

The argument is intensified by drawing out the absurdity of viewing vision as a property in a manner analogous to the argument put forward in Chapter II in relation to motion and this leads to the affirmation that all there is in the act of vision is the visual perception itself. The crux of the argument, then, is that the seer, the act of seeing and that which is seen have relational conventional existence but are, from the ultimate point of view, empty of any inherent existence. Garfield sums up this conclusion expressed in verse six, stating: 'Vision and its subject are thus relational, dependent phenomena and not substantial or independent entities. So neither seeing nor seer nor the seen (conceived of as the object of sense perception) can be posited as entities with inherent existence. The point is just that sense perception cannot be understood as an autonomous phenomenon, but only as a dependent process.'[12]

The opponent is allowed one final objection, with the argument that as consciousness is real and comes about as a result of sense perception, the sense perception must itself be real. The reply made is simply that all of the other senses, including the mind, exist in the same way as vision has been

---

[12] Garfield, *Fundamental Wisdom*, 140

shown to exist, i.e. conventionally and not absolutely, and that therefore no further argument is required.

Whilst this small and tightly argued chapter is ostensibly about sight primarily, Nāgārjuna's point at the end of the chapter is well made as the argument given does indeed allow of a much wider application. Drawing attention to this, T.R.V. Murti comments: 'In either case the intention is to provide an account of the cognitive process without having to suppose an immutable substrate (ātman) underlying the states.'[13]

3.2.5 Chapter IV Examination of the Aggregates

Frequently in the *Mūlamadhyamakakārikā* the line of reasoning is developed according to the arguments of Nāgārjuna's notional opponent, arguments which are often presented in the form of an implicit horizon rather than explicitly stated. The implicit argument behind Chapter IV seems to be an objection that Nāgārjuna supposes will be made to his analysis of vision in the preceding chapter, namely that even if it is granted that vision and/or the object that is viewed are without substantial existence, such existence can still be ascribed to the human subject who sees. In this chapter the category of form is examined, though Nāgārjuna's wider purpose is betrayed by the title of the chapter: the aggregates, whilst comprising all of reality, most frequently occur in discussions of the concept of *anattā*, or not-self, in discussions about the nature of human beings.

Equally, as Garfield points out, though *rūpa* is most often translated as form, the meaning here is rather matter and accordingly the place of the chapter in the overall argument becomes clearer when it is read with these two qualifications in mind. Garfield states: 'It is important to realize that this taxonomy is to be understood pragmatically: There is no deep doctrinal or philosophical point that hangs on dividing the properties or capacities of humans up in just this way. In fact, most often the only important point about analysis in terms of the aggregates is that humans are composite. The precise nature of the best decomposition is of interest to psychology and to soteriological practitioners, but is at bottom, from the standpoint of the tradition, an empirical matter.'[14]

Central to the philosophical analysis of form as a category in this chapter is the notion of causality, and the argument begins by locating form, *rūpa*

---

[13] T. R. V. Murti, *The Central Philosophy of Buddhism: A Study of the Mādhyamika System*, (London: Unwin, 1960), 185

[14] Garfield, *Fundamental Wisdom*, 142

qua matter, in the context of the search for its cause. Nāgārjuna takes it for granted that his opponent shares with him a belief in dependent origination, a fundamental Buddhist doctrine, and thus it is inconceivable to suppose that form is without a cause. Equally, both the existence of form and its putative cause are debated in terms of inherent existence. This in turn leads Nāgārjuna to the logical contradictions with which he hopes to refute the possibility that there might be any such inherently existent phenomena.

Immediately the reader is led into the logical conundrum that lies at the heart of the chapter: form must have a cause as everything that exists is dependently originated, yet if there is such a cause, conceived of as existing inherently, then it lacks a corresponding effect, as form is not then itself inherently existent. Garfield seeks to elucidate the point being made in the following terms: 'But since in the context of inherent existence merely conventional existence counts as no existence at all, an inherently existent cause with a merely conventionally existent effect would count just as much as an ineffective cause. So neither can we make sense of an inherently existent cause of the existence of material form if material form is held not to be inherently existent.'[15] The point being made is the incoherence of asserting an inherently existing cause of matter, whether matter is itself conceived of as inherently existent or not.

If form is conceived of as existing inherently, then a cause is superfluous. If from a similarly ultimate point of view form does not exist, then the issue of its cause simply fails to arise.

In the middle of the chapter a hermeneutical move similar to that made with regard to vision occurs: Nāgārjuna underlines that form as an abstract category with independent existence is incoherent and should be considered only in relation to concretely existing phenomena:[16]

> 5. Form itself without a cause
>   Is not possible or tenable.
>   Therefore, think about form, but
>   Do not construct theories about form.[17]

The putative opponent is allowed a further implicit objection in the idea that while phenomena may be empty, the matter of which they are composed is not.

---

[15] Garfield, *Fundamental Wisdom*, 144
[16] Cf. Garfield 146
[17] MMK 4:5

Nāgārjuna replies to this argument in verse six:

> The assertion that the effect and cause are similar
> Is not acceptable.
> The assertion that they are not similar
> Is also not acceptable.[18]

This is also ruled out on the basis of an analysis of the causality that would be involved. If cause and effect are deemed to be the same, i.e. if matter causes itself, as they would have to be for matter to be inherently existent, then the conclusion begs the question[19] and the opponent's objection is logically invalid. If they are different, i.e. if matter is caused by non-material causes, and here again the target is the notion of either or both cause and effect existing inherently, then the logical paradoxes already cited apply.

This is further echoed in verse eight which points out that any objection to the contingent or 'empty' view of form being advanced would either involve asserting that form is without cause, thus again begging the question, or stating that it is caused by something else which exists inherently, leaving the interlocutor with the task of explaining that particular phenomenon and so on, leading into an infinite regress. All of this results in the position that form is without inherent existence and also is dependent on its actual instantiation in concrete phenomena, thus rendering it empty of being from an absolute sense but existing in its emptiness in the contingent realm.

3.2.6 Chapter V Examination of Elements

Chapter V continues seamlessly from the arguments advanced in the preceding chapter on aggregates with the focus now on the ontological status of phenomena and their properties, the properties in question being conceived of as defining characteristics of phenomena. The argument begins by asserting the contingent nature of space – space *in se* cannot be conceived of as an entity that subsequently comes to bear characteristics. The point of this logical move is to show that everything that exists has characteristics, as prior to the existence of something with characteristics there is nothing present in any sense at all: space, too, is empty of inherent existence.

---

[18] MMK 4:6

[19] It is of particular interest that Nāgārjuna here relies on the logical incoherence of the opponent's argument to falsify it rather than on the observable character of matter itself.

From verse two the central argument of this chapter is constructed: as everything has characteristics and nothing exists that does not, what sense can it make to posit entities which possess characteristics? To affirm the existence of such would entail positing entities separate from the characteristics they possess. Yet such have been shown not to exist. This point is taken further in verse three where the focus turns to the nature of characteristics themselves. Just as entities that are separate from characteristics cannot be posited, neither can inherently existing characteristics be logically affirmed. If characteristics of things did exist inherently, they would pertain to phenomena that were either characterised or uncharacterised. In the first instance they would be superfluous and in the second the phenomena in question would then cease to be uncharacterised. The central point in all of this argumentation is that it is logically fallacious to separate phenomena from their characteristics, from an ontological point of view. As such, inherent existence cannot be ascribed either to phenomena or to their characteristics – they are relative to each other and dependent upon each other for their existence.

As in previous chapters, the argument is then extended: as all characteristics are conventional in their existence, this must apply also to existence and nonexistence, an argument that is coupled with the denial of the absolute existence of phenomena.

An interesting conclusion comes at the end of the chapter when, for the first time in the text, the logical argumentation engaged in is given soteriological import as the concept of the 'pacification of objectification' is introduced. Commenting on this Garfield points out:

This is the soteriological import of this discussion of fundamental ontology: If one reifies phenomena – including such things as one's own self, characteristics (prominently including one's own), or external objects – and if one thinks that things either fail to exist or exist absolutely, one will be unable to attain any peace. For one will thereby be subject to egoism, the overvaluing of oneself and one's achievements and of material things. One will not appreciate the possibility of change, of the impermanence and nonsubstantiality of oneself and one's possessions. These are the seeds of grasping and craving and, hence, of suffering. The alternative, Nāgārjuna suggests, and the path to pacification, is to see oneself and other entities as non-substantial, impermanent, and subject to change and not as appropriate objects of such passionate craving.[20]

---

[20] Garfield, *Fundamental Wisdom*, 152

3.2.7   Chapter VI   Examination of Desire and the Desirous

The argument advanced in Chapter VI is isomorphic with the argument advanced in relation to phenomena and their characteristics and in a sense can be viewed as a transposition of this argument into the realm of the human. The category chosen for this is that of desire, a category that is of fundamental importance in Buddhist analysis of the human predicament. Following on from the previous argument, the relationship between the subject of desire and desire itself is examined, beginning with a consideration of the notion that the subject of desire exists inherently and is therefore the ground for the existence of desire. This of course poses the conundrum of what leads the subject of desire to be designated in those terms if desire does not really exist. On the other hand, without such a subject desire cannot be affirmed to exist either, all of which leads Nāgārjuna to the assertion that from the ultimate point of view, desire simply does not exist. At the end of verse two it is made clear that the argument works in the same manner if one starts by affirming the existence of desire and seeks to establish the existence of the 'desirous one'. All of this becomes logically clearer when one bears in mind that the assumed opponent is one who views desire, the desirous one or both as entities who exist from the ultimate point of view.

Nāgārjuna next turns his attention to the objection that both can be posited as entities if they are affirmed as arising together as inherently existent. For Nāgārjuna this is fallacious as if the two are viewed as simultaneous, the logical corollary would be that each could in theory occur in the absence of the other, something which has already been shown to be impossible. One is also left trying to explain why the two always occur together. Again the conclusion reached is pressed into wider service in the argument against inherent existence with the affirmation at the end of the chapter:

> So, like desire, nothing whatever
> Can be established either as simultaneous or as nonsimultaneous.[21]

Garfield points out that this final comment, as throughout the text, must be placed in context: Nāgārjuna is not denying that simultaneity occurs but rather that it is impossible to logically affirm the simultaneity or non-simultaneity of two inherently existent phenomena.

---

[21] MMK 6:10b

3.2.8 Chapter VII Examination of the Conditions

Chapter VII comprises a long analysis, the purpose of which is to locate *pratītyasamutpāda* between the Scylla of inherent existence and the Charybdis of complete nonexistence. The logical problem of how phenomena do exist if dependent arising is itself deemed to be empty is also addressed. The chapter opens by considering the logical difficulties that result from viewing arising as itself arisen: if arising is itself dependently arisen, it should have the three properties that Buddhist analysis ascribes to all dependently arisen phenomena, namely arising, abiding and cessation. The crux of these three properties, ontologically speaking, is impermanence. This would, however, mean that as dependent arising is impermanent, things could potentially arise in a non-dependent manner, something which would violate the Buddhist affirmation that everything that exists does indeed come into being dependently.

On the other hand, if dependent arising is viewed as being itself produced, one is left with the conundrum of explaining its existence as well as the problem, from the Buddhist point of view, of affirming the existence, at least potentially, of something that is not dependently arisen. A further attack follows on the opponent's view of dependent arising as existing inherently: if this view is held, then dependent arising must be viewed as occurring with the three properties of all phenomena accruing to it either separately or together. If they occur separately then the ascription of all three to all phenomena is violated; if together, then a logical contradiction arises as the three cannot be true of the same phenomenon simultaneously. An additional interesting point is made in verse three where Nāgārjuna points out that if the three characteristics have further properties, an infinite regress comes about as these properties then have to be explained; if, on the other hand, the three characteristics do not have any properties other than the three marks of arisen phenomena, then they cannot be considered to be phenomena at all.

At this point the opponent's voice sounds with the assertion that dependent arising is itself a product of a more fundamental arising that arises without being itself dependent on anything else, a view that was in fact proposed by some Buddhist schools at the time. Nāgārjuna replies by asking how the arising of the basic arising is to be explained: if it is dependent on something else, an infinite regress occurs; if it is independent then the assertion begs the question. In addition, if the basis is itself deemed to be unarisen, then once again the principle that there is nothing that is not arisen is violated.

The opponent replies by citing the example of a butterlamp which casts light upon itself as well as on everything else:

> Just as a butterlamp
> Illuminates itself as well as others,
> So arising gives rise to itself
> And to other arisen things.[22]

At this point in the chapter, Nāgārjuna embarks upon a sustained critique of the example emphasising that contrary to the opponent's view, the example contains a disanalogy. Two points are crucial to Nāgārjuna's reply: first, the opponent seeks to use the example to illustrate an ontological difference between an arising which is not itself dependently arisen and all other phenomena which are. If transferred to the butterlamp example, such a difference would entail the first arising being illustrated by darkness, with all that is arisen corresponding to the light shed by the lamp. But in the example, everything is illuminated, so the necessary ontological contrast required to sustain the analogy is not present. The second point which undergirds this reply is the commonly assumed view in Buddhist thought at the time that darkness was something which was ontologically existent and not merely the absence of light; accordingly it would have to be darkness, which corresponded to dependent arising and not light.

Three further points are made in reply to the opponent's example. Having cited the view that darkness is an entity in order to show the opponent's example to be defective on its own terms, Nāgārjuna sets out to show these terms themselves to be defective. This he does by extending the previously made point about the analogy requiring the juxtaposition of darkness and light. The crux of the point here is the incoherence of the concept of light reaching darkness conceived of as inherently existing, as this would require the two to be simultaneously present, something which is logically impossible. If, however, such illumination does not require light to reach darkness, then in theory all the darkness in the world should be illuminated by this single butterlamp. Finally, if the essential nature of light is such that it is self-illuminating as well as casting light on other things, the nature of darkness can be deemed to have similarly reflexive powers. As for Nāgārjuna the nature of darkness is to conceal, it would then be self-concealing, rendering it undetectable to perception. The point of all this is summed up by Garfield in the following terms:

> The point of all this is not that we can't see lamps when they are lit or that we can when they aren't. Rather it is that the mechanism by which we see what we see when a lamp is lit is the same whether we are seeing

---

[22] MMK VII:9

the lamp or other things. To put it in contemporary terms, photons reach our eyes from the lamp or from its flame in the same way they do from the other physical objects in the neighborhood. And just as the visibility of the things in the neighborhood is dependent on a host of conditions, so is the visibility of the lamp. So we do not have even an analogy to a case where the status of dependent arising would be distinct from that of the dependently arisen.[23]

At this point Garfield's commentary seems to falter in a way which casts some doubt on the minutiae of his treatment of this particular chapter. In relation to the butterlamp example Garfield states that the point is made specifically in reference to dependent arising, thus disconnecting the line of reasoning from the opponent's previous positing of a basic self-subsistent arising which gave rise to dependent arising which was itself dependent. Here this fault line becomes exacerbated in Garfield's treatment of verse thirteen. The verse itself states:

> How could this arising, being nonarisen,
> Give rise to itself?
> And if it is arisen from another,
> Having arisen, what is the need for another arising?[24]

For Garfield this is clearly a reference to the presumed self-arising of dependent arising. Yet given the structural similarity with the opponent's earlier argument in verse four[25] in which two arisings are also mentioned, it seems far more likely that Nāgārjuna is here bringing his analytic gaze to bear on this particular concept. In this view, then, the point of the verse is twofold: first the inexplicability of the first self-generating basic arising if it is self-arising, and second the superfluity of positing a second level of arising if this first level is in fact itself dependent on other factors.

With this point we are back once again to the main line of argument and in the next verse Nāgārjuna states his conclusion which he will devote the rest of the chapter to defending. This verse states:

---

[23] Garfield, *Fundamental Wisdom*, 167

[24] MMK VII:13

[25] 'The arising of arising only gives rise
To the basic arising.
The arising of the basic arising
Gives rise to arising.' MMK VII:4

> The arisen, the non-arisen and that which is arising
> Do not arise in any way at all.
> Thus they should be understood
> Just like the gone, the non-gone, and the going.[26]

The crux of this verse is an attack on a reified view of arising *qua* entity. As it makes no sense to say that arising occurs in that which has not yet arisen or that which will arise in the future, and its presence as an entity is superfluous in that which is currently arising, it becomes necessary to abandon any view of arising as an entity and to limit affirmation of its existence to the conventional level.

Following on from this Nāgārjuna points out the difficulty of viewing dependent arising as an existing process: if it is such a process then it exists prior to that which is arisen, in which case it cannot serve as an adequate explanation for that which arises as, if it were such an explanation, the phenomenon in question would already have arisen as a result. The point here is that things do not arise as a result of an independently existing process of arising; rather, they arise in dependence on other phenomena and as a result of them, and it is this process which is named dependent arising. Other than this process there is simply nothing that corresponds to dependent arising: it is empty. Further, Nāgārjuna asserts in verse sixteen that phenomena are 'peaceful' in a subtle point which draws once again on the analytical category of the two levels of existence, a point which Garfield draws attention to:

> For phenomena, having no essence, cannot have even these properties essentially. One way of seeing that is this: If we take the import of the threefold nature of phenomena seriously, we see that the phenomena are themselves literally momentary. And if they are momentary, then there is literally no time for them to arise, to endure, or to decay. So from an ultimate point of view, the point of view from which they have no existence as extended phenomena at all, they do not possess these three properties. Hence no single real entity is in flux. In this sense they are peaceful.[27]

This formulation of the ultimate nature of things is followed by a statement of the universality of dependent arising: there is nothing which comes to be except through this process. A problem occurs, however, in the form of an

---

[26] MMK VII:14

[27] Garfield, *Fundamental Wisdom*, 169

infinite regress when arising is taken as that from which phenomena spring – from what does arising itself result? Commenting on the second half of verse nineteen, Garfield maintains that the notion of a nonarisen arising is ruled out as begging the question. It seems more probable, however, that the point being made is that if one phenomenon can be nonarisen why this can not apply to every phenomenon:

> If something nonarisen is arisen,
> Then all things could arise in this way.[28]

At this juncture Nāgārjuna drives home his point in a verse which refers back to the opening chapter's examination of conditions:

> Neither an existent nor a nonexistent
> Can be properly said to arise.
> As is taught before with
> "For neither an existent nor a nonexistent."[29]

What is being underlined here is the incoherence of anything conceived of as existing inherently being dependent on conditions for its existence. If something exists inherently, by definition it exists independently of any conditions. Nor can arising be coherently applied to what is nonexistent as it would then exist.

Having considered arising, Nāgārjuna now turns to the other two marks of phenomena, namely that everything endures and everything ceases. In terms, first, of the ceasing of phenomena, Nāgārjuna sets up a dilemma by pointing out that nothing deemed to be ceasing can be said to be arising. On the other hand, all phenomena are, by dint of their impermanence, deemed to be ceasing. The conclusion, then, is that no phenomenon can be said to be arising. Here, as throughout the text, it remains important to remain cognisant of the level on which Nāgārjuna is speaking – in this instance the level of ultimate rather than conventional existence.

In the next verse (twenty-two) stasis is seen as the instant lying between the other two stages of arising and ceasing but which, because of the nature of arising and ceasing, has itself no duration. Thus, it is argued, there is ultimately no stasis in what we ordinarily deem to be static. Yet neither can such a stasis be derived from what is nonstatic.

---

[28] MMK VII:16b
[29] MMK VII:20

The result of this analysis of the three marks of existence is brought out in verse twenty-three, which comprises both the argument about the marks of arising and the attack on essentialist views of endurance. Garfield sums up the point being made here as follows: 'Since to exist is to exist in time and things that are ceasing are by definition not in a state of continued existence, ceasing phenomena do not provide the kind of continuity with numerical identity that endurance demands. And all phenomena are, upon analysis, seen to be constantly ceasing. So endurance has no possibility of instantiation, and ceasing phenomena cannot have this property as an essential attribute.'[30] The point is given further emphasis with reference to the ubiquity of death and aging, these being adduced as further proof that endurance may not be viewed as something ultimately existing.

In verses twenty-five, twenty-eight and thirty-two, stasis and cessation are viewed in a manner analogous to the treatment of arising earlier in the chapter, in which the possibilities of being either self-positing or explained by an infinite regress are rejected. At this point in the text Nāgārjuna's focus turns to further emphasising the empty nature of the three marks of existence as he leads to the conclusion of the chapter in which he amplifies this point to emphasise the emptiness of all that exists.

Part of his move from the analysis of the marks of existence to the emptiness of all phenomena lies in his furthering of the analysis of cessation. Emphasising that ceasing phenomena cannot logically act as an ontological substratum for the instantiation of cessation, he underlines the impossibility of absolutely existent phenomena serving as such a basis either. The point of this latter move is to show that as cessation clearly does occur, such essentially existent phenomena clearly do not exist at all. This is clarified further in the next verses in which the impossibility of applying arising or cessation to essentially existing entities is further demonstrated. In the case of cessation, Nāgārjuna's preferred example here, it makes no sense to affirm of an inherently existing phenomenon that it ceases. For it to do so would mean that it would inherently exist and not exist simultaneously, something which is clearly an impossibility. Neither would it make sense to affirm of something that is inherently nonexistent that it ceases.

The characteristics of arisen phenomena are taken as the basis for both the ultimate nonexistence of compounded phenomena and the impossibility of affirming that anything essentially exists. Reflecting on this point, Garfield draws an interesting conclusion in terms of the basis of designating this as empty:

---

[30] Garfield, *Fundamental Wisdom*, 172

When from the Mādhyamika perspective one asserts that a thing is empty or that it is dependently arisen, one is not contrasting their status with the status of some other things that are inherently existent. Nor is one asserting that they are *merely* dependent on some more fundamental independent thing. Nor is one asserting that instead of having an independent essence things have as their essence dependence or emptiness, either or both of which exist in some other way. Rather, as far as one analyzes, one finds only dependence, relativity, and emptiness, and their dependence, relativity, and emptiness.[31]

The chapter finishes by affirming the dream-like nature of existent reality and the marks of existence themselves:

> Like a dream, like an illusion,
> Like a city of Gandharvas,[32]
> So have arising, abiding,
> And ceasing been explained.[33]

3.2.9 Chapter VIII Examination of the Agent and Action

This chapter treats of the view which is familiar in the West as a staple of philosophical idealism and was adopted by the Cittamātra School within Buddhism, namely that while existent phenomena in the world were indeed to be affirmed as empty, the subject was deemed to be intrinsically existent. Nāgārjuna begins his consideration of this view by affirming his middle way and by rejecting the extremes of inherent existence on the one hand and a nihilistic denial of any existence on the other.

Central to the issue of the agent and the action, which is the matrix within which this question of the status of the subject is considered, is the problem of change. Action, however conceived, involves change. Yet if the subject is inherently existent, such change would be impossible, which would lead to a situation in which the relationship between agent and action would be

---

[31] Garfield, *Fundamental Wisdom*, 177

[32] Mythological creatures in both Hindu and Buddhist thought; in this instance, however, it is more likely that the term is being used in its alternative meaning to denote that part of the continuum of the consciousness of an individual which exists in the intermediate state between death and rebirth

[33] MMK: VII:34

sundered, leading in turn to a doubly absurd scenario in which action takes place without agency and the agent is an agent without ever acting. Yet a similar absurdity would arise also in the case that agent and action were denied any being whatsoever. The point of this preamble comes in verse four in which Nāgārjuna provides the first element of his answer to these objections:

> Without a cause, the effect and
> Its cause will not occur.
> Without this, activity and
> Agent and action are not possible.[34]

The point here is that effect and cause (i.e. change) are necessary to make sense of agency and action. This is impossible in the context of inherent existence but makes eminent sense in the context of dependent arising. On the other hand, a denial of being is every bit as unsatisfactory and fails to provide any casual explanation whatsoever, something which would also be absurd. All of this has a further level of significance for Nāgārjuna, as the Buddhist path also becomes nonsensical without the possibility of action and corresponding effects.

Nāgārjuna now turns his attention to the question of affirming both existence and nonexistence simultaneously of agent and action. Garfield glosses this verse in terms of perspectival designation, essentially in terms of subject and object,[35] yet it is difficult to see the warrant for this in the text, and read in the light of verses such as VII: 30[36] it seems more plausible to see this as a dismissal of the stated perspective on the grounds of the law of noncontradiction.

The rest of the chapter is essentially a recapitulation of the point already adduced leading to an affirmation of agent and action as existing relationally in terms of interdependence. As he has done before in the text, at the end of

---

[34] MMK VIII:4

[35] 'An existent and nonexistent agent
  Does not perform an existent and nonexistent action.
  Existence and nonexistence cannot pertain to the same thing.
  For how could they exist together?'
                                        MMK VIII:7

[36] 'For an existent thing
  Cessation is not tenable.
  A single thing being an entity and
  A nonentity is not tenable.'
                              MMK VII:30

the chapter Nāgārjuna gives this insight a much wider application, relating it here to the doctrine of *anattā*, or not-self, by stressing that what pertains to the relationship between agent and action pertains more widely to the category of appropriation. Garfield points out the significance of this move both in itself and for the wider purposes of the text:

> By "appropriation," Nāgārjuna indicates any cognitive act by means of which one takes an attribute or entity as one's own, or as part of one's self. That includes the grasping of the aggregates as the self or of one's mental states as part of one's identity or of one's possessions as central to one's being. Appropriation in this broad sense is, hence, a central object of concern for Buddhist philosophy and psychology. And the relation between the appropriator and the act of appropriation is an important object of analysis. For in many ways the self that is constructed through appropriation presents itself as the subject of appropriation. But it is merely constructed, and its substantial reality is illusory. Then what indeed does the appropriation? And where there is no appropriator, how does appropriation occur? Nāgārjuna here suggests that this account of the relation between agent and action provides a model for understanding that relation. That is, this analysis provides a perfect paradigm for understanding the nature of subjectivity.[37]

3.2.10 Chapter IX Examination of the Prior Entity

Just as in the last chapter the status of the subject was examined by couching it in questions surrounding the agent and action, in this chapter a further consideration is undertaken in the light of sense perception. The position to which Nāgārjuna is responding here is a further refinement of the previous attempt to posit a subject, this time based on the putative need for there to be an ontological base to which the various perceptual faculties of sense accrue. The logical basis of this argument is essentially the unity of consciousness experienced when sense perception takes place.

Nāgārjuna's reply focuses on the supposed independence of the subject from the senses, an independence which logically follows from the subject being viewed as a basis for them. If such a self is posited as independent from the sense faculties, then how does a person arrive at knowledge of it? (Here the backdrop of the Buddhist designation of mind as a sense cements

---

[37] Garfield, *Fundamental Wisdom*, 182

this argument.) Further, given this independence from the senses, the self itself is superfluous in terms of explaining their existence. In contrast to the above view, Nāgārjuna proposes a view of subject and object in terms of interdependence, a move we have already seen in the consideration of agent and action.

Garfield adds a further gloss in the footnote to this verse (IX:5)[38] in which he points out that the Sanskrit used here couches this verse very much in the context of the category of appropriation, one which has already been encountered as fundamental to the Buddhist analysis of the human predicament. Arguably, when set in this broader context, the verse may be read as simultaneously drawing attention to the interdependence of subject and object and to the ultimate nonexistence of both as well as addressing the question of the relation between agent and action.

Faced with this refutation, the opponent makes a further move and seeks to turn the interdependence put forward by Garfield on its head by using it to argue that each act of perception leads to the constitution of a separate subject of that act:

> While prior to all of seeing, etc.,
> That prior entity doesn't exist,
> Through seeing, etc., by another one,
> That other one becomes disclosed.[39]

Nāgārjuna's response to this is twofold: he argues first of all that such a view would require a self to arise prior to each incidence of perception, and also that this would entail both the multiplication of selves as well as their simultaneous presence when more than one perceptual act is taking place at the same time. More fundamentally, the unity which was the basis for positing such a self in the first place becomes fractured, thus further undermining the argument. Nāgārjuna extends this line of reasoning by asserting the nonexistence of a basis for the perceptual faculties in a self and by denying the inherent existence of the faculties themselves, viewing both, instead, as existing relationally.

---

[38] 'If activity, etc., are not possible,
Entities and nonentities are not possible.
If there are neither entities nor nonentities.
Effects cannot arise from them.'
MMK IX:5

[39] MMK IX:6

At the end of the chapter the analysis is widened out once again and the question of noncontradiction is touched upon in the light of the now clear ontological status of phenomena and the faculties through which they are perceived:

> The apparent paradox involved in saying that things both exist and do not exist in one breath and saying that they neither exist nor do not exist in another – indeed of refusing in another sense to permit even these predications in another mood – arises, Nāgārjuna points out, from the conceptual imputation of inherently existent bases for these predications, which then have to be thought of as having contradictory properties. Absent the bases, we can see these assertions merely as useful analytical tools in various dialectical contexts to help us to see the ultimately empty and conventionally real nature of phenomena. And Nāgārjuna concludes this chapter by asserting that once one ceases hypostasizing the subjective self – that entity that might seem to be, as Descartes notes, the most obviously existent and most easily known entity of all – the temptation to hypostasize other entities dissolves.[40]

3.2.11 Chapter X Examination of Fire and Fuel

Chapter X considers the commonly cited example of the relationship between fire and fuel which was often employed by Buddhist schools such as the Sautrāntika and Vaibhāśika to affirm the reality of a substantially existing self in the context of *pratītya-samutpāda*. In the example, the one-way dependence of fire on fuel was viewed as analogous to the relation between the self and its predicates, specifically in relation to the subject who acts and perceives. The terms of the debate are set out in the opening verse in which fire and fuel are stated to be neither identical with each other nor different *qua* two intrinsically existing entities. In reading this chapter it is pertinent to bear in mind that the relationship posited between the two is unidirectional and that the opponent seeks not simply to affirm the self as an essentially existent base but also to point up the role of the dependently arisen, hence the importance of the non-mutual dependence of fire on fuel.

Nāgārjuna then opens his refutation of this position by pointing out the logical consequences of viewing fuel and fire as separate from each other. If such a scenario were true, the fire would burn ceaselessly, would arise

---

[40] Garfield, *Fundamental Wisdom*, 187

without cause, and the notion of it having a beginning in which it is kindled would be meaningless. Nāgārjuna now sets up a dilemma in which he considers the relationship between fuel and combustion: either the two are identical or they are different. If they are the same then fire is effectively left out of the picture when one views the set of relationships in the non-relational terms of the opponent's reified worldview. If fuel and burning are different then what has not been burned will remain unburned and one is left with the difficulty of explaining how any fuel ever comes to be burned. The point that Nāgārjuna is seeking to illustrate here is, of course, that it only makes sense to view fire and fuel relationally and conventionally, and given that they only make sense in terms of emptiness, the opponent's example simply does not hold water, so to speak.

In verse six the opponent's voice is heard once again citing a further analogy, this time drawing a parallel between the relationship between man and woman: just as men and women are anatomically designed to connect, so fire and fuel are naturally possessed of a similar ability to connect. This, however, entails fire and fuel being independent of each other with all the logical difficulties this raises, not least of which is the struggle to explain the nature of their connection, *a fortiori* given that in the opponent's view their separate essences entail properties that cannot exist together in time.

At this point it is implicitly assumed in the chapter structure that we can conclude that fire and fuel are to be viewed in terms of mutual dependence, and in verse eight Nāgārjuna considers a possible objection to this view. If fire and fuel are mutually dependent, on what foundation do both of them depend, or is one to be posited as the basis of the other?

Returning to the terms of the opponent's view, Nāgārjuna points out that if fire arises in dependence on fuel, then effectively two fires are established as fuel can be designated as such only due to the presence of fire. Equally, if one were to say that only one fire was established in such a way, then there would be something other than fire which made the fuel fuel. The circular nature of such a view is underlined in verse ten in which Nāgārjuna asks the leading question which takes the reader back to the fundamental viewpoint upon which the entire analysis of the text is based:

> If that on which an entity depends
> Is established on the basis
> Of the entity depending on it,
> What is established in dependence on what?[41]

---

[41] MMK X:10

The answer Nāgārjuna is leading up to is, of course, that nothing is established on the basis of anything else, but he engages with the opponent's view further before bringing the reader to this point. In verse eleven he sets out to use the points that have emerged so far in the chapter to maximum effect:

> Now Nāgārjuna draws the general ontological moral from this discussion of the putative counterexample. If an entity is inherently existent, it must be independently established as an entity and with its own nature. So no entity could be established as inherently existent through dependence on any other entity. Only inherently existent entities could be independent. To establish something as inherently existent through its dependence on something else is incoherent. So since entities can be established neither through independence nor through dependence, there is no way to establish anything as an entity in its own right.[42]

Referencing the previous examination of movement, fire and fuel are established as being coherently conceptualised only in relational terms. In addition, whilst the dependence of fire on fuel is affirmed, the option of regarding fuel as a reified entity is ruled out, as is the notion of fire as a property of fuel. Finally, the point is widened to cover other relationships, most significantly that of the self and its properties. Garfield elucidates this point in relation to the chapter's closing verse (MMK X:16): 'This colophon verse reminds us that when existence is understood in terms of emptiness and when entities are regarded as purely relational in character, identity and difference can only be understood conventionally. This applies not only with respect to apparently distinct entities, but also to the relation between parts and wholes, things and their attributes, events and their causes, and as Nāgārjuna emphasises here, self and the objects of awareness. Strict identity and difference as determined by reference to phenomena themselves are only conceivable from the incoherent standpoint of inherent existence.'[43]

3.2.12 Chapter XI Examination of the Initial and Final Limits

At this point in the text Nāgārjuna turns his attention to the question of the beginning and end of things in the context of the view of emptiness he is proposing. This reflection opens with a reference to the Buddha's famous

---

[42] Garfield, *Fundamental Wisdom*, 194
[43] Garfield, *Fundamental Wisdom*, 195

designation of certain questions as unanswerable.[44] Garfield reads this chapter specifically as a reflection on the continuity of the individual whilst recognising that there are other readings in the commentarial literature. In his view, Nāgārjuna makes a move analogous to Kant's position in declaring that any answer given to the question of the beginning of cyclic existence lies outside the bounds of coherent discourse. As such, designations of beginning or ending can only apply as conventional designations referring to *saṃsāric* processes. The insight is widened to rule out the possibility of designating a spatiotemporal middle, as well as ruling out designation of prior, posterior and simultaneous.

As throughout, Nāgārjuna's target here is a view of these designations which takes them to exist inherently and he spells out the logical incoherence of such a view in relation to birth, old age and death specifically in relation to the doctrine of reincarnation which he would have held in common with his opponent. If birth comes first and exists essentially, then there could be no aging and death involved either before or after, something which is untenable in a worldview in which reincarnation is assumed. Equally, if birth comes after old age and death, then these exist without any prior cause. Nor can the three conceived essentially occur simultaneously. In Garfield's view, the conclusion reached by Nāgārjuna is that these terms may not be applied essentially in two senses: first, in terms of absolute rather than conventional being, and second as designating intrinsic delimitations of time or space in the conventional realm.

In verse seven Nāgārjuna proposes what we might term an 'ontology of emptiness' which he advances as the only logically viable option remaining once the logical ramifications of essential beginning and ending have been thought through:

> Not only is cyclic existence itself without beginning,
> No existent has a beginning:
> Neither cause and effect;
> Not character and characterized.[45]

---

[44] Garfield, *Fundamental Wisdom*, 197, Footnote 65
[45] MMK XII:7

3.2.13 Chapter XII Examination of Suffering

At this point in the text Nāgārjuna turns to a topic that is, for Buddhists, of the utmost importance, namely suffering. Throughout the chapter there is, as Garfield points out, an implied criticism on the part of the opponent to which Nāgārjuna is responding: given the assertion of emptiness as an all-embracing category, doesn't this invalidate the four noble truths proclaimed by Buddha himself? Nāgārjuna's answer is ultimately to affirm that it is only through the realisation of emptiness that the four noble truths can be coherently understood, but at this point he sets the stage by considering the nature of suffering. In considering this topic Paul Williams draws attention to the terms of the Mādhyamika approach: 'This is a version, of course, of the old and basic Buddhist claim that we suffer because we do not perceive things the way they really are; the root cause of the human predicament is a very deep form of ignorance. The refutation of the innate conception of inherent existence requires a correspondingly deep and sustained familiarity with meditation on emptiness.'[46] Thus, far from being one topic among others, this chapter cuts to the very heart of the Mādhyamika project in its entirety.

The analysis begins with a consideration of suffering in the light of the tetralemma already encountered earlier in the text:

> 1. Some say suffering is self-produced,
>   Or produced from another or from both.
>   Or that it arises without a cause.
>   It is not the kind of thing to be produced.[47]

Nāgārjuna then sets about refuting each of these examples. Suffering cannot be self-caused, as the universality of the law of dependent arising would be violated, nor can it come from another as this would require the presence of essential difference which, as shown by the preceding analyses of emptiness, simply does not exist. Equally, suffering may not be conceived of as inherently separate from the one who suffers, as her identity *qua* one who suffers is by reason of her suffering. Such an absence of difference along with the relational nature of suffering and sufferer further rules out the option of suffering being produced by another, as here too categories may be invoked only

---

[46] Paul Williams, *Mahāyāna Buddhism: The Doctrinal Foundations* (London: Routledge, 2009), 61
[47] MMK XII:1

relationally. In addition, a view of suffering as caused by another would lead to an infinite regress. Having ruled out these two options, the option of both causing suffering is also negated. As always what is refuted by Nāgārjuna is an essentialist notion of suffering with the corresponding retrieval of the category of suffering as existing conventionally, albeit in a way that is empty of any inherent existence.

3.2.14 Chapter XIII Examination of Compounded Phenomena

In some ways this chapter may appear to be a non sequitur from the preceding analysis of suffering, yet to view it as such is to fail to appreciate the heart of the Mādhyamika analysis: it is precisely the failure to grasp the emptiness of phenomena that lies at the heart of the human predicament. Thus the chapter opens with a reference to the teaching of Buddha himself which is used to frame the assertion of the misleading character of deceptive phenomena:

> 1. The Victorious Conqueror has said that whatever
>   Is deceptive is false.
>   Compounded phenomena are all deceptive.
>   Therefore they are all false.[48]

The sense in which falsehood is employed here is in terms of the way in which compounded phenomena lead us to believe that they exist inherently. Yet the question of what these phenomena actually are once deception has been cleared away also arises, and the response given is in terms of Buddha's affirmation of the truth of emptiness.

Nāgārjuna now cites the reality of change as a basis for affirming this emptiness. The implied opponent, however, makes the claim that by asserting the emptiness of all phenomena, emptiness is now being put forth as their essence. In addition, the problem of what can be coherently seen as changing if phenomena are without essence is cited. For Nāgārjuna to deny the existence of any entityhood whatsoever nullifies the coherence of change and thus undermines the very basis he is using to assert the emptiness of everything.

The reply Nāgārjuna makes is to point out that if phenomena do indeed have entityhood in the absolute sense, then change is in no way coherent and the ongoing process of identity becomes itself incoherent. Things so

---
[48] MMK XIII:1

conceived would be incapable of change and thus the only meaningful ascription that could pertain would be between different things, not between something as it now is and as it was previously. Not only this, but emptiness itself is also empty – the universality of Nāgārjuna's ascription of emptiness to all things applies here as well – it is not an essence that entities have, it is the absence of any such essence: 'Emptiness is important because it is the only way that things can exist. Moreover, emptiness is not an entity. It is not a distinct phenomenon to which other phenomena are related. It is exactly the emptiness of all phenomena. The conventional character of conventional entities and their emptiness are one and the same.'[49]

The chapter closes with a denial of the legitimacy of any discourse beyond the conventional, specifically of what Nāgārjuna describes as 'views', conceived of here as any argument in which the terms of the debate are those of inherent existence or the corresponding nonexistence of phenomena. Nāgārjuna's assertion is that by asserting his position as he does, he is refusing the terms of the debate, and therefore he himself does not hold a view. Moreover, the limits of the conventional realm are the limits of coherent linguistic utterance before one slides into *avidyā*, and Nāgārjuna himself has no intention of crossing such limits. Accordingly, emptiness itself is merely conventional, without absolute essence, and is itself also utterly empty.

3.2.15 Chapter XIV Examination of Connection

In this chapter Nāgārjuna's analysis is further refined and, paradoxically, it could be said that it is in his consideration of the relationship between the compounds of phenomena in this chapter and the previous one, that the radicalness of his conception of emptiness becomes apparent. He begins by taking an example used by earlier Buddhist thinkers, namely vision, and linking it with the broader questions that pertain when the phenomenon of connection is considered. The point that he uses to build his argument here is a point already cited a number of times in the text: without substantial intrinsic being, the difference between things conceived of in a reified sense proves to be incoherent and ultimately empty. In turn, without any such difference, the relations between compounds in phenomena and between different phenomena are also shown to be mere conventional designations. Hence the phenomenon of connection under examination is revealed also to be empty and in a very real sense the question simply vanishes.

---

[49] Garfield, *Fundamental Wisdom*, 211

The point is made another way in the contention that as difference is relational, difference in any essential sense is shown to be nonexistent. If said difference did exist in such a way, by virtue of it doing so essentially it would not be dependent on anything else. Yet the notion of difference is inherently relational – things are only different in relation to other things – thus difference conceived of as intrinsic is simply incoherent and a further instance of the *avidyā* of the unenlightened mind. Connection is thus shown to be contingent and empty. Considering the significance of this move, Garfield connects it to a further sharpening of the concept of dependent origination:

> It is quite tempting when examining dependent, compound phenomena to think that while they themselves might not be inherently existent, and might not be the ultimate entities of the empirical world, it must at least be a fundamental fact that their being constituted of parts, or dependent upon their location in a causal and mereological nexus, exists as a fact. That would seem, in fact, to be the natural way to interpret the doctrine of dependent origination and the emptiness of macroscopic entities. But Nāgārjuna here pulls the rug out from any such analysis, pointing again to the emptiness of emptiness: Not only are compounded phenomena empty of inherent existence, but so is the relation among their constituents and determinants in virtue of which they are compounded.[50]

3.2.16 Chapter XV Examination of Essence

Moving from compounded phenomena to the consideration of essence, the argument being set forth is now placed in a wider Buddhist context with specific reference to the Buddha's teaching of the middle path. In that sense the chapter echoes the refutation by the Buddha of the two extremes of inherent existence and nihilism. The concept of essence is refuted here with reference to its three logical attributes: essence that exists inherently would have to be independent, unmade and without cause. Such a definition means it is nonsensical to speak of essence arising as a result of *pratītya-samutpāda*; yet as for any Buddhist everything that comes about does so precisely as a

---

[50] Garfield, *Fundamental Wisdom*, 219.

result of this process, this would have to mean that essence so conceived simply does not exist.

Commenting on this Murti avers: 'Buddha declares rūpa, vedanā, etc. to be illusory, mere bubbles etc. In the *Majjhima Nikāya*, it is stated: "Depending on the oil and the wick does the light of the lamp burn; it is neither in the one nor in the other, nor anything in itself; phenomena are, likewise, nothing in themselves. All things are unreal; they are deceptions; Nibbāna is the only truth." Basing himself on this text Nāgārjuna says "In declaring that it is deceptive and illusory, the Lord means Śūnyatā – dependence of things".'[51]

Quite simply, then, essence conceived of in the traditional manner is an incoherent concept. This in turn reinforces the argument against the existence of entities and inherent difference. In verse five the dependence of the notion of nonentities on that of entities is underlined, refutation of one leading to the refutation of the other, and the incoherence of normal linguistic usage is cited in 5.b as evidence of the underlying emptiness revealed by this incoherence:[52]

> 5. If the entity is not established
> A nonentity is not established
> An entity that has become different
> Is a nonentity, people say.[53]

Nāgārjuna then drives home his point by stating the incompatibility of any view that involves entities and their Meinongian opposites with the path set out by Buddha. Considering the Mādhyamika view, Williams underlines its position poised between the Scylla of absolute existence and the Charybdis of nihilism: 'When the Madhyamaka speaks of all *dharmas* as empty (*śūnya*) it means specifically that all *dharmas* (and therefore all things) are empty of inherent existence. They have no essence. They are only relative. It is inherent existence which is opposed by the Madhyamaka, not tables and chairs as such, but tables and chairs conceived of as inherently existing and therefore, in the Buddhist context, as permanent and fully satisfying.'[54]

As indicated by the closing words of this quote, from a Buddhist point of view this teaching has strong soteriological implications and its converse

---

[51] Murti, *Central Philosophy of Buddhism*, 50

[52] Oddly this highlighting of the incoherence of normal linguistic usage is not mentioned by Garfield in his commentary on the text. Cf. Garfield 222

[53] MMK XV:5

[54] Williams, *Mahāyāna Buddhism*, 61

has roots in the grasping that is characteristic of unenlightened existence.[55] Thus the middle path is established, affirming existence but of a conventional non-inherent type. The latter half of the chapter reinforces this conclusion by pointing out that any affirmation of essence would render the clearly observable processes of change and extinction both impossible and incoherent. Thus, Nāgārjuna concludes, 'a wise person/Does not say "exists" or "does not exist"'.[56]

3.2.17 Chapter XVI Examination of Bondage

The category of bondage is one that occupies a central place in any Buddhist analysis of the predicament of *saṃsāric* existence and hence of liberation from that existence. In this context Nāgārjuna considers a likely objection to his doctrine of emptiness on the part of the imagined opponent: for the Buddhist path to make any sense, surely the bondage which afflicts all sentient beings must at least be real. Garfield sums up the situation thus: 'From a Buddhist perspective, we are bound: bound to our conceptions of entities and essence, bound to our selves, bound to objects, and principally, bound to cyclic existence itself. Surely, the opponent might ask, mustn't the bondage that accounts for the illusions so ruthlessly analyzed in the previous chapter

---

[55] In the text Nāgārjuna mentions the *Discourse to Kātyāyana* to underline the point being made. Commenting on this, Garfield points out: 'In the *Discourse to Kātyāyana*, the Buddha argues that to assert that things exist inherently is to fall into the extreme of reification, to argue that things do not exist at all is to fall into the extreme of nihilism, and to follow the middle way is neither to assert in an unqualified way that things exist nor in an unqualified way that things do not exist. It represents one of the fundamental *suttas* of the Pali canon for Mahāyāna philosophy. In the *sutta*, the Buddha claims that reification derives from the failure to note impermanence and leads to grasping, craving, and the attendant suffering. Nihilism, he claims, is motivated by the failure to note the empirical reality of arising phenomena. It leads to suffering from failure to take life, others, and morality seriously enough. The middle path of conventional existence leads to engagement in the world without attachment.' Garfield, *Fundamental Wisdom*, 223

[56] MMK XV:10.b
In a slight difference of emphasis, Perry Schmidt-Leukel locates the teaching of emptiness in the context of the Mahāyāna view of deluded perception rather than in a direct engagement with false ontology, a view that is broadly consistent with the view put forward by T. R. V. Murti in *The Central Philosophy of Buddhism*: 'Nāgārjuna's philosophy thus supports the idea put forward in the Perfection of Wisdom Sūtras that all conceptual apprehension of reality is an illusion.' Perry Schmidt-Leukel, *Understanding Buddhism*, (Edinburgh: Dunedin Academic Press, 2006), 122

be intrinsically real? If not, what is the causal basis for all of these illusions and all of this suffering?'[57]

Here, as throughout the text, the opponent's imagined objections to Nāgārjuna's doctrine of emptiness revolve around the notion of inherent existence, in this instance the inherent existence of bondage. Nāgārjuna's response is to argue that far from underscoring the reality of the predicament of saṃsāra and the concomitant reality of transmigration, such a view in which bondage is viewed as essentially existent actually renders these things unintelligible and incoherent. Fundamental to his line of reasoning is the conundrum of permanence and change. Thus he begins by asking:

> If compounded phenomena transmigrate,
> They do not transmigrate as permanent.
> If they are impermanent they do not transmigrate.
> The same approach applies to sentient beings.[58]

Quite simply, then, transmigration is an incoherent concept if any kind of inherent existence is attributed to phenomena, as if they exist inherently they cannot undergo change. Yet if they are impermanent, they do not have temporal endurance anyway, so nothing can coherently be said to transmigrate. Two consequences flow from this: if there is no transmigrator, then there cannot be said to be any transmigration. If transmigration does not exist (with existence conceived of here as innate), then neither can a similarly conceived bondage to cyclic existence be affirmed.

At this point the argument is further refined, as the concept of grasping is introduced. Whilst the term has a fairly wide purview in Buddhist thought, the argument here focuses especially on the nonexistence of the inherently existing subject:

> If one transmigrates from grasping to grasping, then
> One would be nonexistent.
> Neither existent nor grasping,
> Who could this transmigrator be?[59]

As it is the nature of *saṃsāric* existence to seek to establish the reality of self by grasping, whether at the aggregates which comprise the human being or

---

[57] Garfield, *Fundamental Wisdom*, 225
[58] MMK XVI:1
[59] MMK XVI:3

at external phenomena, to say that transmigration is from one grasping to another is the same as saying that the self does not in fact exist,[60] either as one who exists substantially or as the independently existent subject who grasps at phenomena, a conclusion which restates that of the preceding verse.[61]

The argument is widened, now, to encompass compounded phenomena generally: as compounded phenomena existing *saṃsārically* are by definition impermanent and without inherent existence, it would make no sense to say that they pass into nirvāṇa. Undergirding this view are a number of assumptions which link it to the analysis of grasping: 'If compounded phenomena are permanent, grasping is permanent. And if grasping is permanent, saṃsāra is permanent. And if saṃsāra is permanent, then nirvāṇa is impossible. But the philosopher who is positing inherently existent bondage is doing so in order to defend a Buddhist perspective on cyclic existence and nirvāṇa. This is precisely the motivation for the reification – the worry that saṃsāra and nirvāṇa are, if not inherently existent, nonexistent. So this conclusion is inadmissible for such an opponent.'[62]

The fulcrum on which this argument turns is that for compounded phenomena to pass into nirvāṇa they would have to have some kind of permanence as otherwise it would make no sense for their contingent aggregation to perdure. Yet as such (sapient) phenomena come about as a result of grasping, if they are permanent, the grasping which gives rise to them must also be permanent.[63] This point links not only into the analysis of grasping but also to the nature of nirvāṇa and saṃsāra, a topic which is taken up more fully in Chapter XXV.

The question of bondage, then, is located within the broader matrix of *pratītya-samutpāda*, and in verse five Nāgārjuna states his conclusion which asserts that the contingent nature of phenomena renders any inherent notion of bondage or transmigration unintelligible:

---

[60] Cf. Garfield, *Fundamental Wisdom*, 227

[61] 'If someone transmigrates,
Then if, when sought in the fivefold way
In the aggregates and in the sense spheres and in the elements,
He is not there, what transmigrates?'
MMK XVI:2

[62] Garfield, *Fundamental Wisdom*, 227

[63] The analysis here refers to the Buddhist doctrine of reincarnation whereby, as a result of grasping, sentient beings fail to enter nirvāṇa and so are reincarnated.

All compounded phenomena, as arising and ceasing things,
Are not bound and not released.
For this reason a sentient being
Is not bound and not released.[64]

A more precise delineation of Buddhist analysis now comes into focus as Nāgārjuna explores the relationship between grasping and bondage. Refusing to identify grasping with bondage, Nāgārjuna seeks to refute a truncated view of bondage.[65] As grasping is part of saṃsāra, it is impermanent and without any existence from the ultimate point of view. Given this fact, if bondage is indentified with grasping, in what sense can it be said to really bind? Yet neither is there any bondage apart from the root delusion of grasping, so the question arises: in what sense can we speak of bondage as an intelligible concept at all?

To answer this question Nāgārjuna refers back to his previous analysis of motion in Chapter II, specifically the question of when motion may be said to begin and the incoherence of attributing a beginning of motion to that which is not moving or to that which is already moving. The conclusion reached in that analysis was that movement and the mover can only be intelligibly posited in relationship to each other and hence not as inherently existing in and of themselves. A similar conclusion is applied here to bondage and the bound and this is cited as a refutation of the opponent's view that bondage may be affirmed to be non-empty.

In the last two verses of the chapter the delusion of seeking to grasp after nirvāṇa is treated, a view that is delusional in terms of the 'I' that it entails (arguably as a result of *saṃsāric* failure to grasp the non-dual nature of reality) as well as the reification of both nirvāṇa and saṃsāra.[66] Reflecting on this Garfield draws attention to the stylistic nuance present in the Tibetan text:

---

[64] MMK XVI:5

[65] As Garfield points out, part of the refutation of the identification of grasping and bondage is the more comprehensive concept of bondage in which the mutually reinforcing relationship between grasping and delusion is comprised. (Cf. Garfield, *Fundamental Wisdom*, 228)

[66] '"I, without grasping, will pass beyond sorrow,
And I will attain nirvāṇa," one says.
Whoever grasps like this
Has a great grasping.'
MMK XVI:9

There is a stylistic feature in this verse that deserves note: The pronoun "I" (*bdag*) is uncharacteristically fronted in the sentence and is emphasized with the focus particle (*ni*). Nāgārjuna is hence drawing attention to the fact that the individual in whose mouth this verse is put is grasping to his own identity as an agent and as a continuing subject both through saṃsāra and into nirvāṇa. This grasping onto self, he suggests, precludes the nirvāṇa the speaker craves. But Nāgārjuna presents another argument as well: It is also possible to grasp after nirvāṇa – to reify it as a state and to crave it as a phenomenon inherently different from saṃsāra and as highly desirable since it is indeed characterized as liberation from suffering. But this grasping onto the end of grasping is itself a grasping and so precludes the attainment of nirvāṇa.[67]

Thus, paradoxically it is only by relinquishing any grasping after nirvāṇa that one can attain the liberation it promises. Garfield further avers that Nāgārjuna is urging the reader on to the relinquishment of grasping after nirvāṇa as well as of the notion of a subsistent self through the realisation that these too are empty. Whilst for the purposes of the analysis being undertaken here, Garfield's reading of the text is being taken as one side of the proposed Lonerganian dialectic, the commentarial traditions which have grown up around the *Mūlamadhyamakakārikā* do not speak with one voice and the view that nirvāṇa is empty in the sense Garfield intends is far from universally accepted.[68]

3.2.18 Chapter XVII Examination of Actions and Their Fruits

This chapter begins by stating the views of four putative opponents, with each set of views coming closer to Nāgārjuna's actual view. Thus it is not the case that the opponents are presented as being simply in error; rather, their views often have a limited legitimacy pertaining to the conventional realm. Fundamental to the question under consideration in this chapter is

---

[67] Garfield 229

[68] For further consideration of this point, the following texts are significant: Andrew Tuck, *Comparative Philosophy and the Philosophy of Scholarship: On the Western Interpretation of Nāgārjuna*, (New York; Oxford: Oxford University Press, 1990); Kamaleswar Bhattacharya, trans., *The Dialectical Method of Nāgārjuna (Vigrahavyāvartanī)* (Delhi: Motilal Banarsidass, 1992); Nāgārjuna and the IIIrd Karmapa, Karl Brunnholzl, trans., *In Praise of Dharmadhātu* (Boston, MA: Snow Lion Publications, 2007); Schmidt-Leukel, *Understanding Buddhism*, Ch 12

the conundrum of how to conceive of the consequences of actions given the doctrine of emptiness.

The first opponent presents a standard taxonomy of actions and avers that actions must perdure until their consequences come to fruition and that the notion of actions having consequences is fundamental to any conception of the dharma. Accordingly there must be a connection between actions and their fruits. Garfield sums up the question posed by the first opponent as follows: 'The problem is this: Given that the consequence of an action may be far in the future, something must persist to connect the action to the result. This is a kind of karmic analog of doubts about action at a distance. It is the same kind of move that lies behind trace theories of memory in recent philosophy of mind. So this first position is that there must be some permanent entity that remains in existence until the consequences of an action occur.'[69]

In contrast to this first position, the second opponent speaking in verses seven to ten disputes the terms of the argument and denies both the nonexistence and the permanence considered by the previous interlocutor. Using the analogy of the seed which becomes a sprout and then issues in a fruit, this opponent posits a third term connecting actions with their consequences:

> 9. So, in a mental continuum
> From a preceding intention
> A consequent mental state arises.
> Without this, it would not arise.
>
> 10. Since from the intention comes the continuum,
> And from the continuum the fruit arises,
> Action precedes the fruit.
> Therefore there is neither nonexistence nor permanence.[70]

This third term itself must perdure, however, constituting 'a kind of karmic link that is generated by the action and remains in the pyschophysical continuum until the consequence is produced'.[71]

The third opponent bases the argument advanced on the Buddhist soteriological goal of realising the Dharma. Citing one of the many taxonomies common in Buddhist texts, the opponent states that the five pleasures which

---

[69] Garfield, *Fundamental Wisdom*, 233

[70] MMK XVII:9–10

[71] Garfield, *Fundamental Wisdom*, 233

correspond to the five physical senses come about as a result of the virtuous deeds through which the Dharma is realised. If actions and consequences are not linked, what sense is there in following the Dharma at all? As the Dharma is to be attained as the result of virtuous actions, these actions must be inherently existent.

The fourth opponent mounts the most sophisticated of the arguments thus far presented and does so by rejecting the implicit substantialism of the preceding view, positing a more abstract schema in which the relation between the consequence(s) of an action and the action itself is akin to a promissory note.[72] In addition, the consequences of an action cannot be precisely delimited and are operative throughout the different dimensions of existence. In itself, action is not inherently good or bad.

The opponent now proceeds to give advice on the relinquishing of attachment, the crux of which is that such relinquishment is not the straightforward goal of virtuous actions in the way conceived of by the previous opponent – such a view trivialises the nature of attachment. Rather, one abandons such attachment through meditative insight into the ultimate nature of all things. Furthermore, the process of reincarnation takes place not as a direct causal result of discreet actions; rather, all the actions of a person's life form a single determinant which results in rebirth. Interestingly, in the commentary Garfield's discomfort with this notion is obvious as he transposes the point being made here into the realm of actions contained in one life, a point that is unlikely to have been that which Nāgārjuna intended. Commenting on the idea of karmic consequences, he states: 'But of course the implications of this are more general and concern every moment of any life. They can hence be made independently of any discussion of transmigration, though of course they help to demystify that Buddhist doctrine, at least as it is conceived in Mahāyāna philosophy.'[73]

The choice of language is telling and alerts us to the reductionist hermeneutic(s) operating in Garfield's treatment of the text. Yet at the end of the argument the opponent slips into the substantialism Garfield predicates of the previous opponents with the notion that:

---

[72] '16. Action is like an uncancelled promissory note
    And like a debt.
    Of the realms it is fourfold.
    Moreover, its nature is neutral.'
                                    MMK XVII:14

[73] Garfield 238

18. In this visible world,
   All actions of the two kinds.
   Each comprising action and the unexpired separately,
   Will remain while ripening.[74]

The rest of the chapter comprises Nāgārjuna's response to all that has come before, a response which opens with his own formulation of the Buddha's teaching in relation to this topic:

20. Emptiness and nonannihilation;
    Cyclic existence and nonpermanence:
    That action is nonexpiring,
    Is taught by the Buddha.[75]

Actions, like all other dharmas, are empty of ultimate existence and are only conventionally real. On the other hand, they are also stated to be 'nonexpiring'. Garfield suggests that this seemingly contradictory formulation is best understood in the context of two interlocking points. First, the consequences of actions continue and do not cease at a particular moment in time; second, as actions do not inherently exist in the first place, neither do they expire as there is quite simply nothing to expire. Action is empty of essence and does not expire as it has only conventional reality. If action did have absolute reality, it would of necessity be eternal, neither coming into being nor passing out of it. A number of other logically absurd consequences would follow also: 'Nāgārjuna here and in XVII: 24 draws some of the moral consequences of the nihilistic view of action that seems to follow from the conditions set on its existence by the reificationist: Actions would not come into being through agency and so would have no regular relation to any agents. And so one might find oneself experiencing the consequences of some action one had not performed, or find that it was, in some sense, one's own action. One would not take action seriously as one's own responsibility and would not worry about moral infractions.'[76] Further consequences include the blurring of the distinction between good and evil and the continual arising of the consequences of actions.

---

[74] MMK XVII:18
[75] MMK XVII:20
[76] Garfield 240

The second point developed by Nāgārjuna relates to action whose nature is affliction.[77] Here he refers back to the analysis in Chapter XII on the nature of suffering: there, suffering was shown to be empty of inherent being; here, as affliction is being posited as the nature of action, if affliction is empty, then the action being considered must also be empty. The opponent counters with the objections that affliction and action are taught as giving rise to rebirth. If one declares these to be empty, how can this teaching be affirmed? Nāgārjuna's response refers back to Chapter I and affirms the purely relational and conventional character of the agent and the one who experiences – neither has essential existence and neither can be conceived of apart from the other; rather, both are elements of the one individual in the context of their karmic existence. At the same time, since the action has been shown to be empty, it follows that the agent also is empty.[78]

The opponent again objects: if agent and action are affirmed as nonexistent, then one must say the same of the consequences of actions and the one who experiences them.

Unsurprisingly, Nāgārjuna's reply is to state that saying these things are empty is not saying they are nonexistent. In the conventional sense they do indeed exist, but their existence does not extend beyond this. Summing up Nāgārjuna's formulation of this point, Garfield states: 'Again, it is important to emphasize that emptiness, rather than being a kind of nonactuality contrasting with empirical reality, is in fact the very condition of empirical reality and hence the only kind of genuine actuality. Mirages and dreams are actual phenomena, which actually appear and which have consequences. But that does not mean that they appear to us in a nondeceptive way... By analogy, saṃsāra, action, karmic link, and consequence, Nāgārjuna argues, are real empirical phenomena, but are empty of anything more than conventional existence.'[79]

3.2.19 Chapter XVIII Examination of Self and Entities

In this chapter another central concern of Buddhist analysis is treated as Nāgārjuna considers the nature of the self, a question which is widely identified as a core source of delusion in Buddhist thought. He begins by showing the incoherence of positing an inherently subsisting self: if such a self

---

[77] Here, Nāgārjuna seems to introduce yet another implied opponent, though the text gives no direct evidence of this. Cf. Garfield 241

[78] Cf. MMK:VIII

[79] Garfield, *Fundamental Wisdom*, 243

were identical with the aggregates, it would not make sense to posit it as unchanging and independently existent. If, on the other hand, it is affirmed as independent of the aggregates (the senses are included here), we would have absolutely no way of knowing it and therefore no grounds for positing its existence.

The putative opponent objects that without a concept of self it makes no sense to ascribe the properties which comprise a person to a self which bears them and of which they are properties. Nāgārjuna replies that the solution to this question is quite simply to cease from any such ascription and indeed that such a move has significant positive aspects, specifically in the relinquishing of the grasping which is a core element of saṃsāra. The correlative insight which emerges is that the self is ultimately empty, as are the aggregates. Garfield adduces a further significance from these two verses (XVIII: 2–3):[80] 'The relation between the second and third verses of this chapter is also important from the standpoint of the relation between theory and practice, philosophy and soteriology: Nāgārjuna emphasizes the two-way streets in this neighbourhood. Understanding emptiness leads one to grasp less, to become more detached. Relaxing one's tendency to grasp leads to a realization of emptiness. Philosophy, meditation, and the practice of the moral virtues that issue in the relaxation of grasping are conceived of from this vantage point as necessarily mutually supportive.'[81]

Building on this view, the fourth verse states that the extinguishing of the self leads to liberation from saṃsāra, a point which is further developed throughout the remainder of the text. Central to this view is the concept that the source of *saṃsāric* suffering lies in the mind which ascribes absolute existence to phenomena that exist solely in the conventional realm. Garfield comments: 'The diagnosis, though, of the predicament of saṃsāra and the corresponding prescription are clear: Grasping, contaminated action, and suffering are rooted in delusion, and this delusion comes from cognitive error. The root delusion – the fundamental cognitive error – is the confusion of

---

[80] '2. If there were no self,
  Where would the self's (properties) be?
  From the pacification of the self and what belongs to it,
  One abstains from grasping onto "I" and "mine."
 3. One who does not grasp onto "I" and "mine,"
  That one does not exist.
  One who does not grasp onto "I" and "mine,"
  He does not perceive.'
  MMK XVIII : 2–3

[81] Garfield, *Fundamental Wisdom*, 248

merely conventional existence with inherent existence. The realization of emptiness eliminates that fabrication of essence, which eliminates grasping, contaminated action, and its pernicious consequences.'[82]

The chapter proceeds with a consideration of what the teaching about the self propounded in Buddhism actually entails. The crux of this consideration is that the reality of the self from a conventional point of view has been taught, as has the emptiness of the self, each of these acting as a corrective respectively to the tendency to reify the self or to deny it completely. Yet the final option given, that of neither self nor not-self, entails seeing the emptiness of both poles of this debate. Reflecting on the deeper significance of this, Garfield states: 'That doctrine is closely tied to that of the emptiness of emptiness. Both the terms "self" and "no-self" together with any conceptions that can be associated with them, Nāgārjuna claims, are conventional designations. They may each be soteriologically and analytically useful antidotes to extreme metaphysical views and to the disturbances those views occasion. But to neither corresponds an entity – neither a thing that we could ever find on analysis and identify with the self, nor a thing or state that we could identify with no-self.'[83] In this, as in all other cases, the ultimate reality of both self and non-self is emptiness.

This perspective is then widened into a broader consideration of entities which issues in what Garfield calls the 'positive tetralemma' of verse eight:

> 8. Everything is real and is not real,
> Both real and not real,
> Neither real nor not real.
> This is the Lord Buddha's teaching.[84]

In this formulation, the teaching of the two truths, of conventional reality and ultimate emptiness, is applied to all that exists and both perspectives are woven together to underline the ultimate emptiness of everything whilst affirming the conventional reality of entities. In an interesting corollary to this Nāgārjuna states that the various perceptual distinctions that we experience when contemplating reality belong to the mind and not to the nature of reality. Reality itself is not something we can grasp or perceive but it nonetheless

---

[82] Garfield, *Fundamental Wisdom*, 248
[83] Garfield 249
[84] MMK XVIII:8

retains its own characteristics.[85] Commenting on this, Perry Schmidt-Leukel underlines the fundamental nature of this view, commenting simply: 'The whole idea of "real entities", as units which are demarcated in time and space and defined by their mutual relations, is an artificial construct of the human mind.'[86]

For Garfield, in this verse the nature of *pratītyasamutpāda* is now recapitulated but this time against the backdrop of the affirmation of the ultimate nature of reality: 'But in the context of the deeper understanding of emptiness and of the relation between the ultimate and the conventional developed in this chapter, a deeper reading of this verse is in order: Our attention is called to the fact that the analysis of dependency developed here – and consequently of the conventional reality and ultimate nonexistence of the dependent – is at the same time a correct conventional characterization of the nature of phenomena and an ostention of the fact that it is only a conventional designation of a nature that must remain uncharacterizable.'[87]

The chapter concludes by directly stating the nature of reality according to this teaching ('Without identity, without distinction;/Not existent in time, not permanent' (MMK XVIII: 11b)) and also by indentifying the attainment of Buddhahood and liberation from the bondage of saṃsāra with correct insight, specifically in relation to the nature of the self. Considering the significance of this, Murti points out: 'Nāgārjuna states this dialectical predicament thus: when the self is posited, an other (para) confronts it; with the division of the self and the not-self, attachment and aversion result. Depending on these all vices spring up. Attachment begets the thirst for pleasure, and thirst hides all flaws (of the objects). Blinded by this, the thirsty man imagines qualities in things, and seizes upon the means to achieve pleasure. Saṃsāra is thus present as long as there is the attachment to the 'I'.'[88] Thus in a very real sense the teaching propounded here goes to the heart of the teaching being given in the *Mūlamadhyamakakārikā* and, Nāgārjuna would surely want to insist, to the heart of the Dharma itself.

---

[85] '9. Not dependent on another, peaceful and
   Not fabricated by mental fabrication,
   Not thought, without distinctions,
   That is the character of real*ity* (that-ness).'
                                MMK XVIII:9
   (Italics given in Garfield's translation)

[86] Schmidt-Leukel, *Understanding Buddhism*, 120

[87] Garfield, *Fundamental Wisdom*, 252

[88] Murti, *The Central Philosophy of Buddhism*, 270

3.2.20 Chapter XIX Examination of Time

Having established the emptiness of entities and the self from an ultimate perspective, Nāgārjuna now closes off a further line of objection by examining the notion that time may be considered to inherently exist. Central to this is the problem of causality already considered in other places in the text (Chapters I and VII). Nāgārjuna begins by considering the existence of time *qua* past, present and future, and the diachronic necessity that the past must be seen as giving rise to the present and the future. This contention, however, means that the present and future must at some point exist in the past, something which would constitute a logical absurdity. Given the necessity that past, present and future must be successive elements in the posited inherently existent phenomenon of time, without their being present in the past, the present and future simply could not exist. Garfield adds that time is fundamentally relational and that the present is designated as such only in relation to the past and future; therefore if the present is not present in the past, it must be conceived of as existing independently of it, which would effectively mean, given its necessary relation with the past, that it could not exist at all: 'Time is by definition an ordering of events in which moments stand in determinate relations to one another, in virtue of which the location of any moment depends on the location of all of the others. The present is the present only because it is poised within the past and the future. If it were not, it would not be the present. So either the present is in the past, in which case it is nonexistent, or it is independent of the past and the future, in which case it is nonexistent.'[89]

In verse four this argument is widened to include the past and the future as similarly relationally conceived, along with the various dimensions of space. Following this, a second assault on the notion of time as inherently existent is mounted with the consideration of a further dilemma, namely whether time is stationary or changing. If time is stationary, this would entail the simultaneous existence of past, present and future; if changing, then a meta-time would be required as change takes place against the backdrop of time. As neither option allows one to coherently conceive of time as an inherently existent entity, time itself is shown to be ultimately empty of being.

The final verse links the consideration of time with the preceding chapter on entities:

---

[89] Garfield, *Fundamental Wisdom*, 256

> 6. If time depends on an entity,
> Then without an entity how could time exist?
> There is no existent entity.
> So how can time exist?[90]

Garfield views this verse as underlining that it makes no sense to posit time as inherently existent and simultaneously arising from entities which, in any case, have already themselves been shown to be empty of inherent existence. Time, then, is fundamentally a relation between entities; as entities are only conventionally real, the same must apply to time which furthermore has no existence beyond this relation. Time, too, is empty.

3.2.21 Chapter XX Examination of Combination

Nāgārjuna now posits another potential objection to the emptiness of all dharmas, an objection that is a refinement of the previously refuted view of causality. This view avers that whilst the inherent dependence of a phenomenon on a cause cannot be sustained, phenomena may legitimately be viewed as arising from combinations of conditions. The effect of this view is essentially to say that while phenomena may be asserted to be dependent on the web of all other phenomena, it is precisely this dependence itself which may be affirmed as inherently existent.

The refutation of this argument opens with a destructive dilemma of the type used by Nāgārjuna throughout the text: this dilemma hinges on whether the arising effect can be viewed as present in the set of conditions that gives rise to it. If it is already present in them, then it does not make sense to posit the effect as arising at all, as it is already in existence. If it is not present in the conditions, the problem of causality and the relevant link between cause and effect presents itself, *a fortiori* as the relation of dependence in question is supposed by the opponent to be inherent. The dilemma is further amplified by Nāgārjuna: if the effect is in the conditions already, it should be possible to perceive it prior to any arising; if it is not present in any sense in the conditions that give rise to it, what connects these conditions to the phenomenon in question in a way that distinguishes them from other collections of conditions with no causal influence here?

Commenting on the significance of this question, Garfield draws attention to what will arise later in the text as the refutation of all views: fundamentally, this teaching refers to the contention of Mādhyamika philosophers that

---

[90] MMK XIX:6

by affirming emptiness, they are rejecting all metaphysical views wherein anything is posited as lying behind the mutually conditioned and ultimately empty web of phenomena that is reality:

> There is simply no general metaphysical answer to such a question for a Mādhyamika philosopher. A collection of conditions determines its effect simply because when those conditions are present, that effect arises. That fact may in turn be empirically explicable by other regularities. But there is no independent foundation for the network of regularities itself. However, for the substantialist there must be some analysis of the collection of conditions itself that answers the question regarding *how* that collection has the power to produce that effect. And the answer the opponent proposes is that it does so because the effect is inherently present in some sense in that collection.[91]

The critique is then sharpened as Nāgārjuna draws attention to an ambiguity in the designation 'cause'. He has already pointed out that conditions and specific causes together are deemed to bring about effects, and he now points out that if the cause ceases to be such once the effect is brought about, then along with causes which have not yet produced an effect, one must also logically recognise the existence of causes without causal status, something which would be absurd:

> 5. If the cause, in having its effect,
> Ceased to have its causal status,
> There would be two kinds of cause:
> With and without causal status.[92]

On a deeper level, the question being asked here is in what precisely is causality located, what is the nature of the relationship between two phenomena deemed to be causally related? Throughout the chapter the opponent's view against which Nāgārjuna is arguing posits an inherent view of causality, albeit one which allows for the role of more than one phenomenon as causal agent. Yet, as Nāgārjuna scrutinises the coherence of this notion, it becomes apparent that nothing is actually changed by this move on the opponent's part and the nature of the posited causality remains elusive.

---

[91] Garfield, *Fundamental Wisdom*, 259
[92] MMK XX:5

Crucial to Nāgārjuna's critique is the role of time as a category and in the next three verses he examines the logical problems involved in different temporal parsings of the causal relationship. Thus if the cause ceases prior to the effect being produced, then from a logical standpoint the effect is simply causeless. Simultaneity is also logically contradictory however, as whatever the precise nature of causality turns out to be, temporal precedence of cause to effect is a *sine qua non*, a factor which also renders it incoherent to speak about an effect arising prior to the causes and conditions upon which it depends.

The cumulative effect of the above considerations is to problematise the essence (i.e. the dependent relationship between phenomena and the combination of causes and conditions which give rise to them) proposed by the opponent. At this point in the chapter (verse nine), Nāgārjuna replies to a possible answer on the part of the opponent, namely the view that the relation between the cause and effect as two distinct entities is not relevant as the effect is a transformation of the cause rather than a different entity. Nāgārjuna replies that if this is so and the opponent continues to assert the intrinsic causality of the cause, then the effect will continue to arise *ad infinitum* even after the initial supposed transformation has occurred.

Having underlined the logical difficulty with the implied opponent's view, Nāgārjuna returns to the tetralemma which forms the crux of his analysis in this chapter. Having shown the problems inherent in an effect preceding a cause or occurring simultaneously with it, he now examines the problematic nature of the causal link *per se*. In the analysis given, the notion of cause and effect being joined is ruled out under the category of simultaneity; the problem is then that of explaining how cause and effect can be related at all in the absence of such a link, given that in the view being advanced by the opponent they are two separate inherently existent entities with independent self-sufficient essences. If they are not joined, in what sense can one be said to cause the other? In verse eleven,[93] the image of sight is invoked as a metaphor for the problem involved:

Here Nāgārjuna returns to his critique of the idea of a causal nexus. He points out that though that idea has been shown to be incoherent, it is

---

[93] 'Moreover, If not joined with its cause,
What effect can be made to arise?
Neither seen nor unseen by causes
Are effects produced.'
MMK XX:11

the only way that one can make sense of a real causal link or of inherently existent production. So in its absence, we cannot make sense of the production of an effect by its cause. In the last two lines, Nāgārjuna makes use of the strange metaphor of a cause seeing its effect to denote this link (*thongs-ba*). This is clearly a metaphor for this link, suggesting that whether it is forged by contiguity or by some other means at a distance, it will be explanatorily impotent.[94]

The point being made here is similar to the analysis of conditions in Chapter I, namely that the fact that there is no logical way to make sense of causation in the context of inherent existence means that we should simply abandon the idea.

The temporal categories are then restated to underline their inapplicability to any kind of simultaneity between phenomena in causal relationship to each other.[95] The resultant dilemma is then formulated in verse fifteen:

> 15. Without connecting
>   How can a cause produce an effect?
>   Where there is connection,
>   How can a cause produce an effect? [96]

The opponent counters by positing a similar dilemma using the category of emptiness: if a cause is empty of an effect, how can causation occur? If it is not empty of it, then the problems delineated by Nāgārjuna earlier in the chapter pertain. Surely, then, Nāgārjuna's invocation of the category of

---

[94] Garfield, *Fundamental Wisdom*, 263

[95] '12. There is never a simultaneous connection
   Of a past effect
   With a past, a nonarisen,
   Or an arisen cause.

13. There is never a simultaneous connection
    Of an arisen effect
    With a past, a nonarisen,
    Or an arisen cause.

14. There is never a simultaneous connection
    Of a nonarisen effect
    With a past, a nonarisen,
    Or an arisen cause.'
                    MMK XX:12–14

[96] MMK XX:15

emptiness suffers from the same explanatory impotence as his opponent's position?

Nāgārjuna replies simply by pointing out the incoherence of asserting that any non-empty phenomenon arises in the first place; if it is indeed non-empty, then arising does not occur as the phenomenon already exists *in se*. Thus Nāgārjuna deals with the gordian knot that has arisen by simply cutting through it without further ado, a stratagem which is rhetorically heightened by his situating the arisen phenomenon in ultimate perspective in verse eighteen,[97] thus underlining precisely what he means by emptiness: 'Nāgārjuna emphasizes here the double edge of the ontology of emptiness. Even though it is in virtue of the fact that conventional entities are constantly arising and ceasing that they are empty, their emptiness entails that they do not, from the ultimate standpoint, arise, cease, or abide at all. This is an eloquent statement of the interpenetration of the ultimate and conventional truths: The very ground on the basis of which emptiness is asserted is denied reality through the understanding of emptiness itself. The emptiness of phenomena is, after all, asserted on the basis of their momentary impermanence.'[98]

Having asserted this, one further destructive dilemma is set up emphasising the logical incoherence of asserting either the identity or the difference of cause and effect conceived of as inherently existing, moving the prior argument from the category of time to ontology. If cause and effect were viewed as identical, this identity would pertain between that which produces and that which is produced, thus negating the very idea of causality; yet to view them as different leaves no way of explaining the causal relationship at all and causes become indistinguishable from other phenomena that are not in causal relationship to the effect.

Whilst the answer given appears identical to the previous answer, i.e. to point out that the logical problems under consideration pertain only when existence is viewed as inherent, the argument goes further and distinguishes dependent arising from causation, pointing out that the latter does not exist at all from the ultimate perspective and therefore the causal relationship involved in dependent arising itself is ultimately empty. In addition, the critique is extended to cover the second of the two categories allowed by the

---

[97] '18. How can the empty arise?
How can the empty cease?
The empty will hence also
Be the nonceased and nonarisen.'
MMK XX:18

[98] Garfield, *Fundamental Wisdom*, 264

opponent in positing the causal link as inherent, namely the collection of conditions without which the direct causal factor cannot function as such. Here Nāgārjuna points out the incoherence of attributing inherent causation to something that is not itself inherently existent. Tellingly, this is not claimed for the conditions by the opponent and in addition the conditions are a collection of individual phenomena, all of which, in the Buddhist view, will automatically be viewed as dependently arisen. The conclusion reached is twofold: causation itself is empty from the ultimate viewpoint and makes sense only from the conventional viewpoint in the relational terms that pertain to empty phenomena. Combinations of causes and conditions are subject to the same logical points adduced in relation to causality when only one dharma is posited as the causal factor and thus they too are empty.

3.2.22 Chapter XXI Examination of Becoming and Destruction

Prior to the consideration of more specifically Buddhist topics in the closing chapters of the text, Nāgārjuna moves in this chapter to consider another possible objection to his doctrine of emptiness: that the becoming and destruction which comprise dependent arising are themselves inherently existent. Unsurprisingly this is a view that he rejects and in doing so he pursues the same method he has used in previous chapters as he seeks to show the logically untenable nature of holding this view.

He opens the chapter by presenting the conclusion of his argument in advance:

> 1. Destruction does not occur without becoming.
>   It does not occur together with it.
>   Becoming does not occur without destruction.
>   It does not occur together with it.[99]

This verse along with the following verses underlines that becoming and destruction cannot be conceived of in isolation from each other. Destruction must be preceded by becoming as otherwise there would be nothing to destroy. On the other hand, impermanence is an observable facet of reality and is affirmed in Buddhist teaching as one of the three marks of existence, so becoming without destruction cannot be affirmed either. The view that Nāgārjuna seeks to refute here is, as before, that of an implied opponent who

---

[99] MMK XXI:1

is affirming inherent existence, in this case the inherent existence of becoming and destruction. Having established that the two must be held together, Nāgārjuna points out that this is logically impossible if the two are conceived in the manner attributed to the opponent, as the two conceived of as inherently existing could not simultaneously exist together. Thus the situation is arrived at in which it is established that becoming and destruction cannot be held together and yet cannot be conceived of as existing separately either, a point which throws the coherence of asserting their existence at all into question as Nāgārjuna points out in verse six.

At this point Nāgārjuna proposes a destructive tetralemma[100] which sums up the argument so far, an argument which Garfield links with a view of phenomena as comprising a series of evanescent moments conventionally grouped together as a 'thing':

> This verse offers an epigrammatic summary of the previous argument: All phenomena, when analyzed closely, resolve into ephemeral moments, constantly disappearing to be succeeded by later stages of what are conventionally identified as the same objects. So everything that has ever existed has disappeared. Such a thing cannot be coming into existence. But no nondisappeared thing ever comes into existence. For as soon as it exists, it disappears. Similarly such things cannot be in the process of destruction. But nothing that is not ephemeral is destroyed either. Given this ephemeral nature of phenomena, establishing becoming and destruction as distinct, independent processes is impossible. This claim is made directly in XXI: 8.[101]

The point of this is to underline the logical incoherence of seeking to propose arising and destruction themselves as inherently existent, a point which will be expanded on further towards the end of the chapter.

In verse eight, Nāgārjuna draws on the implied opponent's acceptance of the emptiness of entities to point out that this acceptance precludes the view of arising and destruction as inherently existent: if these are to be so conceived, then from the absolute viewpoint as well as the conventional, their

---

[100] 'There is no becoming of the disappeared.
There is no becoming of the nondisappeared.
There is no destruction of the disappeared.
There is no destruction of the nondisappeared.'
MMK XXI:7

[101] Garfield, *Fundamental Wisdom*, 269

existence is to be affirmed; yet the opponent already grants that from an absolute perspective entities themselves do not exist. Thus one is left affirming the existence of becoming and arising from an absolute perspective whilst simultaneously ruling out the existence from this point of view of anything to which these processes could possibly pertain. Nor do the logical difficulties become any less intractable through reverting to a view of entities as existing from the absolute point of view, as then the properties that they would possess would preclude coming into or passing out of being.

In verse ten, the impossibility of conceiving of becoming and emptiness as being either the same or different when viewed from a reified standpoint is brought to the fore. If they exist inherently, by definition they cannot logically be the same thing,[102] yet each applies to every moment of which an entity is comprised, therefore they cannot be conceived of in isolation either.

Verses 12–13 delineate the problems that are involved in viewing dependent arising as concerning discrete entities that exist in and of themselves in a recapitulation of the initial argument set forth in Chapter I. This argument functions similarly here as it seeks to rule out all the various logical options for relating phenomena to each other, thus showing that dependent arising cannot be affirmed at all on these terms.[103]

Moreover, Nāgārjuna avers, the notion of inherent existence applied to any phenomenon at all (in this case to becoming and arising) involves one in what could be termed positions of ontological extremity, namely absolute existence and absolute nonexistence. Applied to the observable arising and destruction of phenomena, one is left affirming becoming and arising in a way which makes such an affirmation logically absurd. Commenting on this,

---

[102] Nāgārjuna's invocation here, as in numerous other places, of the law of non-contradiction renders Garfield's rejection of this law elsewhere when analysing the *Mūlamadhyamakakārikā* highly problematic, cf. Jay L. Garfield, Graham Priest, 'Nāgārjuna and the Limits of Thought,' in *Empty Words: Buddhist Philosophy and Cross-Cultural Interpretation* by Jay L. Garfield (Oxford: Oxford University Press, 1992), 86–105. This said, it must be admitted that Nāgārjuna does seem on occasion to give credence to such an interpretation

[103] '12. An entity does not arise from an entity.
An entity does not arise from a nonentity.
A nonentity does not arise from a nonentity.
A nonentity does not arise from an entity.
13. An entity does not arise from itself.
It is not arisen from another.
It is not arisen from itself and another.
How can it be arisen?'
MMK XXI:12–13

Garfield points out: 'If one thinks that any existent entity must exist inherently, then one is forced simultaneously to embrace the extremes of nihilism and reification. One must reify because any existent must be treated as inherently existent and hence permanent. But upon observing the impermanence of phenomena, one will be driven to nihilism since their impermanence would entail their lack of inherent existence and hence their complete nonexistence.'[104]

At this point the implied opponent interjects and seeks to turn Nāgārjuna's argument on its head by denying that the acceptance of entities entails the ontological extremes used in the *reductio*. Rather, the affirmation of cyclic existence requires the affirmation of entities as there would be nothing to which becoming or destruction could pertain otherwise, but the nature of cyclic existence is such that these entities can be viewed as a continued flux of the 'becoming and destruction of causes and effects'.[105] Given that their existence is impermanent, the ontological extremes mentioned by Nāgārjuna simply do not arise. Nāgārjuna counters by echoing the opponent's conclusion and turning its logical force on itself:

> 16. If cyclic existence is the continuous
> Becoming and destruction of causes and effects,
> Then from the nonarising of the destroyed,
> Follows the nonexistence of cause.[106]

Given that, for the opponent, existence means inherent existence, the impermanence of causes and effects must entail viewing them as nonexistent, thus rendering it absurd to speak of causality in relation to them. Here, however, a slight chink appears in Nāgārjuna's argument, as the opponent at this point seeks only to assert that inherent existence characterises becoming and destruction, not entities themselves, thus it could be argued that the opponent recognises her own form of Nāgārjuna's 'two truths' doctrine. Nāgārjuna has dispensed with the logical terminus of this view already, pointing out the logical untenability of asserting that becoming and destruction exist from an ultimate point of view whereas the phenomena to which they pertain do not. The logical outcome of Nāgārjuna's argument still holds in terms of his affirmation of the law of non-contradiction and the implications that flow from this, but the coherence is not formulated fully, either in terms of formally

---

[104] Garfield, *Fundamental Wisdom*, 271
[105] MMK XXI:15b
[106] MMK XXI:16

spelling out the logical status of this law or in terms of joining up the two elements of his refutation of the opponent's position.

The third element of the refutation of the absolute existence of becoming and destruction is now introduced as the argument turns to Buddhist soteriology. Here the point being made is that if entities exist absolutely, their cessation is impossible, thus logically contradicting the reality of the cessation of suffering, a core point of Buddhist teaching.

The final four verses seek to copper-fasten the argument by examining the logical problems entailed in the view that the cycle of existence comprises a series of momentary phenomena which exist in the context of inherently real becoming and destruction. Given that by affirming the inherent status of becoming and destruction the mutual conditioning of empty phenomena is ruled out, the argument turns on the logical difficulties entailed in explaining how phenomena could be related to each other, regardless of their duration. If a phenomenon which gives rise to another entity ceases before the other entity arises, there can be no connection between them. If it has not ceased, however, then the notion of conventional entities as being comprised of a series of evanescent and causally related momentary phenomena is thrown into jeopardy. On the other hand, if the arising of one phenomenon occurred simultaneously with the destruction of the other, then two distinct, separate phenomena are involved and there is no basis for posing a causal connection between them. If the identity of the two posited phenomena was proposed, then the problems involved in the simultaneity of inherent becoming and ceasing reemerge. Accordingly, the series proposed by the opponent can exist in none of the three temporal dimensions and thus cannot exist at all.

3.2.23 Chapter XXII Examination of the Tathāgata

Chapter XXII marks the beginning of the final section of Nāgārjuna's oeuvre in which he turns his analysis of emptiness to the examination of the fundamental teachings of Buddhism itself. First among these is a consideration of what his teaching of emptiness means in terms of the nature of the Buddha. He opens this consideration against the backdrop of the opponent who would wish to affirm that the Buddha exists inherently and he sets about considering this view by examining how such existence could be predicated in relation to the aggregates which comprise human beings.

The wider context, however, is the relationship between the two truths (conventional and absolute) and questions pertaining to how one may meaningfully speak of the absolute. In his commentary Garfield summarises this problem in the following terms: 'But there is also an ultimate truth about this world: It is empty (of inherent existence). None of these objects or persons exists from its own side (independently of convention). From the ultimate point of view there are no individual objects or relations between them. Just how these two truths are connected, and how we are to understand them simultaneously, is the central problem of Mādhyamika epistemology and metaphysics, and from the standpoint of Mādhyamika, a satisfactory solution is essential for Buddhist soteriological practice and ethics as well.'[107] Thus the ontological status of the Buddha becomes the focus for a wider and more fundamental set of questions and leads up to what is perhaps Nāgārjuna's most startling conclusion in Chapter XXV.

The question implicitly posed is 'in what does the "self" of the Buddha consist?' and this is analysed in the framework frequently known as the 'fivefold analysis':

> 1. Neither the aggregates, nor different from the aggregates,
> The aggregates are not in him, nor is he in the aggregates.
> The Tathāgata does not possess the aggregates.
> What is the Tathāgata?[108]

The self of the Buddha conceived of as inherently existent cannot be identified with the aggregates, as such a self would be both unitary and unchanging, whereas the aggregates by definition are both plural and subject to change. Yet neither can the self be different from the aggregates, as what happens to them is viewed as happening to the self, and from the point of view of Buddhist soteriology, if such difference were to be maintained, what would be the point in seeking to purify the aggregates as advocated by Buddha's teaching?

The third option to be ruled out is that the self is the subject of which the aggregates are properties; this is untenable, as if one removes all the aggregates, the self is nowhere to be found, a fact that also leads to the refutation of the fourth view, i.e. that the self can be found within the aggregates as cited in the fourth option.

Verse two considers a fifth option which in many ways is the central plank of the implied opponent's stance: that the self is both different from and dependent on the aggregates. Yet the dependence on the aggregates put forward in this view is inimical to inherent existence and rules out the idea that the Buddha has an essence that exists inherently and therefore without dependence. Yet neither can the Buddha be viewed as having an essence as a result

---

[107] Garfield, *Fundamental Wisdom*, 275
[108] MMK XXII:1

of a relation to any other essentially existent entity, as if the Buddha does not have an essence in and of himself, a differential relationship with any other essence is logically impossible.

The opponent counters (verse 4b) that if the last two options are ruled out, how is it possible to conceive of Buddha at all? In an effort to reassert the notion of the Buddha's self as different from but dependent on the aggregates, the opponent states that even if prior to realising Buddhahood the Tathāgata did not depend on the aggregates, in order to function as a Buddha such dependence became the case. In Garfield's formulation: 'That is, on the opponent's view, even if the Buddha had no dependence on the aggregates prior to attaining Buddhahood, in order to act as a Buddha, he must depend upon his consciousness, perception, body and so forth. So if we suppose that the Buddha is now inherently existent and omniscient and compassionate and so forth, we must assume that he exists through dependence on his aggregates in some sense.'[109]

Nāgārjuna replies by drawing on his earlier point that there can be no self dependent on the aggregates; were this the case, the self would have to be in some way distinct from the aggregates, yet if all the aggregates are removed, the self is nowhere to be found. Thus no entity can exist independently of the aggregates in saṃsāra. The consequence of this for the opponent's position is that it must then be maintained that the Tathāgata was not dependent on the aggregates in saṃsāra but became so in nirvāṇa in order to function as a Buddha, a position which is simply nonsensical in terms of the trajectory of Buddhist soteriology.

The next two verses draw on the preceding critique of the notion of the self as independent of the aggregates, pointing out that given that this has been shown to be impossible, the idea of a self which appropriates the entities must also be ruled out. Once this is ruled out, Nāgārjuna asks, in what way is it possible for the Tathāgata to exist in terms of any such grasping of the aggregates?

The consequence of this, as verse eight states, is that the idea of the Buddha existing in terms of any essence must be ruled out, a consequence which also rules out any idea of the Buddha existing through differentiation from any other essential entity. The conclusion reached is that the Buddha, too, is empty, a conclusion which is not only radical given traditional Mahāyāna conceptions of the Buddha's nature but also raises the question of how it becomes possible to speak about the absolute viewpoint in which there are no entities and no separate existence whatsoever. Verse eleven formulates this

---

[109] Garfield, *Fundamental Wisdom*, 278

point in a negative tetralemma, the point of which is that statements made about the absolute may only be said to be conventionally true, as language itself belongs to the conventional realm: 'The central claim in this verse is that all assertion, to the extent that it is true at all, is at best nominally true. Discourse about the ultimate character of things is not exempt from this generalization. Predication always requires an entity of which the predicate can be true; and the emptiness of phenomena guarantees that from the ultimate standpoint, there are no phenomena to be empty. The language is hence at best only ostensive.'[110] Language, too, is empty and awareness of this fact is urged as one seeks to speak about the absolute realm.

The analysis then returns to consideration of the Buddha and the middle way between absolute existence and nihilistic nothingness comes into view. To ascribe inherent existence to the Buddha from the absolute viewpoint would involve affirming the absolute existence of the aggregates. Yet as has already been shown, this makes no logical sense from the viewpoint of the absolute in which there are neither essences nor entities. Furthermore, if the aggregates do exist inherently but cease in nirvāṇa, then nirvāṇa is simply annihilation and the Buddha cannot be said to exist in any sense. The choice then becomes between saying that Buddha exists and is not in nirvāṇa or that he both exists and does not exist. From a logical point of view, neither is tenable and thus the concepts involved in the opponent's view end up foundering on the rocks of their own logical implications.

Nāgārjuna's response to this is essentially to dispute the terms of the debate and he points out in verse fourteen that it is inappropriate to apply the terms existence or nonexistence in the way the opponent does to one whose nature is empty, a formulation that echoes the Buddha's own silence when faced with such questions,[111] among which was the question of the existence or nonexistence of the Tathāgata after death. Just as the Buddha's nature is empty from the ultimate point of view, so too is that of the world, leading Nāgārjuna to state in the final verse of the chapter:

> 16. Whatever is the essence of the Tathāgata,
> That is the essence of the world.
> The Tathāgata has no essence.
> The world is without essence.[112]

---

[110] Garfield, *Fundamental Wisdom*, 280

[111] The earliest formulation of these questions is found in the Pāli canon in the 'The Shorter Instructions to Malunkya': Thanissaro Bhikku, trans., Cula Malunkhyaputta Sutta, Majjima Nikaya #63, accessed 9 December 2013, http://www.accesstoinsight.org/tipitaka/mn/mn.063.than.html

[112] MMK XXII:16

The goal as set forth here is to see things as they are by stepping out of the illusory nature of the conventional discourse in which we conceive of things as existing separately, inherently, etc., and it is this 'stepping out' which is the goal of the dialectical approach Nāgārjuna proposes. This, however, leads into a divergence of interpretations between those who interpret Nāgārjuna in terms which eschew the transcendence which is more familiar to the categories of religious thought. Garfield states: 'This crucial final verse emphasizes again the lack of any fundamental nature of entities. Emptiness is the final nature of all things, from rocks to dogs to human beings to buddhas. This fact entails, for Mahāyāna philosophers, the possibility of any sentient being to be fundamentally transformed – to attain enlightenment. But this is so, paradoxically, because ultimately there is no fundamental transformation, because there is nothing to transform.'[113]

Whilst for the purposes of the proposed dialectic it is Garfield's reading that will constitute one of the terms, it must be noted that this is contested territory and that as well as the divergence between some Western interpreters and the mystical interpretations[114] advanced within the various schools of Mahāyāna Buddhism,[115] there is divergence among Western scholars also, some of whom insist that the view proposed here does not mean that emptiness in a purely negative sense is the final word.[116]

3.2.24 Chapter XXIII Examination of Errors

Chapter XXIII sees Nāgārjuna turn his analysis to a particularly subtle form of delusion: namely the view that the defilements and errors that bind us

---

[113] Garfield, *Fundamental Wisdom*, 282

[114] Cf. Bhattacharya, *The Dialectical Method of Nāgārjuna*
Brunnholzl (transl.), *In Praise of Dharmadhātu*

[115] Personal conversation and correspondence with Perry Schmidt-Leukel.
Classical approaches to the text include the commentaries of Buddhapālita, Bhāvavivika, Candrakīrti and Sthiramati. Whilst any of these would have been more convivial to the attempt to establish a dialectic relationship to the thought of Rahner, Garfield's reductionistic reading has been purposefully chosen as providing a more rigorous test of the epistemology set forth by Lonergan in *Insight*

[116] 'It is virtually axiomatic in Mahāyāna Buddhism that the adequate linguistic response in the face of ultimate truth is silence (see for example Vn 9). But among the last and highest things we can say before we must pass over to silence is that reality, in its true nature, is Bodhisattva-like, is a pure Buddha Land, or indeed, *is* Buddha.' Schmidt-Leukel, *Understanding Buddhism*, 124

to *saṃsāric* existence are inherently existent. In his analysis he follows the traditional Buddhist taxonomy which posits three ultimate defilements (desire for what isn't desirable, hatred for that to which one ought not to be averse, and confusion regarding the nature of entities) and four basic errors (that there is a permanent self in the aggregates, belief that happiness can be achieved in saṃsāra, viewing the body as a source of happiness, and affirmation of a permanent self separate from the aggregates). In this schema the errors arise from the defilements and so it is to these that Nāgārjuna turns first. He begins by locating the genesis of these defilements in the tendency of thought to reify entities, resulting in a vicious circle in which having falsely attributed pleasant and unpleasant qualities to the illusory essence of things, we react to them with desire or aversion. Equally, it is our desire and aversion which we conflate with a thing having inherent properties and so we become trapped in a desirous hall of mirrors, so to speak. The consequence of this is that just as the defilements depend on this vicious circle, itself comprised of illusory and empty mental operations, the defilements themselves are also empty of absolute being.

In verse three this conclusion is given added force, as the previous arguments deployed to demonstrate the absence of any kind of permanently existent self are alluded to with the corollary that if there is no inherently existent self to be defiled by the defilements, then the defilements themselves are attributes of an empty subject and as such cannot exist inherently. The putative opponent objects at this point that given we recognise the reality of the defilements, we must also recognise the reality of the subject to which they pertain. Nāgārjuna counters by pointing out that previous analysis has already failed to demonstrate the existence of such a subject and therefore the defilements must be thought about in a way that does not presuppose an inherently existent self. Developing this line of reasoning, Nāgārjuna draws an analogy between the previously considered relation between the self and the aggregates, stating that the same argument applies to the relation between the self and the defilements. Thus the defilements are 1) not the same as the aggregates, 2) not different from them, 3) not their basis, 4) not their core and 5) neither depending on them nor distinct from them. Equally, as the defilements depend on 'the pleasant, the unpleasant, and the errors',[117] things which are themselves empty, they too must be empty.

Verses seven and eight seek to copper-fasten the argument by stating that the six senses are the basis of the defilements and that these two 'should be

---

[117] MMK XXIII:6a

seen as only like a city of the Gandharvas/and like a mirage or a dream'.[118] As the senses are empty (MMK: III), so too are the defilements which depend on them. Furthermore, the characteristics upon which the reification of things is based, i.e. that they are pleasant or unpleasant, must pertain to self, others, or both self and others are themselves empty. These having been shown to be empty, the notion of pleasantness or unpleasantness as inherent properties must also be rejected, a point further bolstered by the interdependent nature of the two properties, with each being defined in relation to the other. The emptiness of these two also renders illusory both desire and aversion, as both are reactions to what does not really exist from the absolute point of view.

An interesting twist to the argument comes in verse thirteen where the first of the four errors is considered from the ultimate perspective. The question asked as a heuristic device is whether, given that ultimately there is nothing that is impermanent, the view that "the impermanent is permanent"[119] may be considered an error at all. The crucial point is that the error here expressed has conventional status only as there is no ultimately existent substratum to be found which would validate its truth from an ultimate viewpoint. A further consequence of the insight corresponding to this error is that as there is no inherently existent self that grasps, the other elements involved in grasping cannot have any absolute being either:

> 15. That by means of which there is grasping, and the grasping,
> And the grasper and all that is grasped:
> All are being relieved.
> It follows that there is no grasping.[120]

This verse has a wider importance also, as Garfield points out, as it extends the line of reasoning to encompass the other errors considered: 'The argument above addresses the first and fourth of the principal errors directly. This verse hints at the generalization of this argument to the other two. If there is no permanent self, there is nothing to do the grasping that generates the view that there is happiness in saṃsāra or to grasp onto the body. Since all of these errors are rooted in grasping and since any inherently existent

---

[118] MMK XXIII:8b

[119] MMKXXIII:13a

Garfield cites this line as referring to the first of the four errors (that there is a permanently existent self) and hence sees the words as referring to an attempt to absolutise one of the aggregates, usually the mind. (cf. Garfield 288)

[120] MMK XIII:15

grasping would depend on an inherently existent grasper, these errors cannot be inherently existent.'[121] Here again the argument pertaining to not-self encompasses both the root delusion and its remedy.

Thus the conclusion reached is that from the ultimate point of view neither error nor the one in error exists. Just as he has done throughout this chapter so far, having stated a conclusion Nāgārjuna goes on to restate it using an alternative logical stratagem, in this instance redeploying the logical difficulties involved in saying that something arises in someone whilst also saying that it develops in them. Error, like everything else that exists, arises, yet via the process outlined at the start of the chapter, error develops in a number of steps also; the problem Nāgārjuna adduces here is how to hold these two together. The analysis outlined means that it must be affirmed that error develops. Yet it also is subject to the law of universal arising: to say otherwise would be to violate this law or to simply leave the presence of error unexplained. Yet holding the two together is illogical, as to say that error develops in someone in whom it is also arising leaves one with more than one error, as well as an error independent of a subject. Furthermore, given the absence of any intrinsic self, the development of error would logically constitute a change in the person, thus further undermining the concept of error arising *in* a subject. This, for Nāgārjuna, constitutes further proof that error too is empty, existing only conventionally.

Adding a third tier to his assault on the ultimate existence of error, Nāgārjuna turns directly to a consideration of error and the process of arising. As already pointed out, according to Buddhist doctrine there is nothing which does not arise, therefore to say that something does not arise is tantamount to denying it exists or involves positing existence in the absence of any explanation, a possibility ruled out by the comprehensive scope of the doctrine of dependent arising. Yet if error does arise, it does so in dependence on something else and therefore cannot exist inherently.

In the final section of the chapter a further line of analysis is considered: if the errors are to exist absolutely, they must logically do so by relating to absolutely existent objects – listed here by Nāgārjuna as 'the self, and the pure/the permanent and the existent'.[122] Yet if these objects exist inherently, the errors cannot be deemed errors at all but on the contrary are shown to be demonstrably true. Garfield sums this up in the following terms:

---

[121] Garfield, *Fundamental Wisdom*, 289
[122] MMK XIII:21a

But why is the opponent forced to think of the objects of inherently existent error as inherently existent? That is, of course, an obviously incoherent position. But the view characterised as an error must have some ontological basis. And the self that is putatively in error has already been ruled out. So the only remaining possibility is that the error is the perception of an inherently real but at the same time deceptive object: a real but nonexistent object. It is this that Nāgārjuna claims is incoherent. Error then can neither be an objectless but inherently existent mental phenomenon, nor can it be a subjectless perception of an inherently real but nonexistent object. So in no way can error be grounded in anything substantial.[123]

Nāgārjuna adds an interesting addendum to all of this, however: the fact that the objects of the four errors do not exist from the ultimate viewpoint does not mean that their opposites exist either. Thus suffering, a transient self, and a body that is not pure are also empty of inherent existence, though these do, of course, have conventional existence. Yet conventional existence does not extend beyond itself and thus Nāgārjuna analyses the objects of Buddhist doctrine, too, in accordance with his 'middle way'. Verse twenty-three sums up all of this in its assertion that 'through the cessation of error/Ignorance ceases'.[124] Yet this cessation does not involve realising the true nature of things; rather, it involves realising that from the perspective of ultimate truth there are no things at all and that all that exists in saṃsāra does so conventionally and without essence.

In the final pair of verses in the chapter, Nāgārjuna steers a middle way, as before, between substantialism and nihilism: if the defilements existed inherently, how could liberation from them be attained, a liberation which is, after all, the whole point of Buddhist teaching? Yet equally, against a nihilism that would posit the nonexistence of the defilements or would seek to deny their character as empty and dependent phenomena, Nāgārjuna states:

> 25. If someone's defilements
> Did not exist through his essence,
> How could they be relinquished?
> Who could relinquish the nonexistent?[125]

---

[123] Garfield, *Fundamental Wisdom*, 290
[124] MMK XIII:23
[125] MMK XIII:25

At first glance, this verse seems contradictory as a refutation as it appears to assert the possibility of relinquishing the defilements on the basis of their existing through a person's essence. Yet here, as throughout the text, the nonexistence that is refuted is a nonexistence conceived of as essential and thus the refutation of the posited nihilism takes the form of denying any kind of essential nonexistence which would negate the conventional existence of the defilements. Here, as throughout, Nāgārjuna carefully walks his middle path in his analysis. On a deeper level, the second half of the verse anticipates the point Nāgārjuna will shortly make when he comes to consider the relation between nirvāṇa and saṃsāra by articulating things from the ultimate, rather than the conventional, perspective. From this standpoint, there are no errors and no subject to which they pertain, hence there is no relinquishment, or indeed need of any relinquishment. All of these elements are merely conventional and, from the ultimate standpoint, have no existence.

3.2.25 Chapter XXIV Examination of the Four Noble Truths

Chapter XXIV is in many ways the climax of the text with the formulation of the central Mādhyamika tenet in verse eighteen. Whilst ostensibly a consideration of the four noble truths, both the nature of emptiness and the relationship between the two truths are central to the argument Nāgārjuna sets forth here. The text opens with objections to Nāgārjuna's teaching on emptiness on the part of the imagined opponent. These consist chiefly in the accusation that what Nāgārjuna is proposing is essentially nihilism and as such leads to a denial of the three jewels in which Buddhists seek refuge: the Buddha, the Dharma and the Sangha. The argument constructs emptiness as a denial of the reality of phenomena, and in particular of dependent arising, issuing in denial of the four noble truths which in turn results in the negation of the three jewels.

Nāgārjuna counters this argument by contending that in reality it is the opponent's position, and not his, which is nihilistic, though he first explicitly grounds what is to follow in the context of the teaching concerning the two truths. Asserting explicitly that the Dharma of the Buddha himself is rooted in the doctrine of the two truths, he locates misunderstanding of the Dharma in a conflation of these two (the conventional and the ultimate). Garfield, commenting on this part of the text, points out that for Nāgārjuna liberation through insight is attained and expressed via conventional devices of language and thought; thus the absolute truth is understood via the conventional. In addition, Nāgārjuna states, the understanding of emptiness is the basis upon which everything else in the Dharma stands or falls:

> 14. For him to whom emptiness is clear,
> Everything becomes clear.
> For him to whom emptiness is not clear,
> Nothing becomes clear.[126]

Thus the argument is made that the opponent has, quite simply, failed to understand and it is on the basis of this misunderstanding that the criticisms of verses 1–5 are levelled.

Verse fifteen introduces the philosophical work of the chapter with the use of a classical Indian rhetorical trope to characterise the opponent's position:

> 15. When you foist on us
> All of your errors
> You are like a man who has mounted his horse
> And has forgotten that very horse.[127]

The image used is that of a man counting his horses and finding there is one missing because he forgets to include his mount, and the charge here is that the nihilism that the opponent has accused Nāgārjuna of is in reality the correct characterisation of the opponent's own position. By attributing an essential inherent existence to phenomena, the opponent, as well as rendering impossible dependent arising, reifies emptiness itself, thus rendering emptiness the 'true' reality, with the conventional realm relegated to the illusory. Not only is this incorrect from the Mādhyamika perspective, it also constitutes a fundamental distortion of the relation between the two truths. Garfield adduces in relation to this point what he views as the defining characteristic of Mādhyamika dialectic, namely that the reification of one of the two truths inevitably leads to nihilism concerning the other, and vice versa.

In verse eighteen, the most crucial in the whole text and indeed in Mahāyāna philosophy more generally, the Mādhyamika philosophy is stated *in nuce*:

> 18. Whatever is dependently co-arisen
> That is explained to be emptiness.
> That, being a dependent designation,
> Is itself the middle way.[128]

---

[126] MMK XXIV:14
[127] MMK XXIV:15
[128] MMK XXIV:18

Thus emptiness is precisely the contingent being that characterises what is dependently arisen, and both emptiness and *pratītyasamutpāda*, as well as being equivalent to each other, are equivalent to conventional designation – all three are different designations of the same state of affairs. Drawing attention to the precise linguistic meaning of the text,[129] Garfield avers that the emptiness predicated of phenomena is true of emptiness itself – this too is merely contingent and arisen: 'Moreover, "emptiness" itself is asserted to be a dependent designation (Tib: *brten nas gdags-pa*, Skt: *prajnaptir-upādaya,*). Its referent, emptiness itself, is thereby asserted to be merely dependent and nominal – conventionally existent but ultimately empty. This is hence a middle path with regard to emptiness.'[130] The implication of this threefold identification is drawn out with the assertion that as dependent origination and emptiness are different characterisations of the same reality, just as there is nothing that has not dependently arisen it follows logically that there is nothing which is not empty, not even emptiness itself.

Having stated his own position, Nāgārjuna turns to an examination of the opponent's position. First, he points out that if phenomena were non-empty as the opponent seeks to assert, dependent arising would be an impossibility, which in turn would mean that the four noble truths would also be rendered incoherent. If suffering, for example, were non-empty, there would be no possibility of attaining liberation from it, the chief goal of the Dharma. Without the possibility of this goal, the Dharma would also be impossible, and in any case if the Dharma were non-empty, there would be no possibility of cultivating it.

Turning to another central Buddhist category, *avidyā*, or ignorance, Nāgārjuna points out that if this too is nonempty, then understanding will not arise, and the same for the various other elements of the Dharma. As verses 29–30 point out, without the Dharma there can be no Sangha and no Buddha. In a further logical absurdity, the notion of the inherent existence of the Buddha and of Enlightenment ends in sundering the necessary relation between the two, meaning that in principle they could occur independently of each other. In addition, given the identity of *pratītyasamutpāda* with emptiness, by denying emptiness the opponent denies dependent arising and hence ends up denying even the possibility of the arising of a Buddha, whether the historical Buddha or further Buddhas in the future, a concept which negates the

---

[129] This question, along with other questions pertaining to the original versions of the text, lies outside the purview of this work – as stated above, for the purpose of the proposed dialectic, Garfield's reading of the text will be taken as one of the terms.

[130] Garfield, *Fundamental Wisdom*, 305

central thrust of the Mahāyāna. Thus, through the insistence on the inherent existence of phenomena, it is the opponent rather than Nāgārjuna who ends up denying the three jewels and falls into the trap of the very nihilism with which Nāgārjuna is here charged.

In addition, Nāgārjuna points out, by positing an essentialist view of phenomena, action as a category becomes unintelligible, as does the concept of karma, predicated as it is upon the idea that actions have consequences. As things would simply exist, the change required for action to be a coherent concept would be impossible, as would any consequences attendant upon actions. Here again the opponent allows only for the two extremes of essential existence or nihilism and eschews the middle path advocated by the concept of emptiness. This is not, Nāgārjuna points out, simply a matter of the logical parameters of two competing philosophical conceptions: as verse thirty-six points out, the opponent's view also clashes with the world as we observe it. In Garfield's formulation:

> Nāgārjuna suggests that to assert the nonemptiness of phenomena and of their interrelations when emptiness is properly understood is not only philosophically deeply confused, but is contradictory to common sense. We can make sense of this argument in the following way: Common sense neither posits nor requires intrinsic reality in phenomena or a real causal nexus. Common sense holds the world to be a network of dependently arisen phenomena. So common sense only makes sense if the world is asserted to be empty. Hence it is the opponent, not Nāgārjuna, who disagrees with the conventional truth.[131]

Here, however, despite the rhetorical validity of the point being made, Nāgārjuna could be charged with an antinomy of thought as he uses common sense as a means of backing up his argument whilst at the same time basing his argument on the concept of *avidyā*: the tendency of the mind to distort reality issuing in precisely the reification with which he charges the opponent.

An additional point pertaining to action is adduced with the assertion that in an essentialist framework, actions would be without a beginning and an agent would thus be so inherently independent of any action(s) actually performed. One would be left affirming the existence of agents independent of any actions. All of this is summed up in verse thirty-eight with the assertion that:

---

[131] Garfield, *Fundamental Wisdom*, 313

> 38. If there is essence, the whole world
> Will be unarising, unceasing,
> And static. The entire phenomenal world
> Would be immutable.[132]

Reflecting on the significance of this formulation, Garfield locates the tendency to reify in the mistaken perception that without such reification existence becomes mired in existential nihilism:

> Perhaps most important from the standpoint of Buddhist phenomenology and, though not hard to see, easy to overlook: We are driven to reify ourselves, the objects in the world around us, and – in more abstract philosophical moods – theoretical constructs, values, and so on because of an instinctual feeling that without an intrinsically real self, an intrinsically real world, and intrinsically real values, life has no real meaning and is utterly hopeless...But if instead we treat ourselves, others, and our values as empty, there is hope and a purpose to life. For then, in the context of impermanence and dependence, human action and knowledge make sense, and moral and spiritual progress become possible. It is only in the context of *ultimate nonexistence* that *actual existence* makes any sense at all.[133]

Here again the tables are turned as the nihilism that seems to the opponent to result from the doctrine of emptiness is shown to be a consequence of the opponent's own reification of phenomena. At the end of his commentary on this chapter Garfield raises an interesting point which could constitute a profound contradiction at the base of Nāgārjuna's thought: if emptiness is a conventional designation, something which would appear to follow from the formulation in verse eighteen, does this not mean that emptiness is not a necessary characteristic of phenomena, thus raising the possibility that phenomena could be both nonconventional and nonempty? Garfield replies by stating that emptiness as conceived of by Nāgārjuna does not function as a 'negation operator', which would lead to the two terms of the designation of emptiness as empty, cancelling each other out, but is rather an ontological

---

[132] MMK XXIV:38

[133] Garfield, *Fundamental Wisdom*, 317
A similar point is made and more comprehensively developed by David Loy in his seminal work *Lack and Transcendence: The Problem of Death and Life in Psychotherapy, Existentialism and Buddhism* (Atlantic Highlands, NJ: Humanities Press, 1996)

predicate, functioning in a nominalistic framework: 'The fact that a phenomenon is without independent nature is, to be sure, a further phenomenon – a higher order fact. But that fact, too, is without an independent nature. It, too, is merely conventional. This is another way of putting the strongly nominalistic character of Mādhyamika philosophy.'[134]

Emptiness as a designation, then, remains within the conventional realm without any ultimate status: it too is empty. Furthermore, the difference between the two realms is that of a perceptual distinction rather than that between two ontologically distinct realms:

> So the doctrine of the emptiness of emptiness can be seen as inextricably linked with Nāgārjuna's distinctive account of the relation between the two truths. For Nāgārjuna, as is also evident in this crucial verse, it is a mistake to distinguish conventional from ultimate reality – the dependently arisen from emptiness – at an ontological level. Emptiness just is the emptiness of conventional phenomena. To perceive conventional phenomena as empty is just to see them as conventional and as dependently arisen. The difference – such as it is – between the conventional and the ultimate is a difference in the way phenomena are conceived/perceived.[135]

At this point in the analysis, the deep coherence of the text becomes apparent as the points set out here all flow directly from the analysis of effects and conditions in Chapter I in which dependent arising, along with all conditions and effects, was shown to be empty. It is on this basis that the threefold identity of emptiness, dependent arising and conventional designation is posited in verse eighteen and also on this basis that emptiness itself is declared to be empty.

3.2.26 Chapter XXV Examination of Nirvāṇa

Chapter XXV proceeds to draw out the implications of the preceding chapter as it considers the nature of nirvāṇa, leading to what is probably the most startling of Nāgārjuna's conclusions. The verse opens with the imagined opponent objecting once again that if everything is empty, does this not preclude the relinquishing of saṃsāra and the arising of nirvāṇa? Moreover, who would do the relinquishing? This objection restates the errors considered

---

[134] Garfield, *Fundamental Wisdom*, 319

[135] Garfield, *Fundamental Wisdom*, 319

in the previous chapter which consist in confusing emptiness with nihilism. Nāgārjuna's response is the same: only emptiness can make sense of the relinquishing of saṃsāra and the arising of nirvāṇa – if these were nonempty, they would be eternal and change of any kind would be impossible. The opponent's error consists in taking the category of emptiness in an absolute sense and confusing it with inherent nonexistence. Only emptiness can make sense of the change involved in being liberated from saṃsāra and entering into nirvāṇa.

In verse three, Nāgārjuna defines nirvāṇa as:

> 3. Unrelinquished, unattained,
> Unannihilated, not permanent,
> Unarisen, unceased:
> This is how nirvāṇa is described.[136]

Garfield points out that it is important to note that both in Sanskrit and Tibetan all of these predicates are negative: nothing can be predicated directly of nirvāṇa as this would imply that nirvāṇa is a phenomenon, an entity, something which Nāgārjuna views as a contradiction in terms given that nirvāṇa is liberation from phenomenal reality. He further points out the difficulty involved in using conventional language to refer to the absolute: given that in the ultimate realm there are no conventional phenomena to serve as the bearers of any predicates and given that nirvāṇa stands in contrast to saṃsāra, there is a risk of wrongly reifying nirvāṇa itself as a phenomenon in order to enable predication. To do so, however, would be to misconstrue the nature of nirvāṇa by turning it into an inherently existing entity; correlative with this is the fact that language reaches its limits as soon as one seeks to move beyond the conventional. As Garfield states: 'One forgets that once one transcends the bounds of convention, there is no possibility of assertion.'[137]

Verses 4–18 rehearse the various reasons nirvāṇa cannot be coherently viewed as a phenomenon and does so in the context of the same tetralemma that has been used as an analytic framework throughout the text. The first point adduced is that nirvāṇa cannot exist, as if it did so it would, like everything that exists, be subject to both aging and death; this is a contradiction in terms, Garfield points out, as nirvāṇa is supposed precisely to be liberation from these factors. Equally, if nirvāṇa existed it would be compounded, as everything that exists comes about through the coming together of different

---

[136] MMK XXV:3

[137] Garfield, *Fundamental Wisdom*, 324

compounds in the process of dependent arising. Garfield points out that this has a deeper significance also: were nirvāṇa a compounded phenomenon, its recognition as a phenomenon would logically entail its conventional existence and it would therefore be the subject of reification on the part of all of those in saṃsāra who have not attained enlightenment (most people!). The inevitable reification of such a phenomenon would be the result of the grasping desire which is the root of *saṃsāric* bondage and suffering, a desire that is itself based on the illusion that things exist inherently. As nirvāṇa stands by definition in contrast to saṃsāra, for the above reasons it could not be compounded and therefore it cannot be said to exist.

At this point in the text the first of the four options in the tetralemma is given more formal consideration: namely whether or not nirvāṇa can be said to exist. We have already seen in the context of the argument relating to whether nirvāṇa could be compounded that Nāgārjuna's answer to this question is negative. Here he gives a further reason: nirvāṇa is defined as freedom from *saṃsāric* existence in its entirety, an existence which comes about through dependent origination. It follows, then, that nirvāṇa is free of dependent origination and hence is nondependent and thus cannot be said to exist in terms of dependent arising. Garfield qualifies this by pointing out that there is a sense in which nirvāṇa *can* be seen as dependent as it is attained through practice of the Dharma, but as there are no phenomena in nirvāṇa, it cannot depend on anything else for its existence in the way that *saṃsāric* phenomena do. This, Garfield avers, raises the question of whether nirvāṇa can be said to exist at all, and it is to this question that Nāgārjuna turns in verse seven:

> 7. If nirvāṇa were not existent,
> How could it be appropriate for it to be nonexistent?
> Where nirvāṇa is not existent,
> It cannot be a nonexistent.[138]

The reasoning here seems cryptic at first, but the point being made is that if nirvāṇa cannot be said in any sense to exist, nonexistence as a property cannot be predicated of it either; of what would such a property be predicated? In addition, where there is a subject for such a predicate, this subject would by definition be implicated in dependent arising.

Garfield states:

---

[138] MMK XXV:7

But when, in trying to characterize nirvāṇa, one is tempted to say that it is a nonexistent, this is in response to the difficulty we have just noted in asserting that nirvāṇa in fact exists. The temptation is to assert then that it is real, but has some kind of ghostly reality as a substratum of the property "nonexistent." But that is simply incoherent – an attempt to have it both ways. So the predicate "does not exist" cannot, in this case, even be applied. If there is no nirvāṇa at all, there is no such basis of predication. Even this apparently negative discourse about nirvāṇa is then blocked, to the degree that it is taken literally as positive attribution of a negative predicate.[139]

This insight is developed further in verse eight as Nāgārjuna points out that as nirvāṇa is deemed to be nondependent, there is no concept that could be either instantiated or not instantiated – that which is nondependent is quite literally '*no-thing*'. Conversely, were there such a concept, it would be implicated in dependence and therefore would be *saṃsāric* by definition.

Nonexistence *qua* a positive property predicated of a distinct phenomenon is not the same as 'non-being', however, and whilst nonexistence in the above sense cannot be applied to nirvāṇa, this is not the same as saying that nirvāṇa does not exist at all. This question is the substratum of verses nine and ten in which nirvāṇa is further described in a relationship of contrast to saṃsāra:

> 9. That which comes and goes
>   Is dependent and changing.
>   That, when it is not dependent and changing,
>   Is taught to be nirvāṇa.'
>
> 10. The teacher has spoken of relinquishing
>   Becoming and dissolution.
>   Therefore, it makes sense that
>   Nirvāṇa is neither existent nor nonexistent.[140]

The point being made here in relation to nirvāṇa is twofold: first, attention is drawn to the significance of the reifying mind in relation to the difference between nirvāṇa and saṃsāra, something which will be developed further in verse nineteen. The crux of Nāgārjuna's reasoning in relation to this is that the difference between nirvāṇa and saṃsāra is a difference of perception. As

---

[139] Garfield, *Fundamental Wisdom*, 327
[140] MMK XXV:9–10

already mentioned, the question of whether this perceptual difference is the entirety of the difference between nirvāṇa and saṃsāra is a disputed one, but in Garfield's reading of the text the difference is indeed solely that between illusory perception and accurate perception.

In addition to this, given that both existence and nonexistence as positive predicates are contingent on the arising and passing away involved in *pratītyasamutpāda*, neither can be coherently applied to nirvāṇa. Nor can both be applied to nirvāṇa at the same time (the fourth term of the tetralemma) as, says Garfield, this would quite simply be contradictory. Further, such dual predication would involve nirvāṇa in the dependence of contingency as well as entailing compounded existence, both of which have already been shown to be inapplicable to nirvāṇa. In verse fifteen, then, the final term of the tetralemma is ruled out as it is denied that nirvāṇa could be neither existent nor nonexistent, as this would imply the possibility, albeit unrealised, of applying both of these predicates to nirvāṇa, a possibility already deemed inadmissible. A corollary to this point is provided in verse sixteen with the question 'by whom is it expounded/"Neither existent nor nonexistent?"'.[141] The question here is the location of the one who would make such an assertion: this has not happened on the part of someone who is in nirvāṇa and, Garfield points out, there is no particular reason for believing such an assertion on the part of one who is in saṃsāra given the delusional character of *saṃsāric* existence and perception.

Having said all this, Nāgārjuna applies the definition of nirvāṇa he gave in verse three to the Buddha after his enlightenment:

> 17. Having passed into nirvāṇa, the Victorious Conqueror
> Is neither said to be existent,
> Nor said to be nonexistent.
> Neither both nor neither are said.[142]

This Nāgārjuna takes to be the ontological status of the Buddha post-enlightenment and it leads to the crescendo of his analysis of nirvāṇa as he states:

> 19. There is not the slightest difference
> Between cyclic existence and nirvāṇa.
> There is not the slightest difference
> Between nirvāṇa and cyclic existence.[143]

---

[141] MMK XXV:16

[142] MMK 25:17

[143] MMK 25:19

As we have seen, neither saṃsāra nor nirvāṇa can be conceived of as having an essence and thus there can be no difference between them, nothing which marks off an ontological boundary between the two. In considering this, Garfield avers that what is being expressed here is that nirvāṇa is simply seeing reality as it ultimately is, and that the difference between nirvāṇa and saṃsāra is simply one of perspective, between seeing with the ignorant mind of delusion and seeing with the enlightened mind of a Buddha. Garfield states:

> At this point, Nāgārjuna…draws one of the most startling conclusions of the *Mūlamadhyamakakārikā*: Just as there is no difference in entity between the conventional and the ultimate, there is no difference in entity between nirvāṇa and saṃsāra; nirvāṇa is simply saṃsāra seen without reification, without attachment, without delusion. The reason that we cannot say anything about nirvāṇa as an independent *nonsaṃsāric* entity, then, is not that it *is* such an entity, but that it is ineffable and unknowable. Rather it is because it is only saṃsāra seen as it is, just as emptiness is just the conventional seen as it is…[144]

Whilst the coherence of asserting that nirvāṇa cannot be conceived of as an entity is clear, Garfield extends this view by stating that nirvāṇa is *only* saṃsāra correctly perceived, in a way that begs the question and arguably goes beyond the limits of what Nāgārjuna himself is saying in the text. Garfield moves beyond the negative tetralemma employed by Nāgārjuna to make a reductionist identification that Nāgārjuna does not make, namely between the ultimate ontological status of things in saṃsāra and nirvāṇa itself. In contrast, Murti opines that all the various schools of Buddhism 'never took Nirvāṇa as nothing, but as an *asaṃskṛta dharma*, some sort of noumenal unconditioned reality behind the play of phenomena'.[145]

Schmidt-Leukel also disagrees with Garfield's analysis here, stating in relation to Nāgārjuna's identification of saṃsāra and nirvāṇa that 'this is not to imply a reduction of Nirvāṇa to the level of Saṃsāra, as some contemporary secularized interpreters of Buddhism seem to suggest. Rather it is Saṃsāra which is lifted up, in a sense, to the level of Nirvāṇa. For the emptiness of everything means not only that Nirvāṇa is unconditioned, unoriginated and unterminated, but that all reality is (see MMK 25:9). However, this is not to be taken as a back-door affirmation of a monistic metaphysical system, but

---

[144] Garfield, *Fundamental Wisdom*, 331
[145] Murti, *Central Philosophy of Buddhism*, 272

rather as the front-door affirmation that everything – without exception – is inconceivable and indescribable'.[146]

In Garfield's analysis, however, the point is clear: nirvāṇa is simply saṃsāra correctly perceived without the distorting influence of the unenlightened mind: it is simply a state of perceiving things as they really are, free from delusion. He goes on to interpret verse twenty-one[147] as ruling out the legitimacy of conceiving of the universe over and against nirvāṇa by pointing out that there is no standpoint outside the universe which enables a coherent conception of the totality of saṃsāra. Arguably Nāgārjuna's words here could be read differently, i.e. that the verse points out the incoherence of viewing nirvāṇa in terms proper to the differentiated phenomenal existence of saṃsāra, thus positing an ontological boundary between the two and effectively conceptualising nirvāṇa as a phenomenon alongside others. The question also arises that if the point being made by Garfield is true, then surely the cognitive moves involved in the linguistic use of the terms saṃsāra, nirvāṇa, etc. are themselves suspect. Garfield formulates the point with a different emphasis, however: 'But there is no vantage point from which the universe is one place among many. That is why talking about what lies beyond it is nonsense and why reifying or characterizing nirvāṇa temporally is one example of that nonsense.'[148]

Leading on from this last verse, Nāgārjuna once again makes use of the strategy already employed in his use of the negative tetralemma to underline that once one steps outside the conventional realm, normal linguistic assertion must cease and nothing can be predicated directly. Finally, reification of the soteriological tools used in order to set sentient beings free from delusion is also ruled out, leading Garfield to describe the Dharma itself as 'a way of engagement with nonentities by nonentities'.[149] Thus Nāgārjuna closes this pivotal chapter of the work, stating:

---

[146] Schmidt-Leukel, *Understanding Buddhism*, 121

[147] '21. Views that after cessation there is a limit, etc.,
And that it is permanent, etc.,
Depend upon nirvāṇa, the final limit,
And the prior limit.'
                    MMK 25:21

[148] Garfield, *Fundamental Wisdom*, 333
In interpreting verse 21 in this way Garfield fails to consider the view that nirvāṇa could be conceived of as a meontological reality; in this respect the meontological conception of Absolute Nothingness provided by Nishida in the context of the thought of the Kyoto School could provide a useful point of orientation for further research on this question

[149] Garfield, *Fundamental Wisdom*, 334

> 24. The pacification of all objectification
> And the pacification of illusion:
> No Dharma was taught by the Buddha
> At any time, in any place, to any person.[150]

3.2.27 Chapter XXVI Examination of the Twelve Links

The penultimate chapter of the text comprises a traditional Buddhist analysis of what might be termed the anatomy of interbeing, only this time located in the context of emptiness as set out in the preceding chapters. The intent of the chapter is soteriological: namely how to use the nature of interdependent existence to attain nirvāṇa. The chapter opens by citing ignorance as the first step in the chain of being, which leads one to perform the three kinds of actions (physical, verbal and mental), which in turn lead to further rebirths. Thus in verse one the actions that human beings perform are cited as the primary reason for their *saṃsāric* bondage. In many respects this is a positive statement as it places within the individual's grasp the means of escape from the *saṃsāric* predicament. Acts in turn leave their mark in the form of dispositions which lead to the formation of consciousness and it is this that transmigrates, leading to the mind–body formation that comprises a human being. Once this *nama–rūpa* (name and form) formation exists, the six senses arise (here, again, mind is deemed a sense) and this in turn leads to contact with phenomenal reality.

Nāgārjuna underlines that such contact is dependent on the senses along with the consciousness that gives rise to form and name (*nama–rūpa*). Garfield comments: 'From the phenomenological point of view, we can say that the domain of perceptibles and the structure of perceptual experience and knowledge depends upon our ability to represent and individuate objects, and that sensory contact is sensory contact in the first place only in virtue of its role in experience, which is in turn dependent upon the entire perceptual process. To put the matter crudely, an amputated sense organ in contact with an object is hardly in contact in the appropriate way'[151] Thus in verse five where consciousness is understood as the apprehension of objects, Nāgārjuna states:

---

[150] MMK 25:24

[151] Garfield, *Fundamental Wisdom*, 337

> 5. That which is assembled from the three –
> Eye and form and consciousness,
> Is contact. From contact
> Feeling comes to be.[152]

Contact or feeling, in turn, gives rise to the craving for the repetition of pleasant experiences and for the ending of unpleasant ones, a desire that leads to the impetus to possess both the sources of pleasure and the means of eliminating displeasure, what Nāgārjuna terms grasping. It is this grasping which makes of the individual one who grasps, i.e. a grasper, and thus sets her on the road to 'old age and death and misery and / Suffering and grief and / Confusion and agitation'.[153] Grasping also leads to an excessive valuation of what is grasped, thus locking the grasper into the bondage of attachment. Finally, Nāgārjuna cites this grasping as that which causes the person to come into existence, stating:

> 7. When there is grasping, the grasper,
> Comes into existence.
> If he did not grasp,
> Then being freed, he would not come into existence.[154]

From the entry into existence proceed the five aggregates which comprise a human person and all the suffering that goes with such an existence. Towards the end of the chapter Nāgārjuna recapitulates the chain of links, again drawing attention to action as the root of the whole cyclic process, though the concept of action invoked here (verse ten) corresponds, according to Garfield, to the concatenation of action and dispositions rather than referring to positive action alone. Central to the process of escaping from the performance of such karmically harmful actions is the acquisition of wisdom: 'But in order really to modify our actions and dispositions to act, we need wisdom – in this context an understanding of the real nature of things, which for Nāgārjuna means the view of all things as empty. This view, Nāgārjuna asserts, must be internalized through meditation, so that it becomes not merely a philosophical theory that we can reason our way into, but the basic way in which we

---

[152] MMK XXVI:5
[153] MMK XXVI:8b–9a
[154] MMK XXVI:7

take up with the world. Accomplishing that, he asserts, leads to the cessation of that activity responsible for the perpetuation of the suffering of saṃsāra.'[155]

Moreover, the context for such cessation through meditation is that of the emptiness of all that exists – what is empty, being devoid of any inherent existence, may be changed, thus emptiness provides a soteriological ground for the hope of liberation from suffering. Thus Nāgārjuna concludes the chapter, saying:

> 12. Through the cessation of this and that
> This and that will not be manifest.
> The entire mass of suffering
> Indeed thereby completely ceases.[156]

3.2.28 Chapter XXVII Examination of Views

The final chapter is both a restatement and an application of the conclusions previously reached regarding emptiness, as well as containing one of the most controverted points made in the text as Nāgārjuna applies emptiness to all views taken of reality. The backdrop is the various alternate views which deny emptiness, views that would be deemed erroneous across the spectrum of Buddhist thought. Garfield points out that having previously shown that the elimination of errors is crucial to the attaining of nirvāṇa, the task Nāgārjuna sets himself in this concluding chapter is that of showing how to eliminate such errors. Not surprisingly, for Nāgārjuna the *fons et origo* of all other errors is the belief in the inherent existence of either the self or other entities.

The analysis begins with a consideration of the question of the continuity of the person over time and this question is linked with the nature of assertions about the world, as Nāgārjuna states in verse one: 'All of these views / Depend on a prior limit.'[157]

The prior limit in question is that of a putative point when either the self or the world can be said to begin and prior to which existence simply cannot be asserted. Equally, statements of a similar nature about the future also require a putative point beyond which the world or the self must be conceived

---

[155] Garfield, *Fundamental Wisdom*, 340
[156] MMK:XXVI:12
[157] MMK XVII:1b

of as being outside the realm of existence. As will be shown, for Nāgārjuna such a semantic move is simply incoherent.

In verse three the problem of personal continuity is introduced explicitly:

> 3. To say "I was in the past"
> Is not tenable.
> What existed in the past
> Is not identical to this one.[158]

To assert identity between one's existence in the present and what constituted an individual in the past would require a complete identity of properties, something which is manifestly not the case given the numerous mental and physical changes which occur in a person over time.

Verse four imagines a person engaging in introspection and designating an element perceived in introspection as the self. Nāgārjuna, in response, draws attention to the interesting phenomenon which occurs in all acts of perception, namely the duality that occurs between what is perceived and the one doing the perceiving, something which pertains to introspection as much as to the perception of external entities. If anything is to be designated the self, Nāgārjuna states, it must be the appropriator of that which is appropriated in the noetic act. Yet this too fails as a proposed unchanging and permanently existing self as the appropriator cannot exist apart from a phenomenon that is appropriated and indeed is conditioned by such, and these objects constantly change, a point which also rules out any attempt to identify the self with the act of appropriating.

An additional problem with any attempt at identification of the appropriator or the appropriating with the self is that one would be obliged to include future acts of appropriation as constituent elements of it, thus involving the absurd paradox of identifying the unchanging self with acts of appropriation that have yet to take place. Nor can this problem be circumvented by proposing an independent existence for the appropriator, as if this were so then acts of appropriation could occur in a nonappropriator, something which, as well as being logically incoherent, would render the change required to achieve nirvāṇa impossible. As Garfield comments:

> The target position here is one according to which the existence of appropriation as a real, persistent feature of cyclic existence is used as the basis for attributing personal identity to a continuing self. That self is

---

[158] MMK XXVII:3

not supposed to be the appropriating itself, but rather a separate entity independent of it. Nāgārjuna points out, though, that it is, and for the proponent of this view, it must be possible not to appropriate – otherwise nirvāṇa would be impossible. So, there will be a nonappropriator who once was an appropriator. But if appropriation is the basis of the identity of the one who has been liberated with the one who was not, that appropriation should persist in the nonappropriator, which would be contradictory.[159]

In verse eight Nāgārjuna asserts that separate from the act of appropriating there can be no self at all, but immediately moves to deny that one can conclude from this that there is no self in any sense:

> 8. So it is neither different from the appropriating
> Not identical to the appropriating.
> There is no self without appropriation.
> But it is not true that it does not exist.[160]

Thus neither is it correct to say that the person who exists is in no way identical with her past. If this were the case then the current existence of a person would have to be conceived *ex nihilo* and the diachronic existence intrinsic to human life would not be tenable: 'If this were so / Without death, one would be born.'[161] While Garfield seems to limit the application of this principle to the question of succession within a single lifespan in his commentary, it seems clear that Nāgārjuna here applies the principle more widely, locating it in the context of reincarnation, a schema that is presupposed in the Buddhist worldview as virtually axiomatic. Such a rupture, Nāgārjuna states, would render unintelligible the phenomenon of human action and, Garfield points out, the conventional identity that is based upon it. Thus one person would perform an action and its direct consequences or fruits would be experienced by someone else in a way that bore no causal relationship.

Against the backdrop of the analysis of the emptiness of the past undertaken earlier in the text, one would be left with the situation whereby the current existence of the person would be simultaneously dependent on something that no longer exists (i.e. her past self) yet without any causal relationship

---

[159] Garfield, *Fundamental Wisdom*, 345
[160] MMK XXVII:8
[161] MMK XXVII:10

pertaining between the two. Summing all this up in a tetralemma in verse thirteen, Nāgārjuna states:

> 13. So, the views "I existed," "I didn't exist,"
> Both or neither,
> In the past
> Are untenable.[162]

Moreover, as pointed out in verse fourteen, all of these arguments apply logically to similar questions of identity projected into the future. Here, as throughout the text, it is important to bear in mind that the aim is not to deny the conventional existence of the self – quite the contrary is the case – but to show the logical incoherence of the phenomenon of personal continuity if the self is conceived of as existing inherently. Throughout the text Nāgārjuna's analysis always occurs against the backdrop of the teaching of the two truths according to which he seeks to affirm the reality of the conventional whilst showing its emptiness from the absolute standpoint.

An alternative view is now considered in the text, namely whether the self could be considered to exist permanently by virtue of being divine. The philosophical backdrop to this is the classical Indian view that the essential self of a person, atman, participates in Divinity (Brahman), the denial of which by Buddhist thinkers led to the chief demarcation of their views from those of the various Hindu thinkers at the time and still forms a crucial dividing point between the two religions today.

Nāgārjuna begins by setting out the parameters of the debate: if a human were divine, then permanence could be legitimately predicated; if not, then impermanence would apply. In verse seventeen, the question of a person being part divine and part human is ruled out as violating the law of non-contradiction, a move which also rules out any attempt to say that the being of a person is neither permanent nor impermanent.

Verse nineteen introduces a further objection to any attempt to think of the self in terms of inherent essence:

> 19. If anyone had come from anyplace
> And then were to go someplace,
> It would follow that cyclic existence was beginningless.
> This is not the case.[163]

---

[162] MMK XXVII:13

[163] MMK XXVII:19

Garfield points out that here the word 'beginningless' denotes inherent existence, so the verse pertains to the question of soteriology and the question of the status of saṃsāra. The argument runs that if a person's absolute identity is to be asserted, this can only be so through the person participating in an unchanging essence. If this is the case, however, then change in any comprehensive sense, such as liberation from saṃsāra and entry into nirvāṇa, becomes an impossibility. Accordingly, a person would be *essentially* in saṃsāra and this would mean that the state of being in nirvāṇa would itself be inherently existent. This Nāgārjuna rules out on the basis of the fundamental Buddhist axiom that such transformation *is* possible, and this in turn further demonstrates in the context of the argument the illegitimacy of conceiving of the self in essentialist terms.

Verse twenty contains the most absolute formulation of the implications of the emptiness of self so far in the chapter, stating:

> 20. If nothing is permanent,
> What will be impermanent,
> Permanent and impermanent,
> Or neither?[164]

As there is no inherently existing entity, no subject is available to bear a definitive predicate of any kind, permanence and impermanence included.

Verse twenty-one[165] returns to the question of a prior limit, this time in relation to the world, and avers that viewing the world as limited or unlimited precludes conceiving of anything beyond the world. Garfield puts the argument thus:

> It is not, that is, a question about whether there is anything beyond the world. For suppose that the world is limited. That suggests that there is something beyond it. But that just means that we haven't come to the end of the world. The whole world includes that stuff that lies beyond. Or suppose that the world is unlimited. That suggests that there is nothing beyond the world. But that just means that everything that is

---

[164] MMK XXVII:20

[165] '21. If the world were limited,
How could there be another world?
If the world were unlimited,
How could there be another world?'
MMK XXVII:21

in the world is, in fact, in the world, which is trivial. The question regarding the limits of the world, so Nāgārjuna suggests, is nonsensical.[166]

As already stated, whilst for the purposes of the dialectical analysis being undertaken in this work Garfield's reading of the *Mūlamadhyamakakārikā* will be taken as normative, the analysis he proposes at this point does appear to be particularly problematic. First he reads the limitedness in question as being a quantitative rather than qualitative limitedness, placing it in the context of a reductionist materialism ('The whole world includes the stuff that lies beyond'). Support for the view that such a characterisation of the world does not amount to a reduction of nirvāṇa to saṃsāra can be found in texts such as the *Udana* in which the Buddha is portrayed as saying:

> There is, monks, an unborn—unbecome—unmade—unfabricated. If there were not that unborn—unbecome—unmade—unfabricated, there would not be the case that escape from the born—become—made—fabricated would be discerned. But precisely because there is an unborn—unbecome—unmade—unfabricated, escape from the born—become—made—fabricated is discerned.[167]

This presupposition of the exclusively material nature of reality runs contrary to the classical Buddhist view. As Perry Schmidt-Leukel states, considering the question of emptiness in the wider context of the Prajñāpāramitā sūtras: 'Is this a denial of ultimate reality, of the "Deathless" which constitutes the original goal and basis of Buddhism? Thus have the "Perfection of Wisdom" Sūtras at times been understood – or better: misunderstood, for the texts themselves point to a different answer. Their claim that everything, including Nirvāṇa, is empty is based on the conviction that everything is as inconceivable and ineffable as Nirvāṇa. The illusion or dream consists in our assuming that the definable and discrete entities we construct with our concepts and mental images show us reality as it really is.'[168]

Thus Garfield may be legitimately charged here with eisegetically proposing a materialist reductionism that is not what Nāgārjuna himself intends. This raises the question of how this verse can be alternatively read. Here, one

---

[166] Garfield, *Fundamental Wisdom*, 350

[167] Thanissaro Bhikku, trans., *Udana* 8:3, accessed 7 December 2013, http://www.accesstoinsight.org/tipitaka/kn/ud/ud.8.03.than.html

[168] Schmidt-Leukel, *Understanding Buddhism*, 117

may state that with the exception of his treatment of nirvāṇa, Nāgārjuna's concern throughout has been with what we would term phenomenal reality and that accordingly the purport of this verse is that there is no phenomenal reality that lies beyond the world. This reading remains legitimate whether one follows Garfield in his view that the liberation of nirvāṇa constitutes simply a perspectival alteration in the way one perceives saṃsāra or whether one views nirvāṇa as being an absolute non-phenomenal reality.[169]

Nāgārjuna continues his line of reasoning by comparing the nature of phenomenal reality to the burning of a butterlamp: rather than worldly reality comprising any kind of essentialist reality (the context considered in the question about the limit of the world), such reality is correctly viewed as a sequence of events: 'But the world, Nāgārjuna suggests, is more like a flame. It is a series of distinct flickering events. While each event is momentary, the sequence continues. But there is no entity that persists and can be said to be eternal or momentary.'[170]

The question of the finitude or infinity of the world becomes simply a question of whether phenomena in the sequential series that comprises reality continue to arise and perish: if they cease to perish, the world becomes infinite; if they cease to arise, it becomes finite. The terms infinite and finite as used by Nāgārjuna here correspond to permanent and impermanent, again implying a qualitative rather than quantitative horizon of interpretation in contrast to that implicit in Garfield's commentary cited above. Finally, the possibility of applying both terms to the world is ruled out as being contradictory and hence nonsensical.

Garfield closes his commentary with a verse that has given rise to much scholarly discussion. The nub of the argument lies in the very last line of the verse:

---

[169] Cf. Schmidt-Leukel: '"Eternity", "non-eternity", "both" or "neither" – these terms are utterly inapplicable to ultimate bliss, says Nāgārjuna, for such designations depend upon descriptive ideas and demarcated concepts (see MMK 22:12–15; 25:1–18). Understanding the emptiness of everything means understanding that not only is Nirvāṇa indescribable, inconceivable and ineffable, but so is all reality. In that regard there is no difference between Nirvāṇa and Saṃsāra…Yet this is not to imply a reduction of Nirvāṇa to the level of Saṃsāra, as some contemporary secularised interpreters of Buddhism seem to suggest. Rather it is Saṃsāra which is lifted up, in a sense, to the level of Nirvāṇa. For the emptiness of everything means not only that Nirvāṇa is unconditioned, unoriginated and unterminated, but that all reality is (see MMK 25:9). However, this is not to be taken as a back-door affirmation of a monistic metaphysical system, but rather as the front-door affirmation that everything – without exception – is inconceivable and indescribable.' Schmidt-Leukel 121. Also page XXX above

[170] Garfield, *Fundamental Wisdom*, 350

> I prostrate to Gautama
> Who through compassion
> Taught the true doctrine,
> Which leads to the relinquishing of all views.[171]

Nāgārjuna's words about the relinquishing of views are usually interpreted as referring to all false views, and especially those which posit phenomena as existing inherently, views which have been the target of his analysis throughout the text. In this view, the teaching of the Buddha, the Dharma and Nāgārjuna's own views are not included in this relinquishment. Garfield points out, however, that there is an additional interpretation of this line which is not posited in opposition but rather goes along with the first interpretation. In this reading of the text all views, including those put forward by Nāgārjuna, are relinquished as the practitioner apprehends emptiness not intellectually but directly through non-dual awareness. In this context no view is appropriate because there is, quite simply, nothing which could be the object of any view.

The term 'view' here refers to the subject–object structure of conventional apprehension in which objects falsely appear as having substantial existence. Once the practitioner becomes enlightened, however, these mental constructions are dissolved in the awareness of the ultimate emptiness of all dharmas. Yet, as outlined throughout the text, emptiness is itself empty: it is not a dharma that in any sense exists, but rather is simply the absence of any essential existence. There is, then, nothing to perceive, nothing to view. It is in this context that all views are relinquished and this is linked to what Nāgārjuna has already said about the impossibility of predicating anything of reality seen from the absolute perspective. Just as language can only be ostensive in approaching things as they are ultimately, once this perspective is grasped meditatively, language and thought both fall away and the reifying conceptualisation that characterises the deluded mind sunk in *avidyā* ceases. Accordingly there are no views, nothing to view, and no possibility of predication. Reality seen as it ultimately is lies beyond the realm of description or reification.

Garfield, while stating that we cannot be absolutely sure what Nāgārjuna intends by this verse, refers to a number of different places in the text in support of this interpretation, in particular the opening verse. This verse,

---

[171] MMK XXVII:30

he points out, parallels the closing verse in the Tibetan text in the language used[172] as well as in its characterisation of the Dharma:

> I Prostrate to the Perfect Buddha,
> The best of teachers, who taught that
> Whatever is dependently arisen is
> Unceasing, unborn,
> Unannihilated, not permanent,
> Not coming, not going,
> Without distinction, without identity,
> And free from conceptual distinction.[173]

The parallel pairs the characterisation of dependent reality in the dedicatory verses with the reference to 'the true doctrine' in the closing verses, and in particular the relinquishing of views mentioned in the closing verse with the reference to what is dependently arisen as being 'free from conceptual distinction' in the opening.

It is in the apprehension of reality in freedom from conceptual distinction that the relinquishing of all views takes place, as without conceptual distinction they become quite simply impossible. The perception of emptiness, then, entails an end to all reification.

Garfield buttresses this analysis by pointing out the logical problems which would be involved if emptiness *could* be the object of any view. For it to be so, it would have to fit into the subject–object framework of perception and therefore it would have to, in some sense, exist. Yet such existence would entail it existing either absolutely or conventionally. If absolutely, then emptiness would become a logically incoherent concept, as what has essential emptiness is the exact opposite of the meaning Nāgārjuna has given to emptiness throughout the text. If its existence were conventional, a logical problem would also occur, as emptiness has been defined as the opposite of the delusory appearance of phenomena seen conventionally in which they appear to have substantial existence along with a substratum, properties, etc. Emptiness is the designation of this separate reified existence as an illusion, therefore emptiness could not logically exist in such a way.

The impossibility of emptiness existing in either of the two ways outlined means that there is nothing to perceive; as Garfield states: 'Since we can't

---

[172] Cf. Garfield, *Fundamental Wisdom*, 354
[173] MMK: Dedicatory Verses

view emptiness even as empty, in view of its very emptiness, we can't have a view of emptiness.'[174]

This is what is meant by the 'reinquishing of all views', and as such constitutes a denial neither of the Dharma nor of Nāgārjuna's own perspective, as these exist and are required on the conventional level. In this respect, Garfield turns to the common metaphor of the Buddha's teaching as a raft one uses to cross a river in a way which links the two interpretations of this verse with the doctrine of the two views used by Nāgārjuna: 'This interpretation would be consistent with the raft metaphor popular in Buddhist philosophy (one discards the raft after one has crossed the river; it would be foolish to continue to carry it overland; similarly, Buddhist teachings are soteriological in intent and are to be discarded after their goal has been attained).'[175]

The first interpretation of this verse, then, would correspond to conventional truth, whilst the second, which entails the relinquishing of all views, Nāgārjuna's included, would correspond to the absolute level of truth, the point at which description of any kind is no longer possible and at which the mind, in experiencing emptiness directly, ceases from the reifying activity of subject–object consciousness. This view is summed up eloquently by Garfield in the closing words of the commentary: 'And if the doctrine of the two truths and their identity is correct, these readings are mutually entailing. To assert from the conventional standpoint that all phenomena are empty and that all views according to which they are not are to be relinquished is to recognize from the ultimate standpoint that there are no phenomena to be empty and that no view attributing any characteristic to anything can be maintained. Even the emptiness of emptiness is empty.'[176]

3.3 Analysis of Nāgārjuna's *Mūlamadhyamakakārikā* According to Lonergan's Metaphysical Method

In terms of the epistemological structure laid out by Lonergan in *Insight*, the primary move in seeking to analyse Nāgārjuna's opus is to locate it within the threefold structure of experience, insight and judgement. The experience that underlies Nāgārjuna's thought can itself be characterised as threefold: i) experience of the nature of individual existents (in Buddhist terms the three marks of all dharmas) grasped both logically and meditatively, ii) the

---

[174] Garfield, *Fundamental Wisdom*, 356

[175] Garfield, *Fundamental Wisdom*, 356

[176] Garfield, *Fundamental Wisdom*, 358

conflict between the various logical statements by which these are ordinarily characterised, and iii) the use of language that is involved in making such statements.

In terms of the relationship between these three factors, the insight formulated by Nāgārjuna is that reality is mutually conditioning, that nothing exists inherently and that such emptiness of inherent existence is itself simply a conventional designation. This insight comes in a sense at one remove and operates in the context of what we might term an apophatic application of Lonergan's method. The insight does not emerge straightforwardly from the *prima facie* relationship between these positive data of experience, but rather is formulated as a result of this relationship. What this means in effect is that rather than a relationship grasped between mental phenomena that are affirmed at face value, bringing them together exposes this 'face value' as being unreliable and not a true characterisation of them. The true characterisation that emerges leads to an interrelation which is affirmed as true and which simultaneously recasts the way in which the data in question are interpreted.

In terms of the underlying metaphysical moves made by Nāgārjuna, it is a question of multiple applications of this same set of moves with the aim of showing the comprehensiveness of the perspective that emerges from it. The insight itself emerges from the logical conflicts which result when the above data of experience are brought together and the relationship grasped turns on the fact that in their true nature none of the above can be affirmed in terms of the naïve realism which seems intrinsic to them, but rather all three are empty, characterised by śūnyata. In this sense we may say that in Nāgārjuna's analysis, conjugate potency, form and act serve as a springboard to a higher viewpoint which in turn leads to the affirmation of central potency, form and act.

Crucial to analysing this aspect of Nāgārjuna's thought in terms of Lonergan's framework is Lonergan's distinction between 'things' and 'bodies'. 'Bodies' Lonergan defines as 'the highly convincing instances of the "already out there now real" that are unquestioned and unquestionable not only for animals but also for the bias of common sense'[177] and these form the object of perception *qua* mere extroversion within the conventional realm which is identified by Buddhist analysis as deluded consciousness (*avidyā*). 'Things', in contrast, are 'the intelligible unities to be grasped when one is within the intellectual pattern of experience' and as such belong to the pattern of

---

[177] Lonergan, *Insight*, 267

experience in which the correct functioning of the intellect is added to the perceived sensory data.

It is one of the aims of Nāgārjuna's dialectic to effect this transition from perceiving bodies to things on the conventional level, but this transition then leads beyond itself to the affirmation of the emptiness of things as their true nature is grasped. The insight that things lack any inherent being but come about solely as a result of *pratītyasamutpāda* (determined arising) leads to their ultimate disappearance when reality is viewed from the absolute level, with a corresponding end to all possibility of predication. Indeed, viewed from the absolute perspective there is 'no-thing' to perceive as there are no distinct phenomena with ontological boundaries between them and the very concept of perception breaks down and yields to the meditative apprehension of non-dual consciousness.

Within Nāgārjuna's framework, no further questions emerge that are unanswered by the schema he has laid out and, accordingly, the insight is affirmed as true (the third of Lonergan's noetic moves, i.e. judgement). *Pace* Nāgārjuna, however, when placed alongside Lonergan's development of his own metaphysics, the reflexive nature of consciousness which is posited as constituting the spiritual in *Insight* does emerge as a question that is unanswered in the *Mūlamadhyamakakārikā*, as does the classical question 'why is there something rather than nothing?'. Certainly it may be argued that Nāgārjuna sets before himself the task of analysing the nature of existent dharmas, thereby precluding the move which Lonergan makes in his transition from contingent being (denoted by the term 'proportionate being' in *Insight*) to Absolute being (God). Rather, Nāgārjuna's leap is one of perception and ultimately one beyond the subject–object duality of perception leading to non-dual awareness, but there is no explicit leap from contingent to absolute being.

It may be argued that something approaching this move lies behind the identification of nirvāṇa and saṃsāra, but the reluctance traditional in Buddhism to apply any firm definition to nirvāṇa applies here, too. If the more reductionist approach of secular scholars like Garfield is rejected, however, interpreting the *Mūlamadhyamakakārikā* against the backdrop of the *Buddhavacana* (texts viewed as containing the words of Buddha) may enable us to see the identification as involving such a transition. Certainly, as seen above, scholars such as Murti and Schmidt-Leukel view what is intended here as entailing this kind of transition. Thus, seen in a wider context, it does seem plausible to view Nāgārjuna as intending such a transition, albeit not in terms of any causality, *a fortiori* given his rejection of causation as a category.

Accordingly the stipulations of the virtually unconditioned that are foundational to the third stage of Lonergan's noetic structure are satisfied, but the reflexivity of consciousness remains as something unexplained within the framework of emptiness, as does the meta-question pertaining to existence *per se*. This forms a real point of divergence between Lonergan and Nāgārjuna, especially as it is precisely the reflexivity of consciousness which constitutes the self-affirmation of the knower in Lonergan's framework, a self-affirmation which he denotes as the self-verifying criterion which underpins his theory of knowledge. It is the reflexive grasp of the structure of human knowing which provides the basis for Lonergan's assertion that the theory of knowledge he produces is the only one which is not arbitrary, as the foundation of the reflexive grasp of consciousness by itself is, by definition, self-verifying. Crucial to this move on Lonergan's part is the inclusion of the knowing self as an intrinsic factor in the ability to affirm that intelligent knowing does indeed lead to an accurate grasp of reality as it is. Seen in this light, although Nāgārjuna does provide a very extensive metaphysics in terms of the nature of dharmas, for Lonergan he is still operating with a latent rather than an explicit metaphysics as he does not examine the structure of mind which provides the basis for all other logical operations. That such inclusion of the knowing knower is necessary is affirmed by Lonergan in his definition of being as the 'objective of the pure desire to know', a definition which itself is made in terms of ostension and not direct predication.

These three stages (experience, insight, judgement) relate in Nāgārjuna's thought to the metaphysical nature of things as they are *in se* and stand in striking contrast to things as they are experienced in terms of ordinary perception. This accordingly leads Nāgārjuna to formulate his doctrine of two truths (conventional and absolute), a move which in Lonerganian terms constitutes a higher viewpoint, i.e. one that combines two conflicting insights in the form of a new insight that comprises both. Here, then, the doctrine of two truths combines the insight into the true nature of existent dharmas with the conventional perception of these that people experience and formulates the concept of the conventional and absolute perspectives.

Interestingly, the noted divergence between things as they are perceived by the mind mired in *saṃsāric avidyā* (ignorance) and things as they are *in se* forms a point of convergence between Lonergan and Nāgārjuna, with both contrasting perception as mere extroversion with correct perception in which the use of intelligence is a necessary component. This also provides an answer to the charge that Nāgārjuna deals not with things as they are but only with things as they appear to us in his use of destructive dialectic. It is precisely his engagement with, and assault on, things as they seem to us that leads him beyond ordinary perception to the ostensive characterisation of things as they are from the absolute perspective (with all of the caveats pertaining to any attempt to directly characterise this in linguistic predication that he sets out).

In contrast to Lonergan, however, Nāgārjuna goes beyond Lonergan's posited isomorphism between the structure of knowing and the structure of the known in his negative characterisation of things as they are *in se* with his eschewing of all possibility of predication and the elision of all ontological boundaries of distinction when reality is viewed from the absolute perspective. Further, his inclusion of the experience of the meditative grasp of emptiness in his analytic framework provides an additional point of divergence from Lonergan, who does not explicitly allow for this kind of knowing in which the discursive mind falls silent and all reification ceases.

At first sight it would seem that this divergence can be accommodated within Lonergan's framework once it is remembered that in Buddhist terms mind is viewed as a sense; this in turn would mean that such meditative knowing could be placed in the experiential category which comprises the first stage of Lonergan's threefold pattern of knowing. There is, however, a problem with this move, as the meditative state described by Nāgārjuna is one in which the subject–object distinction does not pertain, nor do the distinctions between existent phenomena as they are normally experienced: 'For the practitioner who directly realises emptiness, nothing is present to consciousness but emptiness itself. For such a consciousness, there literally is no object since there is in such a consciousness no reification of the kind that gives rise to subject-object duality. Moreover, since such a consciousness is directed only upon what can be found ultimately to exist and since nothing can be so found, there is literally nothing toward which such a consciousness can be directed.'[178]

Thus there is no subject of experience and 'no-thing' which is experienced. This is something which, whilst reported frequently enough in Buddhist writings, falls beyond the normal categories of experience in Western philosophy and thus it cannot be classed as an experience in the sense intended by Lonergan in which there is a subject who experiences various sensory phenomena, data, etc. Moreover, without a dualistic experience of data by a subject, no relationship can be grasped between them leading to an insight, and the third stage does not occur either. Thus this meditative apprehension cannot be accommodated within Lonergan's framework. Yet it is not a phenomenon that doesn't fit as it cannot be conceived of in phenomenal terms at

---

[178] Garfield, *Fundamental Wisdom*, 354

all, nor does it constitute knowing in the usual sense. To this degree it doesn't falsify the claim that all experience and knowing fit within the framework, but rather shows the non-comprehensiveness of these categories by positing a state which falls outside them, so to speak. In Nāgārjuna's terms, it could be said that Lonergan's system proves perfectly adequate at the conventional level but fails to encompass the absolute perspective. The two are not incompatible as no contradiction occurs (for such to occur, it would have to be possible to reify the meditative state), but it does speak directly to the question of whether Lonergan's framework can serve as an integrative framework for Buddhist–Christian encounter, something which will be discussed further in Chapter 4.

Nāgārjuna's final position, as stated above, rests on the ostensive negative characterisation of the nature of being resulting from the insights that emerge from his destructive analysis of the predication that results from knowing as mere sensory extroversion. This corresponds in a sense to Lonergan's concept of objectivity as a nexus of judgements based on the fulfilment of the virtually unconditioned in the relation between experience and insight, except that the objective position arrived at by Nāgārjuna involves no nexus and no positive judgements, and the meditative apprehension referred to is not an experience![179]

Thus it can be concluded that Lonergan's epistemological framework does prove adequate to the task of making sense of Nāgārjuna's metaphysics on the conventional level, and even on the absolute level when this is restricted to the philosophical moves made. In this respect it provides a way of analysing the noetic moves which underpin this analysis. It falls short, however, in

---

[179] Nāgārjuna's most direct reference to the role of meditation in apprehending the absolute nature of reality occurs in MMK XXVI:10–12:

'10. The root of cyclic existence is action.
Therefore, the wise one does not act.
Therefore, the unwise is the agent.
The wise one is not because of his insight.
11. With the cessation of ignorance
Action will not arise.
The cessation of ignorance occurs through
Meditation and wisdom.
12. Through the cessation of this and that
This and that will not be manifest.
The entire mass of suffering
Indeed thereby completely ceases.'

terms of the meditative appropriation of things as they are on the absolute level and thus proves not to be comprehensive and fails to provide a complete integrative framework for Buddhist–Christian encounter, its more limited usefulness notwithstanding. The task that now remains is to investigate to what degree Lonergan's framework can accommodate the challenge of dialectically relating Rahner's thought in the *Foundations* to Nāgārjuna's analysis in the *Mūlamadhyamakakārikā*, a question which will form the subject matter of Chapter 4.

4 Dialectic Application of Lonergan's Epistemology

4.1 Verification of Lonergan's Claims

The principal aim in this final chapter will be to test the validity of Lonergan's claim to comprehensiveness for his epistemological system. This will be examined by seeing whether the proposed epistemology can integrate the two very different systems of thought that have been under examination in previous chapters. Crucial to this endeavour is Lonergan's concept of a universal viewpoint, conceived of as the dialectical interrelation of all different branches of knowledge. Fundamentally, as Tekippe has pointed out, the universal viewpoint is 'simply the implication of a developed knowledge of the structure of cognition'.[1]

Moreover, the lynchpin of this position is the posited isomorphism between the structure of knowing and its contents. Knowing is affirmed as having a universal threefold structure of experience, insight and judgement, a structure that is operative in every act of knowing that is not simply mere extroversion. Being is defined at one remove as the object of this intelligent act of knowing and therefore it will have the same threefold structure as the act of knowing itself (this corresponds to the Thomistic categories of potency, form and act). In affirming this Lonergan is taking it as read that there is no access to being outside of consciousness and it is precisely because of this that being exists of necessity in isomorphism to the noetic structure by which it is grasped.

The positing of being itself as possessed of this threefold structure constitutes the orientating point of departure for the proposed dialectical relation between Rahner and Nāgārjuna. The positing of such a structure should mean that parsing the two systems of thought according to the framework Lonergan has laid out should enable us to meaningfully interrelate them despite their *prima facie* incompatibility.

Specifically, this dialectical interrelation will take the form of i) plotting the various elements of the two systems of thought on Lonergan's

---

[1] Tekippe, *Lonergan's Insight: A Comprehensive Commentary*, 318

epistemological graph, so to speak, and ii) an attempt to grasp the relationship between corresponding elements of the two systems. This dialectical relating is framed by two further basic questions: first, has the foregoing analysis in Chapters 2 and 3 proved consonant with Lonergan's claim that his threefold structure is present in all knowing? Second, does interrelating the two systems of thought on this basis prove to be both meaningful and fruitful?

The Lonerganian analysis of Rahner's *Foundations of Christian Faith* did indeed prove viable (cf. Chapter 2, 42–55) and the threefold structure was found to be present within Rahner's formulations. Equally, the threefold structure also proved viable in analysing the *Mūlamadhyamakakārikā*, with one significant exception. Nāgārjuna, in his analysis, emphasises the importance of meditative apprehension of the insights pertaining to the emptiness of dharmas and this in turn involves the practitioner perceiving reality as it is, without ontological distinctions and in the context of non-dual consciousness. This is something which cannot be accommodated within Lonergan's threefold system and poses a very real challenge to Lonergan's claim for the universality of his categories. In non-dual consciousness there can be no subject or object of experience and thus no experience *per se*, *a fortiori* given that entering into this state involves letting go of the mind's habitual tendency to perceive reality as being comprised of separate phenomena. Moreover, as the experience of separate phenomena is not present, there can be no possibility of a unifying insight which grasps the interrelation between them. This in turn renders the third stage – judgement – redundant also: there can be no virtually unconditioned established and further questions by definition cannot arise (language, too, as a facet of the discriminating mind has fallen silent). This is significant as this awareness is reported by Nāgārjuna as a state that the practitioner can enter, yet the expected intelligibility in terms of the threefold noetic structure Lonergan proposes is not present.

Moreover, as well as pertaining to the meditative grasp of reality as it is from the absolute viewpoint, the same difficulty applies in relation to nirvāṇa itself as it is analysed in the text. This is particularly significant as the Buddha's parinirvāṇa is a fundamental basis of Buddhism as a system of thought and practice. One may of course dispute the truthfulness of Nāgārjuna's claim that such a state is possible (though what Nāgārjuna describes here corresponds to the various dyhanas, or meditative states, which are widely reported in Buddhist literature), but as long as the claim is advanced, it must be accommodated within Lonergan's epistemological framework.

At this point in the analysis it seems appropriate to recapitulate the aims of the dialectic to be established. Lonergan claims that his epistemological system is fully comprehensive and so far this has been shown to be tenable. The question then arises in preliminary form of the significance of attempting to relate Rahner and Nāgārjuna's thought (or indeed any other two disparate positions) on the basis of this system. This question may be formulated in semantic terms: first, can Lonergan's system provide a meaningful framework for the metaphysical analysis of the two texts, and second, does it prove useful in seeking to interrelate them? The answer to the first question is yes: Lonergan's framework does prove applicable to Nāgārjuna's thought in terms of the presence of the threefold structure Lonergan takes as axiomatic, with the exception of Nāgārjuna's formulation of the meditative grasp of reality free from conceptual reification. Given that the same structure can also be applied to analysis of Rahner's foundations, the attempt to dialectically relate the two systems of thought can be undertaken on the basis that the threefold structure Lonergan advances has been shown to be common to both of them. The second question is that of the fruitfulness of such an interrelation and to answer this the focus of the analysis must therefore now turn to attempting such an interrelation.

4.2   Structure of the Proposed Dialectic

In *Insight* Lonergan proposes the structure of the known, based on the isomorphism of the contents of the act of knowing with the stages that occur in this act, as what he terms an 'integral heuristic structure'. As he states in the preface to *Insight*: 'Thoroughly understand what it is to understand, and not only will you understand the broad lines of what is to be understood, but you will also possess a fixed base, an invariant pattern, opening upon all further developments of understanding.'[2] The point being made here is that the schema that arises from self-affirmation of the knowing knower that is constituted in the act of seeking to understand understanding provides an *a priori* structure for what is to be known. Accordingly, given this pattern, a structure exists by which further developments can be plotted, in this case the proposed dialectic interrelation of Rahner and Nāgārjuna's thought on the basis of these three stages (though as will be shown, the other building blocks of Lonergan's system also prove of relevance in the proposed dialectic).

The method adopted will consist in relating the elements of both texts identified as experience to each other and then proceeding to do the same for the elements designated as insight and judgement. The elements of both

---

[2] Lonergan, *Insight*, 28

that correspond to the other concepts advanced by Lonergan will then also be brought into the dialectic.

4.2.1 Experience

The elements of experience in Rahner's system relate principally to the various experiences in the consciousness of the subject which lead to an awareness of those elements of consciousness designated as transcendental (pure openness to being, self-presence of the subject to herself, experience of knowing, loving, freedom, etc.). These are then experienced as intelligible only in the context of the positing of an Infinite Horizon of Being and are further experienced as being made explicitly intelligible in God's revelation in history. This revelation is in turn experienced as true on the basis of its correspondence with the fundamental experiences of the subject as present to herself and the affirmation of this correspondence is then experienced by the subject as faith. In this sense, the relation between the transcendental experience of the individual and the revelation of God in history may be conceived of as a hermeneutical circle, with the correspondence of revelation to the fundamental constitutive experiences of human existence leading back to experience lived in the context of this awareness.

Nāgārjuna's experiential context corresponds more to a threefold progressive structure not dissimilar to that of Hegelian dialectic. The first stage is experience of existents (dharmas) as impermanent, unsatisfactory and lacking any substantial essence which preserves them in being (the three marks of existence as formulated in Buddhist teaching: Anicca, dukha and anatta).[3] The second experiential stage is that of the conflict between these characteristics of dharmas and the mind's habitual way of conceptualising them, i.e. as substantially existent, stable and ontologically separate from each other. The experience of this conflict leads to the realisation that the habitual perception of the mind is in fact deluded and that dharmas are empty of any separate essential existence (the point at which experience passes over into insight), and the practitioner then seeks to meditatively grasp this and starts to progressively experience dharmas as they actually are rather than as they are incorrectly conceptualised by the reifying mind.

---

[3] Though *duḥkha* is identified here with unsatisfactoriness, it is a somewhat more complex concept which defies simple univocal translation into English. For further discussion of this point see Peter Harvey, 'Ennobling Truth/Reality, The Second' in *Encyclopaedia of Buddhism*, ed. Damien Keown and Charles S. Prebish (Oxon: Routledge, 2007), 324–326

Having delineated the elements of both systems that correspond to the category of experience, the question becomes that of the relation between them, and this in the context of Lonergan's 'higher viewpoint'. Lonergan defines this concept in the following terms: 'Still further insights arise. The shortcomings of the previous position become recognized. New definitions and postulates are devised. A new and larger field of deductions is set up. Broader and more accurate applications become possible. Such a complex shift in the whole structure of insights, definitions, postulates, deductions, and applications may be referred to very briefly as a higher viewpoint.'[4]

In brief, then, the higher viewpoint is formulated on the basis of the shortcomings in a position that are shown up when it is brought into contact with new data and/or positions, and this, by implication, in the context of an enlarged field of experiences (those upon which the various insights are based). In addition, in the context of the attempt to dialectically relate two disparate positions, the previously formulated insights pertaining to the positions taken separately serve as a heuristic device in the search for new insight(s) which grasp the relation between the various components of the enlarged field of experience.

Placed in relation to each other, the two experiences on which Rahner and Nāgārjuna build their analyses do not prove to be mutually incompatible as the object of experience in each case is different. For Nāgārjuna, the primary object of experience is the actual nature of phenomena as they are, leading to his questioning of the mind's habitual tendency to reify the objects of perception. Rahner, in contrast, turns to the transcendental elements present in the mind itself; in this sense his move may be deemed to be reflexive as it is the mind itself which is the object of experience here. Seen in this light, Rahner seeks to affirm absolute being on the basis of the transcendental constituents of the mind, while Nāgārjuna, when parsed in Lonerganian terms, simply affirms the contingency of proportionate being.[5] Thus far the two experiences are simply different and complementary and the full implications of their relation to each other comes into focus only when they are considered in terms of how they come to bear on each other in a process of mutual questioning.

Both Rahner and Nāgārjuna have already been shown to be internally consistent, but shortcomings in both do emerge when they are brought into dialogue. Nāgārjuna's formulation of the difference between the actual nature of what exists and the mind's delusory reification of this in terms of stable

---

[4] Lonergan, *Insight*, 13

[5] As noted above (p.192, p.196), the practitioner's meditative grasp of reality free from reification may not be viewed as an experience for the reasons already noted

phenomena is persuasive. But if this is so, this applies to Rahner's subject also: if the subject is empty and is experienced as stable only as a result of the mind's delusion, the search for a context in which transcendental experience is coherently intelligible becomes null and void. In this view, the experiences upon which Rahner bases his affirmation of Absolute Being are simply deluded insofar as they demand the intelligibility that a stable subject requires. Equally, if the operations of the mind are delusional, they cannot provide the basis for the transcendental *analogia entis* which leads Rahner's subject to affirm God as the infinite horizon of being.

On the other hand, Rahner's attention to the role of mind points up Nāgārjuna's failure to examine this in his own thought and to recognise that all experience takes place mediated through the mind. Furthermore, the emergence of mind as a noetic category in the dialectic raises the problem of using mental operations to determine that the mind is in fact delusional in its habitual perception. Nor is Nāgārjuna cognisant of the cultural relativity of the perceptions against which he argues. The backdrop for these perceptions was the identification in Indian thought between atman (the quintessential self of a thing) and Brahman (the eternally existing ultimate reality). It is highly questionable whether the implicit backdrop of these categories is inherent to the mind as opposed to culturally conditioned and contingent. This then raises the question: to what extent is the mind delusional and measured against what criterion? The habitual perception of things does, after all, prove largely accurate in terms of the subject's negotiation of the world as she experiences it. Thus, placing the two positions side by side does pose serious questions to both, and it is these questions which constitute both the context and the impetus for the attempt to relate both the experiential data cited and the insights based on them in the second stage of the dialectic.

The first two questions adduced here do not pose any insurmountable problems. Arguably, the ontological status of the subject is not directly relevant in considering the transcendental elements of her consciousness. Regardless of how one conceives of this ontological status, consciousness continues to function with the various transcendental elements cited by Rahner. Moreover, in the context of a dialectic based on Lonergan's epistemology, his insistence that being is that which is intelligently understood proves germane. Acceptance of this principle means that it is not sufficient to state that consciousness simply functions with these transcendental constants without seeking a corresponding intelligibility. Nor does the insistence that the subject is empty, with this emptiness denoting a lack of inherent existence, in any way affect this search for intelligibility – the data of consciousness remain.

In addition, the contention that the mind is deluded in its habitual reification of phenomena, in which it conceives of them as substantially existent, does not affect the basis of Rahner's *analogia entis* founded as it is upon the transcendental aspects of the mind rather than on the contingent status of phenomena. Accordingly, Nāgārjuna's emptiness in itself in no way vitiates Rahner's move to the affirmation of an Infinite Horizon of Being as that which makes these transcendental elements intelligible and, ultimately, gives rise to them.

The location of Rahner's analytical moves within the data of consciousness itself provides a link to the further question of the status of mental operations given Nāgārjuna's insistence that the mind is habitually deluded.

Here, as in Chapter 3, the exact nature of Nāgārjuna's claim has to be carefully parsed. The precise error he delineates is that of confusing conventional perception with things as they ultimately are, something which he says we are naturally prone to do, and it is this mental habit that he designates as deluded mind. Conventional perception taken conventionally is indeed accurate (chairs are not mistaken for bananas, for example); the error lies in viewing the conventional reality of a dharma as being ultimately true of it, i.e. that the chair exists in its conventional form when viewed from the absolute perspective and exists as an inherently existent phenomenon. The nature of the delusion pointed up by Nāgārjuna, then, may be viewed in terms of a confusion of two perspectives, or as Lonergan would put it, between two kinds of knowing. Specifically the error lies in the illegitimate extrapolation of one perspective (conventional) into the realm of the other (absolute). Hence Nāgārjuna's affirmation of dharmas as empty: conventional designation is merely conventional and conventionally true; ultimately it is empty, i.e. devoid of any ultimate phenomenal reality.

Given that this is so, the difference between true and deluded perception is a contest within the mind that takes place according to the mind's own criteria of logic and truth. Arguably this gives grist to Rahner's transcendentalism and exposes a lack in Nāgārjuna's thought insofar as he does not give direct attention to the role of the mind as the context for his analysis, nor to what enables the mental perception that the mind is operating in a deluded manner, a perception that would seem to require *a priori* categories of truth and logic. Seen in this light, the answer to the question of the criterion or criteria against which a given mental operation may be judged to be erroneous seems to lie, at least in part, in the transcendental conditions of the mind itself, though the role of the data perceived by the senses is also crucial.

4.2.2 Insight

In terms of the second stage of insight, Rahner sees Christian theology as the attempt to grasp the relationship between the various facets of human experience in terms of their full logical implications. This involves, as has been seen, the affirmation of God *qua* the Infinite Horizon of Being against which alone the various transcendental elements that are present in human consciousness make sense. In turn, this Infinite Horizon also constitutes the horizon of the future as by definition it must correspond to the various transcendental desires that are found as integral constituents of human consciousness as their fulfilment. Specifically, doctrine, which Rahner proposes in a role that corresponds to the category of insight put forward by Lonergan, entails the attempt to formulate the self-disclosure of God in the transcendental aspects of human existence as well as in history given in the revelation in Jesus who is viewed as God's Logos. This self-disclosure itself is viewed as constituting the fundamental insight which makes sense of the disparate phenomena of human experience. Thus revelation is seen as a making explicit of these underlying transcendental constants and their implications in a transcendentally based *analogia entis* which forms the basis of the subject's affirmation of God. All of this comes into focus with a particular clarity in Rahner's treatment of the resurrection, which he sees as the unity of the transcendental and categorical. Thus, for Rahner, insight may be said to rest on the mutually complementary twin foundations of the transcendental and the categorical self-disclosure of God to humanity. This nexus of insight further elucidates the experience of the ongoing presence of the Spirit in the Church, as well as in the life of the individual, and is present in condensed form, so to speak, in the word of God in which constitutes a fusion of experience and insight.

For Nāgārjuna, the analysis of experience leads in a converse direction, as he formulates his insights in terms of the nature of both reality and the mind which perceives it. Thus the fundamental Buddhist doctrine of mutual conditioning is reaffirmed, though arguably in Nāgārjuna's analysis it is taken as a category that is given and which he then finds confirmed in his analysis of the nature of phenomena rather than something which he argues for explicitly. More fundamental than this, however, is his assertion that all dharmas are empty of essential existence, and here he does make a convincing case in his analysis of the nature of phenomena. This emptiness leads in turn to the insight that as nirvāṇa and saṃsāra are both empty, there can be no difference between the two, and that as the mind is habitually structured by the categories pertaining to conventional existence which are ultimately delusory, no direct predication is possible about things as they ultimately are, only ostension. In line with this ostensive approach, the question of whether

Nāgārjuna sees the difference between nirvāṇa and saṃsāra as simply perspectival or whether saṃsāra is nirvāṇa in a more fundamental sense that is in line with traditional Buddhist conceptions of nirvāṇa is not one that is settled in the text by any formulated insight and consequently must be left aside for the purposes of formal dialectic.

The question arises, then, of what kind of meaningful interrelation is possible between these insights. Are they compatible and is there any way of arriving at a higher viewpoint that also solves the difficulties that arise when they are placed side by side? The search for such a higher viewpoint comes with the caveat that the resulting insight may not be one that would be recognisable to either Nāgārjuna or Rahner within the enclosed context of their own systems of thought, though it may not, by definition, be logically incompatible with these systems either. Fundamentally, in placing Nārgājuna and Rahner together in the context of Lonergan's dialectic, the interrelation hinges on a meeting of Nāgārjuna's analysis of reality and consciousness with Rahner's transcendentally grounded *analogia entis*.

The first point that emerges is that the two insights, like the experiences on which they are based, are not *a priori* incompatible. Nāgārjuna's analysis pertains to dharmas, what in Lonergan's terminology is deemed 'proportionate being', i.e. all that is not God. Rahner, on the other hand, is concerned with the affirmation of an Absolute horizon of being which by definition is not a phenomenon and so not a dharma. Fundamentally, then, the two again turn their respective analytic gazes in different directions. Moreover, as pointed out above, Nāgārjuna's emphasis on the emptiness of all dharmas is perfectly consistent with the traditional Christian affirmation that God is the only being whose essence is to exist and correlates with the Christian view that all other beings exist in dependence on God (with the addendum that along with this affirmation is the traditional insistence that God is not a phenomenon and so cannot be conceived of as an object over and against other existents).

At this point, the question may be legitimately raised as to whether Nāgārjuna would allow such a correlation; the question itself, however, is not one that can or should be answered in the context of a dialectic such as is being attempted here. We cannot know for sure how Nāgārjuna would have responded to issues that lie beyond the remit of his analysis in the text, or indeed of his cultural and religious horizon *per se*, and for the purposes of the attempted dialectic we must remain within the context of the text under consideration. Moreover, there is a sense in which, as with a work of literature, the death of the author pertains, too, in the attempt at formal dialectic.[6]

---

[6] Roland Barthes, *Image, Music, Text*, trans. Stephen Heath (London: Fontana, 1977), 142–48.

Fundamentally, what emerges in a primary interrelation is the complementarity of the two positions. Affirming that dharmas are empty, or in traditional terminology that contingent being really is contingent, proves consonant with standard Christian doctrine and theology and actually may be seen as a helpful foregrounding of this element of Christian cosmology. Certainly, the affirmation of an Infinite Horizon of Being (God) would have been alien to Nāgārjuna, but the complementarity stands on the grounds that Nāgārjuna analyses phenomena and Rahner's Infinite Horizon is, by definition, non-phenomenal. This means, in turn, that there is nothing in Nāgārjuna's system which would preclude the self-disclosure of such an Infinite Horizon – it is simply a question that Nāgārjuna does not consider.

The interrelation becomes somewhat more problematic, however, when Nāgārjuna's affirmation that there is no difference between saṃsāra and nirvāṇa is considered. Depending on how this affirmation is understood, a correlation with Rahner's Infinite Horizon may or may not be appropriate. Moreover, a question is raised, if the correlation is pursued and Nāgārjuna's identification of nirvāṇa and saṃsāra is accepted, as to the relationship between Absolute and contingent being in Rahner's thought. Conversely, Rahner's Infinite Horizon of Being rebounds on the concept of nirvāṇa in Nāgārjuna's thought when it is placed in the context of Rahner's *analogia entis*. Is Nāgārjuna's insistence on not predicating any qualities of nirvāṇa a legitimate contention or simply a failure to understand and to apply logic correctly?

At this point the above-noted restrictions that pertain to the dialectic being attempted here come into play. To be sure, the exact nature of nirvāṇa in its relation to saṃsāra and the exact meaning intended by Nāgārjuna in his text are disputed questions in the wider literature, but as stated at the outset, for the purposes of this probative testing of Lonergan's epistemology, Garfield's reading of the text is the one taken as constituting the Nāgārjunic pole of the dialectic. Given, then, Garfield's insistence that the difference between nirvāṇa and saṃsāra is simply one of perspective, no correlation can be established with Rahner's Infinite Horizon, and the relation between Absolute and contingent being in Rahner's thought, whilst interesting in itself, does not arise as a question at this point. Nor does Rahner's Infinite Horizon affect the concept of nirvāṇa here, as nirvāṇa is simply a way of perceiving proportionate being.

This does not, however, solve all problems. If nirvāṇa is saṃsāra correctly perceived as it really is in absolute perception, this means perceiving it free of all reification and free of all the phenomenal distinctions that pertain in conceptual perception. This entails, then, the non-dual meditative grasp of reality that we have already seen constitutes a problem within Lonergan's schema.

A further point that emerges is that both Rahner and Nāgārjuna begin their respective analyses in what Nāgārjuna terms the conventional realm of perception. Nāgārjuna arrives at the affirmation of nirvāṇa as absolute perception of saṃsāra as it really is via a series of logical steps wherein he affirms that as both saṃsāra and nirvāṇa are empty of essence, there can be no essential difference between them. At this point, once again, we can ask in the light of Rahner's transcendentalism what it is that makes these logical steps possible, as well as querying what enables the conception, however ostensive, of nirvāṇa at all. After all, whilst a ruthless *via negativa* is followed in relation to nirvāṇa, Nāgārjuna still deems it possible to rule out certain logical options in relation to it.

As happened in the first stage of the dialectical interrelation, placing Rahner and Nāgārjuna side by side shows up a weak point in Nāgārjuna as questions relating to the transcendental emerge once again. Some kind of transcendental element of mind seems to be required both to enable Nāgārjuna to take the logical steps that enable his identification of saṃsāra and nirvāṇa and to conceive of nirvāṇa at all, *a fortiori* given the limits he places on the conceptual mind's grasp of it. At this point Rahner's contention that individual existents can be perceived only against a backdrop of Infinite Being becomes relevant by extension. Nirvāṇa may not be a phenomenon or an individual existent, but it can be conceptualised as being different from other things that can be conceptualised, and as such the question of how this is possible arises.

More broadly, this question proves to be double edged, as the same can be asked of the conditions of possibility that enable the conception of Rahner's Infinite Horizon of Being. Does this mean that Rahner himself falls foul of his own positing of a need for an Infinite Horizon against which other things can be perceived distinctly and gets caught in an infinite regress? The answer to this lies in Rahner's insistence that the concept of the Infinite Horizon of Being is the mind's objectification of what is present in its transcendentality and is not to be univocally indentified, even less confused with this: 'A person knows explicitly what is meant by "God" only insofar as he allows his transcendence beyond everything objectively identifiable to enter into his consciousness, accepts it, and objectifies in reflection what is already present in his transcendentality.'[7]

In contrast, nowhere in Nāgārjuna's use of the term nirvāṇa is there any suggestion that nirvāṇa fulfils a similar role as a *pleroma* of Being that

---

[7] Rahner, *Foundations*, 44

enables perception. The upshot, then, of placing Nāgārjuna and Rahner side by side at this point is to further point up the absence of a formulation of the transcendentalist conditions of mind in Nāgārjuna's opus that emerged in the first stage of the dialectic, and more broadly to emphasise Nāgārjuna's failure to analyse how his analysis is possible in the context of the workings of the mind, despite relying on these workings for its formulation and coherence.

One may further ask if the affirmation on Nāgārjuna's part that there is no difference between nirvāṇa and saṃsāra affects Rahner's theological thought, even when Nāgārjuna's assertion is interpreted as a way of perceiving proportionate being. This is clearly not something that Rahner deals with in *Foundations* and it is doubtful that he would have been aware of such a thought, even less of the possibility of the non-dual grasp of reality without conceptual distinctions with which nirvāṇa has been identified. To fully pursue the theological implications that might follow is not possible within the confines of this current work, but it certainly does emerge as a question which would be worth asking and pursuing in the context of further research on this topic, particularly in dialogue with Buddhist practitioners. Within the present work, an opinion may be hazarded that this insight would not substantially affect Rahner's work as it would not directly affect the transcendental elements upon which Rahner bases his affirmation of God.

4.2.3 Judgement

The third stage of Lonergan's threefold schema relates to two specific concepts: the fulfilment of the virtually unconditioned and the presence or absence of further unanswered questions once the insight has been affirmed as true. The crux of the virtually unconditioned is whether or not the insight fulfils the conditions of its possibility. In both cases this has been shown to be the case, though as has been noted, further questions remain about Garfield's reading of Nāgārjuna's insistence that there is no difference between nirvāṇa and saṃsāra. To this can be added the question of Nāgārjuna's failure to address the role of mind in his analysis, and specifically the transcendental conditions that make his analysis possible.

4.2.4 Further Dialectical Equivalents

As was apparent from the reconstruction of Lonergan's *Insight* in Chapter 1, he develops the threefold schema of intelligent knowing to include other concepts, some of which also emerge as metaphysical equivalents when Rahner and Nāgārjuna's works are placed side by side, whereas in other instances what is notable is the lack of correspondence. The first of these elements is the presence of what Lonergan terms 'implicit metaphysics' in both thinkers. For Rahner this is present in God's self-communication in the depths of human existence (the corresponding explicit metaphysics takes place in God's self-disclosure in the person of Jesus), whereas for Nāgārjuna one may cite his analysis of dharmas and the absence of any analysis of the mental moves this involves. This is more problematic in Nāgārjuna than in Rahner, as in Rahner's case 'implicit metaphysics' accrue to the situation of the human subject, whereas in Nāgārjuna's analysis they permeate his own analysis.

The Remote Criterion of Truth *qua* the template for the correct unfolding of the unrestricted desire to know is also present in both thinkers – in Rahner's case in the explicit role he accords the Church as the norm for human subjectivity, whereas in Nāgārjuna's work the criterion takes the form of the correct use of logic required for accurate analysis and perception.

One of the lynchpins of Lonergan's system is his use of the concept of isomorphism, typified in his assertion that, as that which is intelligently known, being corresponds in structure to the three stages of intelligent knowing as the object of these three stages. This concept of isomorphic correspondence can be found *mutatis mutandis* in Nāgārjuna's thought as it can be argued that absolute reality stands in isomorphic correspondence to the knowing that pertains in the meditative grasp of reality free from all conceptual reification, with the caution that, by definition, this cannot be termed knowing in any normal sense of the word. A more direct isomorphism pertains in Rahner's assertion that as God constitutes us as subjects in will, freedom and love, God also wills, is free and loves.

Lonergan attaches particular importance to the role of inverse insights which he defines as the absence of intelligibility where one would expect this to be present. For Rahner this is the place occupied by sin, which he views as characterised by absurdity and the absence of any intelligibility, in a move strongly reminiscent of Augustine's definition of evil as *privatio boni*. In Nāgārjuna's thought, the meditative non-dual grasp of reality free from all phenomenal distinction and conceptual reification may perhaps be conceived of as an inverse insight, as it proves impossible to locate this state in the threefold structure of experience, insight and judgement, though further investigation would be required to establish whether this conception is legitimate and whether it is not Lonergan's categories themselves which prove inadequate at this point.

One of Lonergan's particularly helpful moves is his distinction between analytic propositions and analytic principles, with the former being statements limited only by the requirements of logical coherence, while the latter require existence in actuality as well as coherence. In Rahner's *Foundations* his evolutionary viewpoint in which there is an evolution from matter to spirit and ultimately to self-transcendence into God may be deemed an analytic principle, whereas arguably all of Nāgārjuna's analysis falls within this rubric of logical coherence and actuality.

Crucial to Lonergan's aim in writing *Insight* is the importance he attaches to insight into insight, the attainment of which he views as the transition from knowing *qua* mere extroversion to intelligent knowing. This transition is strongly present in the analysis of both thinkers but in different ways: in Rahner it takes the form of the transition from the categorical to the transcendental and ultimately to God, whereas in Nāgārjuna it is present in his use of the destructive tetralemma which leads him to the affirmation of the emptiness of conventional reality and the limiting of discourse about absolute reality to ostension.

Linked with this insight into insight is the concept of the reflexivity of consciousness in Lonergan's opus; indeed, it is this reflexivity that Lonergan identifies with spirit and the same concept is found in Rahner's work in which he deems spirit to be being which is present to itself. This, however, constitutes a further question that remains to be answered in Nāgārjuna's framework and falls within the larger group of questions relating to mind that he fails to address.

Concomitant with Lonergan's exposition of the transition from knowing *qua* mere extroversion to intelligent knowing in which insights and judgements are also present is the transition from conjugate potency, form and act to central potency, form and act. The conjugate forms here relate to knowing as 'taking a look', the kind of knowing that stands in contradistinction to intelligent knowing. The transition from these to the pattern of potency, form and act present in intelligent knowing is present in both thinkers – for Rahner, this transition occurs when human life becomes Christian life, lived in the illuminating insight of God's self-disclosure; for Nāgārjuna, the transition is from conventional perception in which phenomena are viewed as non-empty and subsistent to an affirmation of the emptiness of all dharmas and the ostensive awareness of the absolute nature of reality. Once again, however, the categories break down in the transition present in Nāgārjuna's thought as the leap in perception beyond duality to the absolute involves the erasure of potency, form and act in any form whatsoever. Finally, the category of knowing *qua* mere extroversion is present in both thinkers, in Nāgārjuna as naïve realism and in Rahner as lack of faith.

Locating the presence of these other elements in both thinkers serves to further highlight commonalities of structure and approach. Both thinkers are concerned with moving beyond an engagement with reality based on knowing *qua* mere extroversion, and move from this to intelligent knowing in which different affirmations about reality are made (in Rahner's case the affirmation of the Infinite Horizon of Being, in Nāgārjuna's the emptiness of all dharmas). Yet the differences in their approaches are also instructive in the search for a higher viewpoint that encompasses both thinkers' insights. Nāgārjuna's metaphysics are implicit insofar as he does not consider the role of the mind in his analysis and the implications of this role, nor does he address the question of the reflexivity of consciousness which would arguably prove the most difficult to accommodate within his schema. Rahner, meanwhile, posits a direct isomorphism between the transcendental constituents of human consciousness and God and also uses the reflexivity of consciousness as a way to further ground his move to Absolute Being. These features will have implications in the attempt to formulate a higher viewpoint which will be the next stage in the dialectic.

4.2.5 Higher Viewpoint

The attempt to formulate a higher viewpoint which encompasses the insights of both Rahner and Nāgārjuna in a sense takes place with the distant goal of Lonergan's universal viewpoint in sight. This Lonergan defines as 'a potential totality of generically and ordered viewpoints'.[8] In other words, what Lonergan intends by this expression is a complete dialectical interrelation of all the different components of human knowledge based on a grasp of the structure of being:

> There is then a universe of meanings and its four dimensions are the full range of possible combinations
>
> 1 of experiences and lack of experience
> 2 of insights and lack of insights
> 3 of judgements and failures to judge, and
> 4 of the various orientations of the polymorphic consciousness of man.
>
> Now in the measure that one grasps the structure of this protean notion of being, one possesses the base and ground from which one can proceed to the content and context of every meaning.[9]

---

[8] Lonergan, *Insight*, 564
[9] Lonergan, *Insight*, 567

As noted in Chapter 1 there are real problems with this idea of a universal viewpoint, but it does retain a measure of validity when it is seen as a utopian goal which can orientate the dialectic process. Thus far, the attempt has been made to interrelate Rahner and Nāgārjuna in the manner envisaged by Lonergan here and on the basis of this to evolve an insight which encompasses the insights of both thinkers. The insight which has emerged is a combination of both individual insights which have been found to be compatible. Effectively this means Rahner's theology with Nāgārjuna's metaphysics of proportionate being, to use Lonerganian terminology.

At this point an objection may be raised in terms of the conflict of the two thinkers' respective worldviews (Christian and Buddhist, respectively) and this is an objection which has validity once one steps outside the confines of this dialectic. Specifically, the higher viewpoint generated here has validity only within the attempt to dialectically relate the analyses contained in Rahner's *Foundations* and Nāgārjuna's *Mūlamadhyamakakārikā*. Once the purview of the analysis steps outside this confinement, the higher viewpoint generated would have to be subjected to questioning from both wider constellation of insights that constitute both traditions, not to mention other works written by the two authors themselves.

Accordingly, then, the current interrelation would constitute only one moment in a much wider dynamic of dialectical interrelation between the two religions. The significance of the current moment, then, lies not so much in the higher viewpoint that has resulted from it, as in demonstrating that, its limitations notwithstanding, Lonergan's system does indeed provide a coherent epistemological structure for the work of interreligious dialogue. Specifically, it proves useful in terms of enabling meaningful interrelation by establishing a metaphysical equivalence between two viewpoints where such exists and pointing up the asymmetry when the converse is the case. By unearthing the metaphysical commonality present in both positions it enables their various elements to be plotted in relation to each other in a common context, as well as facilitating the reader's engagement with them by linking these elements with the corresponding structure of the noetic process within the reader herself.

Moreover, it enables the somewhat more controversial task of adjudication between positions in terms of their comprehensiveness or lack thereof. In this instance, for example, Rahner's position has a comprehensiveness Nāgārjuna's does not as it can incorporate the latter, whereas the converse is not the case.

A direction is also provided for further research by the new questions that the interrelation generates: How does the notion of *pratītyasamutpāda* relate to the view of God as creator? What relation do enlightenment and the attainment of nirvāṇa have to salvation conceived in Christian terms? What is the relationship between Buddha and Christ?[10] Obviously these questions lie outside the dialectic that has been attempted here, but they do emerge from it. Of course these questions can (and have) been arrived at by other means, but the application of Lonergan's method provides a particularly straightforward means of arriving at them and would have a particular benefit when less well-trodden paths are being pursued. The application of the method also proves beneficial when the two thinkers in question appear initially to be incompatible, as, arguably, is the case when Rahner and Nāgārjuna are first placed side by side, or when the intricacy and vastness of two positions mean that an obvious route into comparative analysis and interrelation does not present itself.

In addition, the current dialectical experiment provides a demonstration of how one insight may supply an element lacking in another when they are interrelated. In the course of the dialectic, the interrelation of the two positions and the mutual questioning this involved led to an awareness of a weak point in terms of Nāgārjuna's failure to analyse the mental operations by which he arrived at his conclusions and the conditions of possibility that enabled these. Within the context of the higher viewpoint, this lack is supplied. Again what is being argued is not that Lonergan's method provides a unique way by which this can be done, simply that it provides a particularly effective and ordered means by which these questions can emerge and answers to them can be sought.

The insight generated opens, as Lonergan stated, on to additional insights. Rahner insists in his work that the presupposition of any soteriology is the fundamental unity of human kind; the lack of ultimate essential ontological difference between existents as formulated by Nāgārjuna provides a particularly helpful way of showing how this unity may be conceived, to cite one example. The bringing together of seemingly incompatible positions and their interrelation according to Lonergan's method, then, does indeed prove singularly fruitful both in terms of an ordered means of interrelating them and also in terms of opening avenues for further developments. In so doing it provides a concrete means of throwing up bridges between different positions which appear at first sight to have little or nothing in common

---

[10] On the broader question of commensurability in Buddhist-Christian dialogue, see Paul Knitter and Peter Feldmeier, 'Are Buddhism and Christianity Commensurable? A Debate/Dialogue between Paul Knitter and Peter Feldmeier Author(s): Paul Knitter and Peter Feldmeier,' *Buddhist-Christian Studies*, 2016, Vol. 36 (2016):165–84

and provides a way of navigating the intricacy and panoramic scope often involved in such positions.

4.3 Significance of Lonergan's Method for the Theology of Religions

As has become apparent, some minor problems notwithstanding, Lonergan's epistemology as proposed in *Insight* has indeed proved to be a viable and successful means of dialectical interrelation between the two positions chosen to test its validity. The structure he proposes was found to be present in both Rahner and Nāgārjuna's thought and as such formed a commonality that functioned as a bridge between them, something that is particularly significant given the *prima facie* appearance of incompatibility between two positions.

In addition to the establishment of a bridge between the two examples chosen for the dialectic, however, the commonality of Lonergan's transcendentally-based epistemology has a wider and more comprehensive application. The positing of the threefold pattern of intelligent knowing as a noetic structure solves the problem of establishing a common backdrop against which differences can be perceived and intelligibility adduced from religious discourses that are not the interpreter's home tradition, contra the view that one must view such differences in terms of incommensurability of discourse.

A good example of this lies in the significance of Nāgārjuna's treatment of the meditative appropriation of emptiness. At first sight this could be mistaken for the subject observing emptiness as a conceptual object, with non-duality viewed as the subject becoming one with external reality and the absence of ontological distinction between things viewed as the perception of their interconnectedness. The true fruitfulness of Lonergan's approach in relation to this example becomes apparent with the failure to apply the three stages of knowing to what Nāgārjuna describes. This realisation disentangles what is being proposed by Nāgārjuna here from the misconceptions which could occur when the state in question is interpreted through the usual categories, without the awareness that what is being alluded to is something which is radically different from anything that can be accommodated within these.

A further significance lies in the positing of the third stage of judgement as an integral part of intelligent knowing. The twofold criterion of the satisfaction of the virtually unconditioned and the absence of any questions that remain unanswered provides a working model of objectivity which does not exclude or elide the consciousness of the subject. As such it is an objectivity that is not vitiated by the awareness of the distinction between noumenal and phenomenal reality and does not collapse the process of acquiring knowledge into a relativistic subjectivity either.

Accordingly, such a model allows for the coherence of affirming one's own faith as true on the basis of this twofold criterion in a way that is not over and against the religious other. Rather, it leaves the question of the ultimate relationship between the different faiths as an open question, with the conceptualisation of this relationship taking the form of the kind of dialectic demonstrated above. As such, the logical problems involved in each of the options of Race's threefold hypothesis[11] are largely avoided and the question of the relationship between the different faiths does not prejudice the more concrete engagement advocated more recently by scholars reacting against the meta-approach adopted by the theology of religions.

4.4 Lonergan's Epistemology and the Move to a Comparative Approach

Recent years have seen a move away from what has been termed the Theology of Religions to Comparative Theology typified by the work of Francis X. Clooney and James Fredericks, which can be seen in some respects at least as a reaction against the theorising of the former approach. Speaking of the comparative approach, Clooney states: 'We are better off if we remain patiently and persistently committed to actual instances of learning, specific experiments, deriving our insights from the actual comparisons and not from a theory about religions or about the methodology of comparison. The comparative theology that I am recommending foregoes the optimism of its ancestors and leaves to others the large judgments about religions.'[12]

Clooney's proposal is not without its merits, specifically in terms of the insights generated from comparative reading of religious texts, and was perhaps an inevitable outcome of the sometimes agonised debates between the proponents of the various positions of Alan Race's threefold hypothesis. There is, however, an antinomy at the heart of Clooney's 'theory averse' approach, namely that there is no interpretative locus that is free of a methodology and of *a priori* views of how the different religions relate to each other.

---

[11] Alan Race, *Christians and Religious Pluralism: Patterns in the Christian Theology of Religions* (London: SCM Press, 1983)

[12] Francis X. Clooney S.J, *Comparative Theology: Deep Learning Across Religious Borders*, (Chichester : Wiley-Blackwell, 2010), 41

While it is true that to derive insights only from meta-theoretical considerations is unsatisfactory, to eschew these questions completely does not remove them from the equation; rather, it simply leaves them to operate implicitly, removed from the questioning that may provide additional insights and avenues of approach. It is in the context of seeking a passage between the Scylla of what appears to be an increasingly stalled debate between exclusivism, inclusivism and pluralism and the Charybdis of an approach which leaves theoretical suppositions unexamined that Lonergan's approach proves particularly useful. Fundamentally the split between the two approaches is a split between what could be called the theory and practice of engagement with the religious other, and any attempt to transcend this split must involve an integration of these two elements. Lonergan's claim that his system is self-verifying and non-arbitrary proves relevant at this point.

Lonergan states in *Insight* that his approach is the only one which is not arbitrary, based as it is on the mind's own operations, and while this claim may justifiably be criticised for being somewhat overblown, it is not totally devoid of merit. Basing any approach on the mind's operations effectively provides a foundation that is self-verifying as to dispute the validity of the mind's operations involves making use of them, a point made by Newman in *A Grammar of Assent*.[13] Moreover, it supports the claim that the system Lonergan sets forth is one that is implicit in every instance of human thought *a priori* and as such would not involve the imposition of an alien theory to the kind of concrete engagement advocated by Comparative Theology. As such, it holds out the possibility of maintaining a theoretical discipline in the work of interreligious engagement while doing so in the context of concrete engagement.

As demonstrated in the above dialectic, the use of Lonergan's system to explicitly parse the relationship between Rahner's and Nāgārjuna's thought proved also to be an effective way of relating the content and of generating comparative insights (e.g. the complementarity of the Transcendental Horizon and the affirmation of the emptiness of dharmas). Such a dialectical method holds out the possibility of what could be termed 'a third way', integrating theoretical and experiential engagement across religious discourses.

The theoretical components generated in such an approach thus far relate only to the methodology of the dialectic and the question may legitimately be posed as to the relation of such an approach to the meta-questions considered in the theology of religions. The eschewing of theory promoted by comparative theology has been challenged by a number of scholars. Writing

---

[13] Newman, *Grammar of Assent*, 47

in the collection of essays *The New Comparative Theology: Interreligious Insights from the Next Generation*, Kristin Beise Kiblinger has drawn attention to the inescapable nature of these meta-questions. Speaking of the comparative theologians' desire to move directly to the interreligious reading of classic texts, she states:

> But we cannot skip over getting clarity on our theological presuppositions about the other and just jump into the practice of reading, because so much hangs on *how* we read, which is determined by our theology of religions in the first place. This is why theology of religions is properly prior to comparative theology (even if comparative theology in turn leads to theology of religions adjustments). The theology of religions obviously implies reading strategies…When comparative theologians describe the kind of reading they have in mind…they clearly point to unadmitted theology of religions inclinations, in spite of their professed distaste for theology of religions.[14]

A widening of the application of Clooney's recommendation that insights be devised from the practice of reading, however, when combined with Lonergan's theoretical framework may serve as the foundation for a 'theology of religions from below'. In such a model, the choices afforded by theology of religions would constitute one of the theoretical components of the dialectic and would assume the character of a heuristic device that may be verified or negated in the course of the dialectic rather than a pre-empting of the outcome.

Contra Kiblinger, such an approach would maintain the validity of an experiential-expressivist approach,[15] rooted as Lonergan's approach is in the first stage of experience, and in which doctrines function as the insights that grasp the relations between the data of experience. Speaking of what she terms the 'older sort of inclusivism' which she views as obsolete, she states: 'Inclusivists of this stripe commonly espouse an experiential-expressivist understanding of doctrine, to use George Lindbeck's term. This theory of doctrine de-emphasizes particular expressions by conceding "priority… to a pre-verbal world of experience". Claims of distinctiveness are easily dismissed and particularities of language are not taken seriously, because

---

[14] Kristin Beise Kiblinger, 'Relating Theology of Religions and Comparative Theology,' in *The New Comparative Theology: Interreligious Insights from the Next Generation*, ed. Francis X. Clooney S.J. 29

[15] C.f. Lindbeck, *The Nature of Doctrine*, 31–32

various expressions can all be seen as inadequately approximating the same experience.'[16]

Certainly Kiblinger is right to cite the elision of differences and the *a priori* adoption of a monistic single-essence approach as problematic, yet it is hard to see why these invalidate an experiential-expressivist approach *per se* or indeed are intrinsic to it. An experiential-expressivist approach could just as easily fit into the kind of unitive pluralism advocated by Paul Knitter, in which many different experiences are related to each other in their implications and recognised in their full distinctiveness, and such a model can incorporate the linguistic component of experience without vitiating the basic approach. Knitter characterises such an approach, stating 'the many are called to be one. But it is a one that does not devour the many. The many become one precisely by remaining the many, and the one is brought about by each of the many making its distinct contribution to the others and thus to the whole...So there is a movement not toward absolute monistic oneness but toward what may be called "unitive pluralism:" plurality constituting unity'.[17]

Adopting Lonergan's dialectical method in the context of such an approach neither eschews the meta-questions nor prejudges the outcome of any enquiry into them and answers the criticisms Kiblinger levels at the experiential-expressivist approach. It further provides a method that enables the relating of 'the many' to each other and allows a probative, rather than deterministic, approach to the question of the ultimate relation of the various religions to each other.

---

[16] Beise Kiblinger, 'Relating Theology', 27

[17] Paul Knitter, *No Other Name?: Critical Survey of Christian Attitudes Towards the World Religions*, (London: SCM Press, 1985), 9

Conclusion

The dialectic attempted in this work was undertaken with the specific aim of testing the validity of Lonergan's claims regarding the comprehensive applicability of his epistemological system. Throughout the concern was with a direct application of his method to the two texts which were taken as the respective poles of the dialectic. The result of this attempt has been the conclusion that Lonergan's claims are indeed verified, with some caveats, and that his epistemology as outlined in *Insight* does provide a means of dialectically relating the two positions chosen. Moreover, the dialectical relation proved useful in enabling two very different positions to be brought into a relationship of mutual intelligibility, and held out the possibility of the mutual enrichment of both.

To attempt the above experiment within the constraints of a text this size meant prescinding from the wider questions involved in adoption of Lonergan's position; these do, however, merit some reflection at this point and serve to adumbrate possible directions for further development of this research.

Fundamentally, according to Lonergan, the nature of the system he sets forth is grounded in the making explicit of the common inner dynamics which pertain to the unfolding of human thought involved in intelligent knowing. These he formulates in terms of the three stages of experience, insight and judgement, with the final stage contingent on the fulfilment of the criterion of the virtually unconditioned and the absence of any further questions left unexplained. To the degree that these are correctly followed, intelligent knowing takes place, while error comes from their violation, whether wittingly or, as is more often the case, unwittingly. The making explicit of these common dynamics means, in turn, that an intrinsic structure underlying all intelligent knowing can be observed and this provides a bridge between any combination of disparate positions. As all coherently intelligent human thought shares the same structure, the elements that function in the same way can be correlated, thus allowing meaningful comparison as well as extending the possibility of formulating a higher viewpoint which encompasses various different positions.

This approach further serves to both expose and negate the naïve realism which Lonergan describes as knowing *qua* 'taking a look' that can lead to a presumption of incommensurability when different positions are placed side by side.

The adoption of such an approach in the context of interfaith dialogue has a number of significant advantages. As a schema which maps out the stages of intelligent knowing, it allows the detection of errors resulting from defective reasoning and also serves to guard against the danger of projection when encountering a religious tradition that is not one's own. It further acts as a 'control' enabling both parties in a dialogue to ensure that mutual understanding has indeed occurred, and also providing an epistemological grounding in the structure of human cognition itself for any insights that may emerge from such a dialogue.

On a practical level, the methodology that emerges from this schema provides an ordered means of structuring dialogue which is, moreover, not arbitrary as it is grounded in structures common to the various positions to begin with. Such interrelation opens up possibilities of mutual complementarity and enrichment, while facilitating the recognition of both similarity and difference.

More broadly, by grounding the affirmation of truth claims transcendentally, Lonergan's epistemology enables adherence to them in a pluralistic context in a way that does not involve outright rejection or negation of other views that may have their own validity. As such, it is an approach that has the potential to address the crisis in plausibility structures[1] that has emerged as the reality of pluralism in the religious and philosophical realm becomes more apparent. Such an approach is particularly vital given the tendency to retreat into fortified forms of certainty when faced with the sense of disorientation that such pluralism brings to many. This reaction is particularly apparent in the current global growth of fundamentalism and, less sharply, in the attempt to thicken group boundaries via 'hot button issues' or the retreat into notions of incommensurability as a way of solving the problem of the religious 'other'. As such, Lonergan's approach holds out the possibility of an epistemologically grounded affirmation of truth claims which nevertheless can remain open to different views and which contains an inner impetus towards dialogue.

In addition to the challenges of religious pluralism, religious belief finds itself challenged by the secularist rejection of the very concept of religious belief, and this, too, demands an answer in terms of the basis of the truth claims advanced by believers. Many believers will of course answer this question by adverting to the formative experience(s) which have given rise

---

[1] For more on this cf. Peter Berger, *The Heretical Imperative: Contemporary Possibilities of Religious Affirmation*, (Garden City, N.Y.: Anchor Press/Doubleday, 1979)

to the religious discourse to which they adhere, but the question of how these experiences may be affirmed as true *per se* will still demand of an answer.

Perhaps more controversially, a further application of Lonergan's method can be found in the possibility of adjudication between contradictory claims, something which can mitigate against a pluralism that becomes so all-encompassing that it is forced to admit religious worldviews which are abusive or inimical to human wellbeing. Here, however, Lonergan's approach would seem to require the addition of an explicitly formulated criterion of human and ecological wellbeing of the type envisaged by Paul Knitter,[2] something which is not sufficiently present in his approach as articulated in *Insight*. On the macro level, the application of this dialectical method to interreligious dialogue is a question of an evolving nexus of insights, which, through their interrelation, holds out the possibility of more comprehensive insights while grounding the process of interrelation in the nature of being as the object of intelligent understanding.

A fundamental question that would require further elaboration for Lonergan's system to have the comprehensiveness he desires pertains to the role of the mind in the critical realist framework he proposed. One of the most intriguing postulates laid down by Lonergan in *Insight* is the isomorphism of the contents of the act of knowing with the process of knowing itself. This does appear to hold up to logical scrutiny: given that our experience through the world comes filtered through consciousness and that being is the object of the unrestricted desire to know (as we cannot affirm the existence of that of which we have no knowledge), it does indeed seem reasonable to say that, *for us*, being is isomorphic with the structure of knowing. Critics such as Etienne Gilson have seen in this type of approach a form of idealism and have disputed the very possibility of a critical realism that does not slide into idealism: 'We have now examined several types of critical realism and in each instance have come to the conclusion that the critique of knowledge is essentially incompatible and irreconcilable with metaphysical realism. There is no middle ground. You must either begin as a realist with being, in which case you will have a knowledge of being, or begin as a critical idealist with knowledge, in which case you will never come in contact with being.'[3]

One could argue, certainly, that to deem Lonergan an idealist is unfair as the critical element of his critical realism simply proposes an isomorphism

---

[2] Paul Knitter, *One Earth, Many Religions: Multifaith Dialogue and Global Responsibility* (Maryknoll: Orbis Books, 1995), 124–35

[3] Etienne Gilson, *Thomist Knowledge and the Critique of Knowledge*, (San Francisco: Ignatius Press, 2012), Location 1628

which is far from a Berkleian insistence that phenomena have no reality outside of the mind. Yet a question does remain, namely what the justification is for affirming the realism involved in critical realism, an element that Lonergan appears to take for granted in *Insight* rather than one he explicitly argues for. To put it bluntly, the insistence on the objectivity of the knowledge yielded by the process of intelligent knowing notwithstanding, what is the basis for positing the correspondence of this knowledge with reality *in se* (regardless of the degree of correspondence posited)? Exponents of *Insight* may argue that this has already been adequately addressed within the schema Lonergan lays out, yet the text does not meet this question head on in such a way that Lonergan's own criteria of judgement are met.

A further lacuna can be detected in what could be termed a naïve view of experience. Curiously for a critical realist, Lonergan gives the impression that the subject experiences the sense or mental data in a pre-interpretive state that seems to correspond to the naïve realism he inveighs against. While it seems clear from his development of his metaphysical schema in *Insight* that this is not what he intends by the concept of experience, for his system to work, it is a category which would require further refinement. Specifically, the category of experience would need to encompass an account of the role of cultural and linguistic conditioning and the role they play in perception. In addition, further research would be required to establish the cross-cultural validity of Lonergan's schema to ensure that it is not applicable only to those cultures in which Western categories of thought and experience have been internalised. Equally broader questions surrounding the role of cultural conditioning in a critical-realist framework would help to establish Lonergan's claims in *Insight* on a firmer basis.

The final question which demands further scrutiny is the practical applicability of the search for understanding as outlined in *Insight* in situations where scotosis is not simply an individual matter but is societally shared. In particular, what traction does this approach have when intelligent knowing, specifically of the social or interreligious other, is overshadowed by conditions of communal strife, scapegoating, ingrained prejudice and the sundry other factors which can inhibit the process of intelligent knowing? While Lonergan touches to some degree on the unconscious blocks to understanding in his adumbration of the concept of scotosis, he does not seem to provide any guidance as to how this may be overcome. As with the other questions raised, this does not vitiate his system or invalidate the claims made, but for the epistemology outlined in *Insight* to be of practical value and use in interfaith dialogue, further research into these questions is needed.

Overall, as the dialectic undertaken in this work demonstrates, *Insight* does hold out the basis for an improved and epistemologically grounded interaction with the interreligious other, with the various dialogical possibilities already noted here. The challenge that emerges, however, is the twofold task of supplying the lacks in philosophical coherence in order to be able to answer possible objections to this approach, and further, to examine how this approach may be used practically in circumstances of societal and religious strife which all too often constitute the backdrop and the impetus to renewed encounter with the other.

None of this is to gainsay the very real achievement of Lonergan in *Insight*, not least in terms of providing a coherent and compelling account of the process of understanding, as well as points of orientation for the journey of mutual understanding between differing viewpoints and/or traditions. At the very least, Lonergan provides an answer to the contention that such understanding is neither possible nor desirable. The ongoing search for wider horizons in the living out of religious worldviews in a way that is dialogical rather than oppositional is a necessary and worthy goal, holding out as it does the possibility of dialogically-based community rather than the construction of oppositional identities. As the current upsurge in inter-communal violence globally demonstrates, such identity projects when combined with social, political and economic stress comprise a lethal cocktail which inevitably leads to further conflict and violence. Moreover, despite proclamations of religion's irrelevance, religion is proving to be a significant component of a number of these situations, thus sharpening the need for dialogue and mutual comprehension.

Seen in this light, the project undertaken in *Insight* has more than simply intellectual relevance but rather can serve to place academic reflection on interfaith dialogue in the very real social contexts in which the meeting of traditions takes place and thus links it with the wider task of peace-building and overcoming conflict. It is this possibility of practical applicability that provides the justification for seeking to extend Lonergan's approach in the ways suggested in order to strengthen its philosophical validity and sharpen its practical application. If further research can supply these lacks, then the project begun in *Insight* has the potential to make a very real contribution to the ongoing search for understanding and cooperation between different faiths, a need that becomes ever more pressing as global society seeks to meet the challenges of a now irrevocably pluralist context.

Bibliography

Albertson, James. 'Review of Insight,' *The Modern Schoolman*, 35 (1957–58): 236–44.

Anderson, Tyson. 'Wittgenstein and Nāgārjuna's Paradox,' *Philosophy East and West*, 35:2 (1985): 157–69.

Barthes, Roland, *Image, Music, Text*. Translated by Stephen Heath. London: Fontana, 1977.

Berger, Peter. *The Heretical Imperative: Contemporary Possibilities of Religious Affirmation*. Garden City, NY: Anchor Press/Doubleday, 1979.

Bhattacharya, Kamaleswar, trans. *The Dialectical Method of Nāgārjuna (Vigrahavyāvartanī)*. Delhi: Motilal Banarsidass, 1992.

Bhikkhu Bodhi, ed. *In the Buddha's Words: An Anthology of Discourses from the Pāli Canon*. Boston, MA: Wisdom Publications, 2005.

Brunnhoelzl, Karl, trans. *Nāgārjuna and the IIIrd Karmapa: In Praise of Dharmadhātu*. Boston, MA: Snow Lion Publications, 2007.

Burrell, David. 'How Complete Can Intelligibility Be? A Commentary on Insight Chapter XIX,' in *The American Catholic Philosophical Association Proceedings for the year 1967*, 250–53. Washington, DC: Catholic University of America, 1967.

Carr, Anne. 'Theology and Experience in the Thought of Karl Rahner,' *The Journal of Religion*, 53:3 (1973): 359–76.

Clooney, Francis X. *Comparative Theology: Deep Learning Across Religious Borders*. Chichester: Wiley-Blackwell, 2010.

Clooney, Francis X, ed. *The New Comparative Theology: Interreligious Insights from the Next Generation*. London: T. & T. Clark Ltd, 2010.

Coppleston, F.C. *Aquinas: An Introduction to the Life and Work of the Great Medieval Thinker*. London: Pelican Books, 1955.

Corcoran, Patrick, ed. *Looking at Lonergan's Method*. Dublin: The Talbot Press Ltd, 1975.

Davis, Avrohom. *The Metsudah Pirkei Avos: A New Translation and Anthology of its Classical Commentaries*. New York: Metsudah Publications, 1986.

Dych, William V. *Karl Rahner*. London: Geoffrey Chapman, 1992.

Easwaran, Eknath, trans. *The Dhammapada*. Tomales, CA: Nilgiri Press, 1985.

Fredericks, James L. *Buddhists and Christians: Through Comparative Theology to Solidarity*. Maryknoll, NY: Orbis Books, 2004.

Garfield, Jay L. *The Fundamental Wisdom of the Middle Way: Nāgārjuna's Mūlamadhyamakakārikā: Translation and Commentary by Jay L. Garfield*. New York: Oxford University Press, 1995.

Garfield, Jay L. and Graham Priest. 'Nāgārjuna and the Limits of Thought,' in *Empty Words: Buddhist Philosophy and Cross-Cultural Interpretation*, by Jay L. Garfield, 86–105. New York: Oxford University Press, 1992.

Gilson, Etienne. *Thomist Knowledge and the Critique of Knowledge*. San Francisco, CA: Ignatius Press, 2012.

Hanh, Thich Nhat. *The Heart of the Buddha's Teaching: Transforming Suffering into Peace, Joy and Liberation*. Berkeley, CA: Parallax Press, 1998.

Harvey, Peter. *An Introduction to Buddhism: Teachings, History and Practices*. Cambridge: Cambridge University Press, 1990.

Hepburn, Ronald. 'Method and Insight,' *Journal of the Royal Institute of Philosophy*, 48:184 (1973): 153–60.

Hick, John and Brian Hebblewaite. *Christianity and Other Religions: Selected Readings*. Oxford: Oneworld Publications, 2001.

Hodgson, Peter C. *Winds of the Spirit: A Constructive Christian Theology*. Louisville, KY: Westminster John Knox Press, 1994.

Honderich, Ted. *The Oxford Companion to Philosophy*. Oxford: Oxford University Press, 1995.

Huxley, Aldous. *Proper Studies*. London: Chatto & Windus, 1927.

Jeanrond, Werner G. 'Karl Rahner, Theologian.' *The Furrow*, 35:9 (1984): 577–81.

Kanaris, Jim. *Bernard Lonergan's Philosophy of Religion: From Philosophy of God to Philosophy of Religious Studies*. Albany, NY: State University of New York Press, 2002.

Keown, Damien. *A Dictionary of Buddhism*. Oxford: Oxford University Press, 2003.

Keown, Damien and Charles S. Prebish, eds. *Encylopedia of Buddhism*. Oxon: Routledge, 2007.

Kilby, Karen. *Karl Rahner: Theology and Philosophy*. London: Routledge, 2004.

Klostermaier, Klaus K. *Buddhism: A Short Introduction*. Oxford: Oneworld Publications, 1999.

Knitter, Paul F. *Jesus and the Other Names: Christian Mission and Global Responsibility*. New York: Orbis Books, 1996.

Knitter, Paul F. *No Other Name?: Critical Survey of Christian Attitudes Towards the World Religions*. London: SCM Press, 1985.

Knitter, Paul F. *One Earth, Many Religions: Multifaith Dialogue and Global Responsibility*. Maryknoll, NY: Orbis Books, 1995.

Knitter, Paul F. *Without Buddha I Could Not Be a Christian*. Oxford: One World Publications, 2009.

Knitter, Paul and Peter Feldmeier. 'Are Buddhism and Christianity Commensurable? A Debate/Dialogue between Paul Knitter and Peter Feldmeier.' *Buddhist-Christian Studies*, 36 (2016): 165–84.

Lane, Dermot A. 'Karl Rahner: Twenty-one Years After.' *The Furrow*, 56:11 (2005): 627–31.

Liddy, Richard M. *Startling Strangeness: Reading Lonergan's Insight*. Lanham, MD: University Press of America, 2007.

Lindbeck, George A. *The Nature of Doctrine: Religion and Theology in a Postliberal Age*. London: SPCK, 1984.

Lonergan, Bernard J. F. *Insight: A Study of Human Understanding*. London: Longmans, Green & Co., 1958.

Lonergan, Bernard J. F. 'Reality, Myth, Symbol,' in Alan M. Olson (ed.) *Myth, Symbol, and Reality*. Notre Dame, IN: University of Notre Dame Press, 1980. 32–3.

Lopez, Jr, Donald S. *Buddhist Scriptures*. London: Penguin, 2004.

Loy, David. *Lack and Transcendence: The Problem of Death and Life in Psychotherapy, Existentialism and Buddhism*. Atlantic Highlands, NJ: Humanities Books, 1996.

Mackey, J. P. 'Divine Revelation and Lonergan's Transcendental Method in Theology,' *Irish Theological Quarterly*, 40 (1973): 3–19.

Marmion, Declan and Raymond Moloney. 'Rahner and Lonergan: A Centenary Tribute.' *The Furrow*, 55:9 (2004): 483–90.

McDonald, Anne. 'Review: The Quest for an English-Speaking Nāgārjuna,' *Indo-Iranian Journal*, 58:4 (2015): 357–75.

Meynell, Hugo A. *The Theology of Bernard Lonergan*, Atlanta, GA: Scholars Press, 1986.

Murti, T. R. V. *The Central Philosophy of Buddhism: A Study of the Mādhyamika System*. London: Unwin, 1960.

Newman, John Henry. *A Grammar of Assent*. New York: Longmans, Green and Co., 1947.

Newman, John Henry. 'A Letter Addressed to the Duke of Norfolk on Occasion of Mr. Gladstone's Recent Expostulation,' *Certain Difficulties Felt by Anglicans in Catholic Teaching*, 2:248, accessed 2 September 2013, http://www.newmanreader.org/works/anglicans/volume2/gladstone/index.html.

O'Doherty, E. F. '*Insight* by Bernard J. F. Lonergan – Review,' *Studies: An Irish Quarterly Review*, 46:184 (1957): 494–6.

Ogden, Schubert M. 'Lonergan and the Subjectivist Principle,' *The Journal of Religion*, 51:3 (1971): 155–72.

O'Grady, John and Peter Scherle, eds. *Ecumenics from the Rim: Explorations in Honour of John D'Arcy May*. Berlin: Lit Verlag, 2007.

Ormerod, Neil. *Faith and Reason: The Possibility of a Christian Philosophy.* Minneapolis, MN: Fortress Press, 2017.

Priest, Graham. *Logic: A Very Short Introduction.* Oxford: Oxford University Press, 2000.

Race, Alan. *Christians and Religious Pluralism: Patterns in the Christian Theology of Religions.* London: SCM Press, 1983.

Rahner, Karl. *Foundations of Christian Faith: An Introduction to the Idea of Christianity.* London: Darton, Longman & Todd, 1978.

Robertson, Jr, John C. 'Rahner and Ogden: Man's Knowledge of God,' *The Harvard Theological Review*, 63:3 (1970): 377–407.

Russell, Bertrand. *History of Western Philosophy.* London: George Allen & Unwin Ltd, 1946.

Russell, Heidi Ann. 'Keiji Nishitani and Karl Rahner: A Response to Nihility,' *Buddhist-Christian Studies*, 28 (2008): 27–41.

Schmidt-Leukel, Perry. *Understanding Buddhism.* Edinburgh: Dunedin Academic Press, 2006.

Schmidt-Leukel, Perry, ed. *Buddhism and Christianity in Dialogue: The Gerald Weisfeld Lectures 2004.* Norwich: SCM Press, 2005.

Siderits, Mark. 'The Madhyamaka Critique of Epistemology – I,' *Journal of Indian Philosophy*, 8 (1980): 307–35.

Siderits, Mark. 'The Madhyamaka Critique of Epistemology – II,' *Journal of Indian Philosophy*, 9 (1981): 121–60.

Siderits, Mark and Shōryū Katsura. *Nagarjuna's Middle Way: Mūlamadhyamakakārikā.* Boston, MA: Wisdom Publications, 2013.

Speake, Jennifer. *A Dictionary of Philosophy.* London: Pan Books, 1979.

Tanaka, Koji. 'On Nāgārjuna's Ontological and Semantic Paradox,' *Philosophy East and West*, 66:4 (October 2016): 1292–1306.

Tekippe, Terry J. *Bernard Lonergan's Insight: A Comprehensive Commentary.* Lanham, MD: University Press of America, 2003.

Tekippe, Terry J. *Bernard Lonergan: An Introductory Guide to Insight.* New York/Mahwah, NJ: Paulist Press, 2003.

Thanissaro Bhikku, trans. 'Cula Malunkhyaputta Sutta, Majjima Nikaya,' accessed 9 December 2013, http://www.accesstoinsight.org/tipitaka/mn/mn.063.than.html.

Thanissaro Bhikku, trans. 'Potthapada Sutta, Digha Nikaya,' last modified 30 November 2013, http://www.accesstoinsight.org/tipitaka/dn/dn.09.0.than.html.

Thanissaro Bhikku, trans. *Udāna: Exclamations; A Translation with an Introduction & Notes.* Accessed 25 February 2014, http://www.accesstoinsight.org/lib/authors/thanissaro/udana.pdf.

Theissen, Gerd and Annette Merz. *The Historical Jesus: A Comprehensive Guide*. Minneapolis, MN: Fortress Press, 1998.

Tuck, Andrew. *Comparative Philosophy and the Philosophy of Scholarship: On the Western Interpretation of Nāgārjuna*. Oxford: Oxford University Press, 1990.

Vass, George. *A Pattern of Doctrines 1: God and Christ: Understanding Karl Rahner Volume 3*. London: Sheed & Ward, 1996.

Williams, Paul. *Mahāyāna Buddhism: The Doctrinal Foundations*. London: Routledge, 2009.

Woodfin, Rupert and Judy Groves. *Introducing Aristotle*. London: Icon Books, 2010.

Index

A Grammar of Assent (Newman) 10, 37, 39–47, 214
a posteriori knowledge of God, Absolute Mystery 57–8
a priori adoption of monistic single-essence approaches 214–16
a priori categories of truth and logic 201
a priori insight 11
a priori views of how different religions relate 213–14
aberration and insight 12, 13, 28
absence of absolutely existent objects 163–4
absence of any intrinsic self 163
absence of doubt 41–2
absence of light 116–17, 185
absence of permanently existent self 161
Absolute Being 208–9
absolute and conventional viewpoints of becoming and destruction 153–4
absolute existence and nonexistence/becoming and destruction 154–5
absolute existence of phenomena 113
absolute fulfillment of transcendence 63
absolute future and God 63, 86–9, 90, 99
absolute horizon and insight 203
Absolute Mystery 56–60, 61, 67–8, 73–4
absolute saviour/Jesus Christ 71–2, 73

absolute truth and the illative sense 46–7
absolutely existent objects, absence of 163–4
absolutes in the examination of nirvāṇa 172
abstraction and the eschatology of Christianity 88–9
abstraction through which first principles are arrived at (Newman) 42
actions
  in accordance with being, God and insight 34–5
  and agent 121–3
  examination of the Four Noble Truths 168
  and their fruits 138–42
  whose nature is affliction 142
actual nature of what exists 199–200
actualisation of human transcendentality/history of salvation and revelation 67–8
actualising the self 56
affirmation
  Absolute Mystery 58–9
  becoming and destruction 152–6
  cessation of a phenomena 120
  Easter experience/Jesus Christ 77
  eschatology of Christianity 87–90
  examination of combination 147–8
  examination of motion 108
  experience 199–200

Four Noble Truths 168–9
general/special transcendent knowledge 32
God and insight 35
Hearer of the Message 55
man as threatened radically by guilt 60, 61
metaphysics as dialectic 26–7, 28, 29
metaphysics as science and dialectic 24–5
nirvāṇa 175–6
see also self-affirmation
affliction 142
agent and action, *Mūlamadhyamakakārikā* 121–3
aggregates 110–12
   examination of errors 161
   examination of the Tathāgata 157–9
aging and death 120, 172–3
   see also death
analogia entis 202–3, 204
analytical propositions and analytic principles 19–20, 207–8
anattā (not-self) 63–4, 110, 122–3, 198
annica teachings of existence 198
'anonymous Christian', formulation 66
Anselm's ontological argument for God's existence 33–4
anthropology 52–3
   Absolute Mystery 56–7
   Hearer of the Message 55
   Jesus Christ 70–71, 74
anthropomorphic projection 25–6
apprehension of reality in freedom/ examination of views 186
appropriation in nonappropriator/ examination of views 180–81
Aquinas, T. 21, 22, 33–4, 35, 55, 58
arising and emptiness 152–6, 167

characteristics of an arisen phenomena 120–21
qua entity/*Mūlamadhyamakakārikā* 117–18
   see also dependent arising as existing process
Aristotle 21, 22
asaṁskṛta dharma 175
assent
   illative sense 45, 46–7
   nature of 44–5
   and religion 43–4
   see also Grammar of Assent
assertion of man as free/responsible 56
Augustine 2, 35, 78, 207
autonomy 59–60
avidyā (ignorance) 131, 167–8, 186
awareness
   Hearer of the Message 55
   insight as knowledge 15–16
   nature of assent 44–5
   reflexivity of knowing 44–5
   unreflective 55
   see also consciousness

baptism 85
becoming and destruction 152–6
'beginningless' 182–3
being *see* notion of being
'birth' of the unconscious (Freud) 48
Bodhisattva ideals 102–3
bodies, insight as understanding 14
bondage
   examination of nirvāṇa 170–72
   examination of the twelve links 177
   and *Mūlamadhyamakakārikā* 134–8
   see also suffering and *Mūlamadhyamakakārikā*

Buddhism
conceptions of not-self 63–4, 110, 122–3, 198
see also Mūlamadhyamakakārikā
butterlamp metaphors 116–17, 185

categorical experience 76–7
categorical knowing 56–7
category of emptiness 150–51
category of time to ontology 151
Catholic Church 79–81
causality
Absolute Mystery 59
and consequences 151–2
context and transcendent knowledge 31–2
examination of the aggregates in *Mūlamadhyamakakārikā* 110–11
examination of combination 149–52
examination of time 146–7
general/special transcendent knowledge 31
man as event of God's free and forgiving self-communication 62–3
cause and effect 149–50, 151
The Central Philosophy of Buddhism (Murti) 133, 134, 145
certitude/certainty 44–5, 47, 74–5
cessation of a phenomena 120
cessation through mediation 178–9
characteristics of an arisen phenomena 120–21
charity 37
Charybdis of asserting too little 24–5
Charybdis of complete nonexistence 115
Charybdis of idealism 14–15
choice of language and consequence 140–41

Christian life 82–6
Christians and Religious Pluralism (Race) 1
Christology 55, 69, 72–3, 89–90
Church 78–82
sacrament 84
Cittamātra School within Buddhism 121–3
Clooney, F. X. 213–14, 215
cognitional theory/insight as knowledge 16
cognitive acts and the method of metaphysics 19
cognitive error 143–4
cognitive process
illative sense and assent 47–8
see also consciousness
cognitive-propositional approaches 53
combination and *Mūlamadhyamakakārikā* 147–52
comparative theology 213–16
complete nonexistence 115
complex assent, nature of 44–5
compounded phenomena and *Mūlamadhyamakakārikā* 130–31, 171–2
concept of self 142–5
concept/conception of the thing 13–14, 21
concretely existing phenomena/ examination of the aggregates 111–12
conditions and *Mūlamadhyamakakārikā* 105–7, 115–21
conjugate potency 21
connection and *Mūlamadhyamakakārikā* 131–2
conscience
assent and religion 43–4
see also notion of good

consciousness
    Absolute Mystery 56–7
    assent 42–3
    contrast between real and notional 40–41
    Enlightenment 174–5
    examination of the prior entity 123
    examination of the senses 109–10
    experience 200
    insight as knowledge 15–16, 17
    Jesus Christ 69–70, 74–5
    man as event of God's free and forgiving self-communication 63–4
    metaphysics as dialectic 25–6
    method of metaphysics 19, 20, 22
    nature of assent 44–5
consequences and action 138–42
consideration of the thing 13–14
contaminated action 143–4
context of external causes/transcendent knowledge 31–2
contingent or 'empty' view of form 112
contrast between real and notional 40–41, 47–9
conventional experience 143–5
conventional reality 144–5
conventional viewpoints of becoming and destruction 153–4
conventional viewpoints of error 163–4
convergence, truth and assent 45, 47–9
cosmos
    Jesus Christ 69–70, 71, 75–6
    metaphysics as dialectic 28
covenantal dynamic 85
creation
    Absolute Mystery 59–60
    Christian life 85
    eschatology of Christianity 89–90

history of salvation and revelation 67
    Jesus Christ 69–70
credence (absence of doubt) 41–2
criterion of truth 26, 38–9, 207
cultural linguistic definition 33–4

darkness/absence of light 116–17, 185
death
    and aging 120, 172–3
    assent 45
    of Christ 76, 77, 85
    Christian life 85–6
    eschatology of Christianity 86–7, 88–9
    examination of nirvāṇa 172–3
    examination of the Tathāgata 159–60
    maturation and 89
    see also saṃsāra/saṃsāric processes
'Deathless' reality 184
deciding about one's self, power of 56
decision-making/Christian life 82–3
decisive existentiell significance/ Christian life 85–6
deconstructionism 103
dedicatory verses in *Mūlamadhyamakakārikā* 104–5
defilements/examination of errors 161–5
definition of being
    insight as knowledge 18–19
    metaphysics as dialectic 26–8
    metaphysics as science and dialectic 23
delusion 143–4, 176–7
denial of the absolute existence of phenomena 113
dependent arising as existing process 118–19

examination of the conditions
   in *Mūlamadhyamakakārikā*
   118–19
examination of the Four Noble
   Truths 167
examination of nirvāṇa 172–3
dependent origination concepts 132
depths of the finite/Jesus Christ 74
desire and the desirous and
   Mūlamadhyamakakārikā 114
destruction 152–6
Dharmas
   actions and their fruits 139–41
   combination 151–2
   dedicatory verses in
      Mūlamadhyamakakārikā 104–5
   essence 133
   the Four Noble Truths 165–6,
      167
   and insight 204
   nirvāṇa 175, 176–7
   'nonexpiring' 140–41
   self and entities 145
   views 185–6, 188
dialectic
   application of Lonergan's
      epistemology 195–216
   between transcendentality and
      categorical experience 76–7
   examination of bondage 138
   examination of the Tathāgata
      159–60
   examination of views 183–4
   history of salvation and revelation
      65, 67
   and metaphysics 22–9
   method of metaphysics 19–22
   self-presence and distance 60–61
discipleship 77
Discourse to Kātyāyana 133–4
discrimination of knowledge and
   attention 25–6

distance, man as threatened radically
   by guilt 60–61
distinctions between things 22–3
divine self-communication *see*
   self-communication
divine self-disclosure 57–8
divinisation 69–70
Divinity (Brahman), examination of
   views 182
doctrines of the final vision of God
   62–3
dogma of Christian faith 52, 53
doubt, absence of 41–2
dual nature of human existence/
   eschatology of Christianity 87–8
dukha teachings of existence 198
Dych, W.
   Absolute Mystery 58
   Christian life 84
   eschatology of Christianity 87–8
   Hearer of the Message 55
   history of salvation and revelation
      64, 68–9
   Jesus Christ 69, 72
dynamic character of the universe/
   method of metaphysics 20–21
dynamism of consciousness/method of
   metaphysics 22
dynamism of the universe
   general/special transcendent
      knowledge 31
   method of metaphysics 22

Easter experience, affirmation of 76,
   77, 85
efficient context and transcendent
   knowledge 31–2
elements and *Mūlamadhyamakakārikā*
   112–13
emotional assessment of good 29
empirical residue 12, 13
emptiness as a designation 169–70

emptiness of everything 175–6
Empty Words: Buddhist Philosophy and Cross-Cultural Interpretation (Garfield) 154
engagement with nonentities by nonentities/examination of nirvāṇa 176–7
Enlightenment 174–5
entities
    examination of becoming and destruction 153–4
    examination of the conditions in *Mūlamadhyamakakārikā* 117–18
    and Meinongian opposites 133
    and self 142–5
    and time 146–7
entityhood in the absolute sense and compounded phenomena 130–31
epistemology
    dialectic application 195–216
    examination of the Tathāgata 156–7
    problems of Christian faith 53
    role of logic, the illative sense and assent 46, 48–9
errors and *Mūlamadhyamakakārikā* 160–65, 179
eschatology of Christianity 86–90
essence
    examination of combination 149–50
    examination of views 182–3
    Kiblinger/monistic single-essence approaches 214–16
    and *Mūlamadhyamakakārikā* 132–4
    realization of emptiness 143–4
    of scripture 80–81
essential nonexistence/examination of errors 164–5
essential self of person (atman) 182

essentialist frameworks and the Four Noble Truths 168
eternal life 76, 77, 87, 88–9
ethics
    metaphysics as dialectic 28
    see also notion of good
Eucharist 84, 86
everything about everything 30
evil
    God and insight 35, 36–7
    as *privatio boni* 207
evolution, cosmic 69–70, 71
ex nihilo and diachronic existence 181
examinations (Buddhism)
    actions and their fruits 138–42
    the agent and action 121–3
    the aggregates 110–12
    becoming and destruction 152–6
    bondage 134–8
    combination 147–52
    compounded phenomena 130–31, 171–2
    conditions 105–7, 115–21
    the conditions in *Mūlamadhyamakakārikā* 115–21
    connection 131–2
    desire and the desirous 114
    elements 112–13
    errors 160–65
    essence 132–4
    fire and fuel 125–7
    the Four Noble Truths 165–70
    the initial and final limits 127–8
    motion 107–8
    nirvāṇa 170–77
    the prior entity 123–5
    self and entities 142–5
    the senses 108–10
    suffering 129–30

Index   235

the Tathāgata 156–60
time 146–7
the twelve links 177–9
views 179–88
excellence and perfection as the cause of everything else 34
exclusivism 213–14
exemplary context and transcendent knowledge 31–2
existence and inherent existence *see Mūlamadhyamakakārikā*
existence and nonexistence 59–60
   examination of becoming and destruction 154–5
   examination of the Tathāgata 159–60
existential nihilism 168–9
existentiell practice of accepting orientation freely 57–8
existentiell significance of Christian events 74–5
experience 198–201
   Absolute Mystery 57–8
   God and insight 35–6
   method of metaphysics 21
   and potency 21, 22, 31
   sense and assent 40–41
experiential-expressivist approaches 53, 214–16
'explicit metaphysics'/insight as knowledge 17–18
extroversion 20, 208–9

faith
   assent 40
   God and insight 37
   history of salvation and revelation 65–6
   Jesus Christ 73–4, 75, 77
false views 185–7
Father, and Logos 78

finality, method of metaphysics 22
finitude
   categorical reality, salvation, and revelation 67–8
   examination of views 185
   Jesus Christ 77
   see also infinite
fire and fuel, *Mūlamadhyamakakārikā* 125–7
'first principles' (Newman) 42
forgiveness 62–4, 77
form
   and essence 132–3
   examination of the aggregates 110–11, 112
   examination of the twelve links 177–8
   potency, form and act 21, 31
formal causality and self-communication 62–3
Foundations of Christian Faith (Rahner) 5, 8, 51–100
   Absolute Mystery 57–60
   analysis according to metaphysics 90–99
   Christian life 82–6
   Church 78–82
   dialectic application of Lonergan's epistemology 195–216
   eschatology 86–90
   Hearer of the Message 55–6
   history of salvation and revelation 64–9
   Jesus Christ 69–78
   man as event of God's free and forgiving self-communication 62–4
   man as threatened radically by guilt 60–61
Fredericks, J. 213
free love 63

free will 35
freedom and liberation
   Absolute Mystery 58–9
   examination of views 186
   Hearer of the Message 56
   history of salvation and revelation 66, 67–8
   Jesus Christ 75
   man as threatened radically by guilt 60–61
   metaphysics as dialectic 28–9
   self-communication 62–4
Freud, S. 48
full certitude 45
fullness of being 70
fundamental cognitive error 143–4
future tense 88–9, 146–7, 179–80
   absolute future and God 63, 86–9, 90, 99
   see also time

Garfield, J. L. 7
   see also Mūlamadhyamakakārikā
general transcendent knowledge 29–32
God and insight 32–7
good *see* notion of good
grace
   Christian life 83, 85
   and Church 78–80
   eschatology of Christianity 87
   man as event of God's free and forgiving self-communication 62–3
   man as threatened radically by guilt 61
'grace as the reason for creation' 89–90
A Grammar of Assent (Newman) 10, 37, 39–47, 214
grasped intelligently
   general/special transcendent knowledge 29–30
   God and insight 34–5
   metaphysics as dialectic 26–7
grasping 143–4, 177–8
guilt 60–61, 65

habitual reification of phenomena 198–201
happiness 160–61, 162–3
Harold, C. F. 40
Hearer of the Message 55–6
"hereditary defect" 61
heuristic anticipation of the solution as known to God 36
Higher Viewpoint (Lonergan) 195, 209–12
historical continuity of God's offer in Christ 81–2
historical revelation 68
historical subjectivity and Jesus Christ 71–2
historicity
   Hearer of the Message 56
   Jesus Christ 74–5
   salvation and revelation 64
history
   Absolute Mystery 57–8
   Christian life 83
   Church 78–82
   eschatology of Christianity 87, 89–90
   evolutionary dynamic of cosmos 69–70
   Jesus Christ 76, 77
   of mediation 68–9
   of salvation and revelation 64–9, 87
Holy Mystery 58–9, 66, 67–8
Holy Spirit 77–8, 84, 85
hope 37, 83
horizon of death/eschatology of Christianity 86–7

human understanding 10–15

identity 182–8
  and compounded phenomena 130–31
  examination of combination 151–2
  examination of views 179–80
ignorance 131, 167–8, 186
illative sense (Newman) 45, 46–8
imagined opponent 165, 166
immediacy of God 63
impenetrability of death 88–9
impermanence 153–5
"the impermanent is permanent" 162
implied opponent 133–5
impossibility of emptiness existing 186–7
incarnation/Jesus Christ 69–71, 73–4
inclusivism 213–14, 215–16
incoherence
  becoming and destruction 153
  denying the phenomenon of awareness 15–16
  emptiness in essence 133
  examination of nirvāṇa 176
  identity 130–31
incompatibility of phenomena existing inherently 106–7
incompleteness of proportionate being 35
independence from the senses 123–4
independence/autonomy 59–60
inference, illative sense and assent 46–7
infinite
  eternal life 76, 77, 87, 88–9
  examination of views 185
  of God 77
  Jesus Christ 74
Infinite Being
  general/special transcendent knowledge 31–2
  God and insight 32–3
Infinite Horizon of Being 56–7, 198, 204
inherent existence and emptiness *see* *Mūlamadhyamakakārikā*
initial and final limits in *Mūlamadhyamakakārikā* 127–8
Insight (Lonergan) 3–5, 7, 8, 9–50
  dialectic application of epistemology 195–216
  general/special transcendent knowledge 29–32
  God 32–7
  and human understanding 10–15
  as knowledge 15–19
  metaphysics as dialectic 25–9
  metaphysics as science and dialectic 22–5
  method of metaphysics 19–22
  preliminary remarks 38–9
integral heuristic structure 17–18, 19, 21
intellectual context and metaphysics as dialectic 27–8
intellectual pattern of experience/method of metaphysics 21
intellectual satisfaction and repose 45
intelligent knowing
  from knowing *qua* extroversion 208
  general/special transcendent knowledge 31–2
  God and insight 34–5
  isomorphic correspondence 207
  metaphysics as dialectic 26–8, 29
  metaphysics as science and dialectic 23
  theology of religions 212–13
intelligibility of being
  general/special transcendent knowledge 30–32

God and insight 32–3, 34, 35
insight as understanding 12
metaphysics as dialectic 26–9
metaphysics as science and dialectic 22–3, 24–5
transmigration and bondage 136–7
'intelligible dependence' 35
interfaith dialogue/Lonergan's structure of knowing 49–50
interpersonal element to transcendental self-interpretation 67
interpretive certitude 44–5
intrinsic intelligence 26–7
intrinsic intelligibility 31–2
intrinsic self, absence of 163
intrinsic sense of a proposition 40
inverse insight 12
investigation and proof, assent 45
invocation of the category of emptiness 150–51
irrationality, God and insight 34–5
irreversibility of intellectualism and assent 45
irreversibility of salvation/eschatology of Christianity 84–5, 87
irrevocability of self-communication 71–2
isomorphism 38–9, 207
   examination of desire and desirous in *Mūlamadhyamakakārikā* 114
   God and insight 34
   metaphysics as science and dialectic 23–4
   method of metaphysics 19, 22
Israel's stance on Jesus 78–9

Jesus Christ 69–78
   Christian life 84, 85
   and Church 78–82
   death of 76, 77, 85
   eschatology of Christianity 87
   history of salvation and revelation 68
judgement 206
   God and insight 35–36
   human understanding 13, 14–15
   insight as knowledge 16–17
   theology of religions 212–13
justification as grace/man as threatened radically by guilt 61

Kant, I. 11, 14–15, 20, 127–8
karma 140
kenosis of God 74
Keown, D. 64
Kiblinger, K. B. 214–16
Kilby, K. 52, 57, 62, 66
Klostermeier, K. 103
Knitter, P. 2, 216
'knowing-as-taking-a-look' (Lonergan) 48–9
'known unknown', metaphysics as dialectic 25

'latent metaphysics'/insight as knowledge 17–18
law of non-contradiction 155–6
law of a subjective apriority 75
Lindbeck, G. 3, 33–4, 215–16
logic, experience 201
logical certitude, Jesus Christ 74–5
Logos 72–3, 78, 202
loneliness 85–6
Lonergan, B. 3–5, 7, 8
   and assent 47–9
   dialectic application of epistemology 195–216
   experience 198–201
   further dialectical equivalents 206–9
   higher viewpoint 209–12
   insight 202–6

interfaith dialogue/structure of
knowing 49–50
judgement 206
move to comparative approach
213–16
significance of method for theology
of religions 212–13
structure of proposed dialectic
197–212
verification of claims 195–7
see also Insight
Lonerganian Analysis of Nāgārjuna *see
Mūlamadhyamakakārikā*
love
Absolute Mystery 58–9
Christian life 83
and Church 81–2
eschatology of Christianity 88–9
God and insight 32–3
see also truth

McDonald, A. 6
Mādhyamika approaches
essence 133
the Four Noble Truths 165–7
suffering 129
Mahāyāna philosophy and the
examination of the Four Noble
Truths 166–8
Majjhima Nikāya 132–3
man as event of God's free and
forgiving self-communication
62–4
man as threatened radically by guilt
60–61
man in the presence of Absolute
Mystery 56–60
marriage 85
mass-velocity 21
material certitude 44–5
materialistic reductionism 184–5

maturation and death 89
mediation
cessation through 178–9
salvation and revelation 67, 68–9
Meinongian opposites to entities/
examination of essence 133
memoria 78
metaphor 116–17, 185, 209–10
metaphysical systems
analysis of Lonergan 90–99
assent 40
as dialectic 25–9
examination of nirvāṇa 175–6
examination of the Tathāgata 156–7
method of metaphysics 19–22
as science and dialectic 22–5
see also causality
metaphysics proper, insight as
knowledge 17–18
metatime 146–7
mind's delusory reification of what
exists 199–200
modus/Absolute Mystery 57
monistic metaphysical systems/
examination of nirvāṇa 175–6
monistic single-essence approaches
214–16
motion/movement and
Mūlamadhyamakakārikā 107–8,
127
Mūlamadhyamakakārikā (Nāgārjuna)
5–6, 7, 8, 102–94, 196
actions and their fruits 138–42
the agent and action 121–3
the aggregates 110–12
analysis 188–94
becoming and destruction 152–6
bondage 134–8
combination 147–52
compounded phenomena 130–31,
171–2

conditions 105–7
the conditions 115–21
connection 131–2
dedicatory verses in 104–5
desire and the desirous 114
dialectic application of Lonergan's epistemology 195–216
elements 112–13
errors 160–65
essence 132–4
fire and fuel 125–7
the Four Noble Truths 165–70
initial and final limits 127–8
nirvāṇa 170–77
the prior entity 123–5
self and entities 142–5
the senses 108–10
suffering 129–30
the Tathāgata 156–60
time 146–7
the twelve links 177–9
views 179–88
Murti, T. R. V. 132–3, 134, 145, 175, 184
mutatis mutandis 207
mystery
Absolute Mystery 56–60, 61, 67–8, 73–4
and myth 25–6, 41

Nāgārjuna 5–6, 7, 8
see also *Mūlamadhyamakakārikā*
nama–rupā (name and form) 177–8
natural revelation 22–3, 68
nature of the self 142–5
see also notion of being
'negation operator' 169–70
The New Comparative Theology: Interreligious Insights from the Next Generation (Kiblinger) 214–15

New Testament 2, 67, 77, 78–9
Newman, J. H. 7, 10, 19–20, 37, 39–49, 214
see also *A Grammar of Assent*
nihilism 154–5, 168–9
nirvāṇa 170–77
and bondage 136
examination of views 180–81, 184
insight 202–3
and insight 204–6
'no-thing' 172–3
'non-being'/examination of nirvāṇa 173
non-contradiction 155–6
non-dual nature of reality and bondage 137–8
nonentities by nonentities, engagement and examination of nirvāṇa 176–7
nonexistence and examination of errors 164–5
'nonexpiring' Dharmas 140–41
nonstasis 119
nothing established on the basis of anything else 126–7
'no-thing' and examination of nirvāṇa 172–3
notion of being
general/special transcendent knowledge 30–31
metaphysics as dialectic 26–8, 29
'objective of the pure desire to know' 54
social nature of man/eschatology of Christianity 87–8
see also definition of being
notion of cause and effect 149–50, 151
notion of dialectic *see* dialectic
notion of evil 35, 36–7, 207
notion of good
general/special transcendent knowledge 30–31

God and insight 36–7
metaphysics as dialectic 26–7, 28–9
potentiality for 36
notion of imagination 42
notion of inherent existence *see Mūlamadhyamakakārikā*
notion of metaphysical equivalence 23
notion of a thing 13–14
notional, contrast between real and 40–41, 47–9
not-self 63–4, 110, 122–3, 198

'objective of the pure desire to know' 17, 54
objectively identifiable thing and Absolute Mystery 56–7
objects of desire 28–9
Old Testament 67, 68
omnipresence of salvation and faith 66
omnipresence of transcendental experience and the history of salvation and revelation 67
ontological argument for God's existence 33–4
ontological aspect of intrinsic intelligence 26–7
ontological difference between arising not dependently arisen and all other phenomena which are dependently arisen 116
ontological divination of man through grace 62–3
ontological extremes used in the *reductio*/becoming and destruction 155
ontological predicate of emptiness as empty 169–70
ontological self-communication 62–3
ontological status of the Buddha post-enlightenment 174–5
ontology and category of time 151–2

opinion 41–2
examination of views 179–88
opponents 133–5, 150–51
optimistic pessimism 83
order that lies within being 32
original sin
man as threatened radically by guilt 61
see also notion of evil; original sin
origins of the subject 60–61
'otherness' 3

'pacification and objectification' concepts 113
past tense 146–7, 179–80
see also time
penance 84, 85
penumbral quality of the illative sense 47–8
perfect act of loving and affirming truth 32–3
"Perfection of Wisdom" Sūtras 134, 184
permanently existent self, absence of 161
personhood definition 55
philosophy
examination of the aggregates in *Mūlamadhyamakakārikā* 110–11
examination of combination 147–8
examination of the Four Noble Truths 166–8
examination of views 182
Hearer of the Message 55
method of metaphysics 20
Pirke Avot (Talmudic tractate) 28
Plato 78
pleroma of Being 205–6
pluralism 213–14
polymorphism of human consciousness 19

242 Index

positing of being 195
positions and counter positions/pure desire to know 18–19
'positive tetralemma' (Lonergan) 144–5
potency
    form and act 21, 31
    method of metaphysics 22
potentiality for good 36
Prajñā-pāramitā sūtras 101, 102–3, 184
pratītyasamutpāda (dependent co-origintaion) *see Mūlamadhyamakakārikā*
Prebish, C. S. 64
present tense 146–7, 179–80
    see also time
primary being (Infinite Being) 31–3
primary intelligible and primate being 32–3
primeval revelation 67
principle of metaphysical causality *see* causality
prior entity and *Mūlamadhyamakakārikā* 123–5
probability of a proposition 41–2
proof and assent 45
property 108
prophet's authority 67
proportionate being
    general/special transcendent knowledge 30, 31–2
    God and insight 35
    insight as knowledge 17–18
    metaphysics as dialectic 28–9
prospective judgements as propositions/insight as understanding 14
protean notion of being/metaphysics as dialectic 27–8
Protestantisms 80–81
pure desire to know
    insight as knowledge 17–19
    metaphysics as dialectic 25–6
    metaphysics as science and dialectic 23
    notion of being 54
'pure openness' 54
purgatory 89
purification/'maturation' and death 89

'The Quest for an English-Speaking Nāgārjuna' (McDonald) 6

Race, A. 1, 213–14
Rahner, K. 5–6, 7, 104
    see also Foundations of Christian Faith
rational being/metaphysics as dialectic 29
real assent 42–3
real, contrast between notional and 40–41, 47–9
reality of evil 36
reality/intelligibility, God and insight 35
realization of emptiness 143–44
reasoning process and real assent 42
reduciotnist identification/examination of nirvāṇa 175
reductio ad absurdum 103
reductionism and the examination of views 184–5
reductionist hermeneutic(s) 140–41
reflexive awareness of knowing 44–5
reflexive expression of what we already know 63
Reformation and Christianity 80, 84
reification
    examination of actions and their fruits 141
    examination of becoming and destruction 154–5
    examination of nirvāṇa 176–7

experience 198–201
reincarnation 140, 181
   see also saṃsāra/saṃsāric processes
rejection of God 65
   see also guilt
religious anguage 33–4
relinquishing of views 185–6
remote criterion of truth 26, 38–9, 207
responsibility 56, 138–42
resurrection 77
revelation 64–9
   Absolute Mystery 57–8
   Jesus Christ 74
role of non-Christian religions in salvation 77–8
role of time as category 149
root delusion 143–4
rūpa (form) 110–11, 132–3

sacrament 77, 84, 85, 86
salvation
   Absolute Mystery 57–8
   Christian life 83, 86
   and Church 78–80
   eschatology of Christianity 86–7
   history of salvation and revelation 66
   Jesus Christ 73, 77–8
   and revelation 64–9
   role of non-Christian religions 77–8
   self-communication 62–3
saṃsāra/saṃsāric processes
   bondage 135–6, 137–8
   errors 160–61, 162–3
   initial and final limits 127–8
   insight 202–3
   and insight 204–5
   nirvāṇa 170–77
   self and entities 143–4, 145
   the twelve links 177

views 182–3
Sautrāntika Schools within Buddhism 125–6
Schmidt-Leukel, P. 2, 134, 144–5, 184
science and metaphysics 22–5
Scylla of asserting too much 24–5
Scylla of inherent existence 115
Scylla of materialism 14–15
secondary intelligibles 34
self and the aggregates, examination of errors 161
self being
   examination of views 182, 183–4
   see also notion of being
"self" of the Buddha 157
self and entities in *Mūlamadhyamakakārikā* 142–5
self as independent of the aggregates/examination of the Tathāgata 158–9
self itself and independence from the senses 123–4
self-actualisation/man as threatened radically by guilt 60–61
self-affirmation of the knower 47–8
   insight as knowledge 15–17, 18–19
   method of metaphysics 19
self-appropriation/history of salvation and revelation 66
self-communication of God to man 59–60, 206–7
   Christian life 83
   freedom and forgiveness 62–4
   history of salvation and revelation 65, 68–9
   Jesus Christ 71–2, 73, 74–5, 78
   man as threatened radically by guilt 61
self-consciousness and Jesus Christ 71
self-determination/history of salvation and revelation 67–8
self-disclosure 57–8

Absolute Mystery 58–9
self-interpretation 52–3
   history of salvation and revelation 67–8
self-negating/man as threatened radically by guilt 61
self-presence 55, 60–61, 69–70
self-transcendence 70
sense experience and assent 40–41
senses and *Mūlamadhyamakakārikā* 108–10
   actions and their fruits 139–40
   errors 161–2
   the prior entity 123
sensitive pattern of knowing 23
sensory pattern of experience/method of metaphysics 21
Shōryū, K. 5–6
sickness 84, 85–6
Siderits, M. 5–6
simple assent 44–5
sin
   Christian life 83
   God and insight 34–5, 37
   and Jesus Christ 77
   man as threatened radically by guilt 61
sola fide 80
sola gratia 80
sola scriptura 80–81
solidarity of humankind 77
soteriology
   actions and their fruits 139–40
   essence 133–4
   and Jesus Christ 77
   nirvāṇa 176–7
   views and Buddhism 182–3
special transcendent knowledge 29–32, 36
Spirit
   and Church 78, 80–81

Jesus Christ 69–70, 76, 77–8
spiritual world and Jesus Christ 71–2
spontaneous assent 41–2
stasis and nonstasis 119
structure of being and knowing, God and insight 34
structure of things 38–9
"subject" in an objective way 55
subject of which the aggregates are properties 157
subject who acts and perceives/fire and fuel 125–6
subjectivity and Jesus Christ 71–2, 75
subject–object structure of conventional apprehension 184–6
suffering and *Mūlamadhyamakakārikā* 129–30, 143–4, 163–4, 170–72
śūnyatā concepts 102–3
'supernatural existential' reality 62, 64
supernatural/transcendentality 66
sūtras 101, 102–3, 184
synthesis between experiential-expressivism and cognitive-propositional approaches 53
synthetic insight 11
'system on the move' (human being) 37
'system on the move' (universe) 22
systematic theology *see Foundations of Christian Faith*

Tarfon (Rabbi) 28
Tathāgata and *Mūlamadhyamakakārikā* 156–60
teaching office of the Church 81–2
Tekippe, T.
   general/special transcendent knowledge 31–2
   grounding human knowing 38
   human understanding 11, 14
   insight as knowledge 16

metaphysics as dialectic 27–8
method of metaphysics 19–20, 22
tetralemma (Lonergan) 171–7, 181–2, 208
   becoming and destruction 153
   combination 149
   self and entities 144–5
   suffering 129
   Tathāgata 158–9
theology of religions 209–16
   Absolute Mystery 56–7
   Hearer of the Message 55
   Jesus Christ 74
   see also Foundations of Christian Faith
'thing in se' 15–16
time
   absolute future and God 63, 86–9, 90, 99
   metatime 146–7
   and Mūlamadhyamakakārikā 146–7, 149, 151–2, 179–80
totality of all that is/Absolute Mystery 57
transcendent knowledge 54, 55, 74–5, 76–7, 201
   Absolute Mystery 56–9, 60, 61
   analogia entis 202–3, 204
   component of subjectivity 56–7
   general/special 29–32
   God and insight 36
   history of salvation and revelation 64, 66, 67–9
   insight as knowledge 17–18
   Jesus Christ 70–71, 72–3, 75, 76
   man as event of God's free and forgiving self-communication 63
   man as threatened radically by guilt 61
   metaphysics as dialectic 29
   and omnipresence 67
   revelation and historical revelation 68–9
   self-interpretation/history of salvation and revelation 67
   see also nirvāṇa
Transcendental Horizon
   Absolute Mystery 58
   history of salvation and revelation 67–8
   man as event of God's free and forgiving self-communication 63–4
transition from knowing qua extroversion to intelligent knowing 208
transmigration and bondage 135–7
Trinitarian terminology and self-communication 64
Trinity, doctrine of 44
'the true doctrine' 185–6
truth
   assent 38, 41–2, 45
   and Church 81–2
   examination of destruction and becoming 155–6
   examination of the Four Noble Truths 165–70
   experience 201
   God and insight 32–3, 35
   illative sense 46–7
   Jesus Christ 73–4
   metaphysics as dialectic 26–7
truth criterion 26, 38–9, 207
twelve links in Mūlamadhyamakakārikā 177–9
'two truths' doctrine 155–6

ubiquity of death and aging 120
Udana text 184
ultimate emptiness 144–5

ultimate existence of error 163
ultimate nature of things 118–19
unconditioned
   God and insight 35
   human understanding 14
   insight as knowledge 17
   metaphysics as dialectic 26
   method of metaphysics 20
unconscious 39, 47–8
   see also consciousness
understanding everything about everything 30
unicity of God's essence 63–4
union/Absolute Mystery 58
'Uniqueness: a pluralistic reading of John 14:6' (Schmidt-Leukel) 2
unity
   and Church 78–9
   Jesus Christ 69–70
   metaphysics as dialectic 26–7
unity of consciousness, examination of the prior entity 123
unity of history, Jesus Christ 77
unity of the human person 23–4
unity of the material and spiritual 24
unity of proportionate being 23–4
unity of the world 69–70
unity of the world concepts, Jesus Christ 73
universal self-communication 77–8
Universal Viewpoint (Lonergan) 26–8, 195, 209–12
universality of God's salvific will 77–8
universality of the offer of grace 78–9
universe
   general/special transcendent knowledge 31–2

metaphysics as dialectic 28–9
method of metaphysics 20–21, 22
   see also cosmos; nirvāṇa; saṃsāra
unknown contents of cognitive acts 19
'unlimited transcendentality' 68
unreflective awareness 55
unrestricted act of understanding 30–31, 32–3, 35
unrestricted desire to know
   general/special transcendent knowledge 30
   method of metaphysics 20
   see also pure desire to know

Vaibhāṣika Schools within Buddhism 125–6
Vass, G. 70
vedanā 132–3
'vestigial empiricism' 14–15
views
   Higher Viewpoint 195, 209–12
   and *Mūlamadhyamakakārikā* 179–88
virtue 37, 83, 140
   see also faith
vision and *Mūlamadhyamakakārikā* 108–9

what exists inherently can (pratītyasamutpāda) *see Mūlamadhyamakakārikā*
what is dependently arisen/dependent arising as existing process 118–19, 167, 172–3
Williams, P. 129, 133
willing and Absolute Mystery 58–9
Wittgenstein, L. 104

www.ingramcontent.com/pod-product-compliance
Lightning Source LLC
Chambersburg PA
CBHW051519230426
43668CB00012B/1672